eview M+L 67:192. Apr '86.

THE NEW GROVE
HIGH RENAISSANCE MASTERS

THE NEW GROVE
DICTIONARY OF MUSIC AND MUSICIANS

Editor: Stanley Sadie

The Composer Biography Series

BACH FAMILY
BEETHOVEN
HANDEL
HAYDN
HIGH RENAISSANCE MASTERS
ITALIAN BAROQUE MASTERS
MASTERS OF ITALIAN OPERA
MODERN MASTERS
MOZART
SCHUBERT
SECOND VIENNESE SCHOOL
WAGNER

THE ᴌNEW GROVE

High Renaissance
Masters

JOSQUIN PALESTRINA
LASSUS
BYRD VICTORIA

Gustave Reese

Jeremy Noble

Lewis Lockwood

Jessie Ann Owens

James Haar

Joseph Kerman

Robert Stevenson

W. W. NORTON & COMPANY
NEW YORK   LONDON

First published in
The New Grove Dictionary of Music and Musicians,
edited by Stanley Sadie, 1980

First published in UK in paperback with additions 1984 by
PAPERMAC
a division of Macmillan Publishers Limited
London and Basingstoke

First published in UK in hardback with additions 1984 by
MACMILLAN LONDON LIMITED
4 Little Essex Street London WC2R 3LF
and Basingstoke

British Library Cataloguing in Publication Data

The New Grove high renaissance masters.—
(The Grove composer biography series)
1. Composers—Europe—Biography
I. Noble, Jeremy   II. Series
780′.92′2   ML390

ISBN 0–333–38237–4 (hardback)
ISBN 0–333–38238–2 (paperback)

First American edition in book form with additions 1984 by
W.W. NORTON & COMPANY
New York and London

ISBN 0-393-30093-5 (paperback)
ISBN 0-393-01689-7 (hardback)

Printed in Great Britain

Contents

List of illustrations

Cover: Four singers with partbooks: painting, 'Concert cham-
pêtre', early 16th century, Italian school (Musée du Berry,
Bourges)

Illustration acknowledgments

We are grateful to the following for permission to reproduce illus-
trative material: British Library, London (figs.1–6, 11); Bayerisches
Staatsbibliothek, Munich (figs.7, 8); Biblioteka Polskiej Akademii
Nauk, Gdańsk (fig.9); Music Library, University of London Library
(fig.10); Seville Cathedral Library (fig.12); Conservatorio di Musica
Santa Cecilia, Rome (fig.13); Lauros–Giraudon, Paris (cover)

General abbreviations

A	alto, contralto	Mag	Magnificat
add.	addition		
Ag	Agnus Dei	Nunc	Nunc dimittis
all	alleluia		
ant	antiphon	off	offertory
appx	appendix	org	organ
B	bass	p.	pars (lp. = *prima pars*, etc)
b	born	pr.	printed
Bs	Benedictus	ptbk	partbook
		pubd	published
c	circa [about]		
c.f.	cantus firmus	*R*	photographic reprint
comm	communion	*r*	recto
Cr	Credo, Creed	RCA	Radio Corporation of America
Ct	countertenor		
		re	response
d	died	repr.	reprinted
ded.	dedication, dedicated to	rev.	revision, revised by/for
edn.	edition	S	San, Santa, Santo, São [Saint]; soprano [voice]
facs.	facsimile	seq	sequence
frag.	fragment	Sup	superius
Gl	Gloria	T	tenor
grad	gradual	TeD	Te Deum
		tr	tract; treble [instrument]
IMS	International Musicological Society	transcr.	transcription, transcribed by/for
inc.	incomplete		
inst	instrument, instrumental	U.	University
int	introit		
		v, vv	voice, voices
Jub	Jubilate	v., vv.	verse, verses
		v	verso
kbd	keyboard	Ven	Venite
Ky	Kyrie		

Symbols for the library sources of works, printed in *italic*, correspond to those used in *RISM*, Ser. A.

Bibliographical abbreviations

AcM	*Acta musicologica*
AMf	*Archiv für Musikforschung*
AMw	*Archiv für Musikwissenschaft*
AnM	*Anuario musical*
AnMc	*Analecta musicologica*
AnnM	*Annales musicologiques*
BrownI	H. M. Brown: *Instrumental Music Printed before 1600: a Bibliography* (Cambridge, Mass., 2/1967)
BurneyH	C. Burney: *A General History of Music from the Earliest Ages to the Present* (London, 1776–89)
CMc	*Current Musicology*
CMM	Corpus mensurabilis musicae
CSPD	*Calendar of State Papers (Domestic)* (London, 1856–1972)
Cw	Das Chorwerk
DTB	Denkmäler der Tonkunst in Bayern
DTÖ	Denkmäler der Tonkunst in Österreich
EDM	Das Erbe deutscher Musik
EECM	Early English Church Music
EitnerQ	R. Eitner: *Biographisch-bibliographisches Quellen-Lexikon*
EitnerS	R. Eitner: *Bibliographie der Musik-Sammelwerke des XVI. und XVII. Jahrhunderts* (Berlin, 1877)
EM	The English Madrigalists
FAM	*Fontes artis musicae*
FasquelleE	*Encyclopédie de la musique* (Paris: Fasquelle, 1958–61)
GfMKB	*Gesellschaft für Musikforschung Kongressbericht*
Grove 4	*Grove's Dictionary of Music and Musicians* [4th edn.]
HawkinsH	J. Hawkins: *A General History of the Science and Practice of Music* (London, 1776)
HMw	Handbuch der Musikwissenschaft, ed. E. Bücken (Potsdam, 1927–) [monograph series]
IMa	Instituta et monumenta
IMSCR	*International Musicological Society Congress Report*
JAMS	*Journal of the American Musicological Society*

Preface

This volume is one of a series of short biographical essays derived from *The New Grove Dictionary of Music and Musicians* (London, 1980). In its original form, the text was written in the mid-1970s, and finalized at the end of that decade. All the composers treated here have been the subject of substantial research since the publication of *The New Grove*, and this is reflected in the changes made for the present reprint. In all cases, the bibliographies have been brought up to date. The texts of the essays on Byrd, Palestrina and Victoria, in particular, have been expanded with further stylistic discussion and musical exemplification; that for Josquin has been revised, with the generous assistance of Herbert Kellman, to take account of recent biographical discoveries (many of them Mr Kellman's own). The work-list for Josquin has been much elaborated, especially by the addition of newly discovered source information. The work-list for Lassus has been expanded by the separate inclusion, in the lists of madrigals, motets etc, of second and subsequent parts of multi-section works. The work-list for Byrd has been appreciably refined, with the assistance of Craig Monson (who also advised on the English sacred music); Joseph Kerman wishes to accord special thanks to Professor Monson, and to Richard Turbet for his assistance with the bibliography.

The fact that the texts of the books in this series originated as dictionary articles inevitably gives them a character somewhat different from that of books conceived as such. They are designed, first of all, to accommodate a very great deal of information in a manner that makes reference quick and easy. Their first concern is with fact rather than opinion, and this leads to a larger than usual proportion of the texts being devoted to biography than to critical discussion. The nature of a reference work gives it a particular obligation to convey received knowledge and to treat of composers' lives and works in an encyclopedic fashion, with proper acknowledgment of sources and due care to reflect different standpoints, rather than to embody imaginative or speculative writing about a composer's character or his music. It is hoped that the comprehensive work-lists and extended bibliographies, indicative of the origins of the books in a reference work, will be valuable to the reader who is eager for full and accurate reference information and who may not have ready access to *The New Grove Dictionary* or who may prefer to have it in this more compact form.

S.S.

JOSQUIN DESPREZ

Gustave Reese

Jeremy Noble

CHAPTER ONE

Life

I Origins and early years

Josquin Desprez, one of the greatest composers of the entire Renaissance and certainly the most important before the second half of the 16th century, was born about 1440. His name appears in various forms in archival sources, including 'Juschino', 'Josse', 'Jodocus Pratensis' and 'Jodocus a Prato'. Josquin was already an adult at the time of the earliest known archival evidence concerning him, which dates from 1459 and refers to him as a singer at Milan Cathedral. He is described as 'Jodocho de frantia biscantori', and it is on the strength of the last word that the conjectural date of his birth is based, since the term 'biscantor' implies an adult singer rather than a choirboy. There are various theories regarding Josquin's birthplace. The best, if negative, evidence comes in a document (Condé FF.78) discovered by Herbert Kellman at Condé-sur-Escaut – now in France, but in Josquin's day in the imperial county of Hainaut, outside the French border. This document states that on 23 August (1521) Josquin had registered as an alien in Condé to safeguard property of his in view of what proved to be his final illness. As an alien he would have been born outside imperial Hainaut, in other words in French territory. In the preface he wrote for a *Livre de Meslanges* (*EitnerS*, 1560c), Ronsard described him as 'hennuyer de nation', and thereby clearly intended to indicate Hainaut as the region of the composer's birth;

1

but this assumption may have been based on Josquin's long connection with Condé, going back at least as far as the 1470s (see pp.4–7 below). In his Songbook (St Gall, MS 463) the Swiss humanist Aegidius Tschudi referred to Josquin as 'belga Veromanduus' (a Belgian of Vermandois, a region in Picardy whose capital was St Quentin), though, like Ronsard, he mentioned no specific town. A safe-conduct of 1479, from the Sforza court at Milan, calls Josquin 'picardus'. Documents connected with his Italian period refer to him as 'de frantia' (1459), 'francese' (1503) and 'gallus' (1510). By far the greater number of his secular compositions have French texts. Culturally and legally Josquin was a Frenchman.

The presumably correct spelling of the composer's name – Josquin Desprez – is established in large part by an acrostic in the opening lines of his motet *Illibata Dei virgo nutrix*, the text of which he probably wrote himself. Letters 1–7 and 9–12 of the acrostic yield 'JOSQUIN' and 'PREZ'; 'DES' is provided by letters 1–3 of line 8. A communication on behalf of Josquin, addressed to Margaret of Austria as Regent of the Netherlands (the letter is dated 23 May, without a year, but has been convincingly assigned to 1508) gives his surname as 'Desprez'. It has been argued that he probably approved this letter himself and that it therefore provides evidence against separating 'Des' and 'Prez'. The remaining 12 lines of the text of *Illibata* seem to present a further acrostic, 'ACAVVESCAVGA', possibly containing a clue to Josquin's birthplace, but the interpretations of Van den Borren (1957), Clarke (1966), Clercx-Lejeune (1972) and Ghislanzoni (1976) remain conjectural.

No written records are known to survive regarding Josquin's family or schooling. According to Claude Hémeré, friend and librarian of Cardinal Richelieu, whose evidence, however, dates from as late as 1633, he was a choirboy at the collegiate church at St Quentin, but Hémeré gave no dates. A lament on the death of Ockeghem by the poet Guillaume Crétin, as well as Jean Molinet's similar lament (set to music by Josquin), indicates that Josquin may have been a pupil of Ockeghem, but this may imply nothing more than an intellectual or spiritual relationship.

A possible clue to Josquin's activity before he went to Italy has been seen in an entry in the Heer Songbook (St Gall, MS 462), but this may be misleading (Kellman). The manuscript contains an anonymous piece, *Guillaume se va chaufer*, to which the compiler, Johannes Heer, applied the title *Carmen gallicum Ludovici XI Regis Francorum*. It was later included in Glarean (1547), without a text and with the title *Lutuichi Regis Franciae jocosa cantio*. Glarean provided a now well-known anecdote relating that Louis XII (reigned 1499–1515) asked that a partsong be composed, in the performance of which he could share. The king had a poor voice, and the composer, so the story goes, wrote a 'jocosa cantio' in which the tenor consisted of a single note. Two problems arise. One is that the Heer Songbook mentions Louis XI (reigned 1461–83), whereas Glarean names Louis XII. The second derives from the fact that the anecdote is part of a section in which Glarean mentions tricks that have been performed by means of musical compositions. He tells the story (recounted on p.7 below) about Josquin's reminding Louis XII of a promise by means of the composition

3

Memor esto verbi tui. He subsequently tells the anecdote of the 'jocosa cantio' but does not name any composer. Modern writers, however, have leapt to the conclusion that Josquin is the composer in question. It is true that Mersenne, considerably later, repeated the story in his *Harmonie universelle* ('Traitez de la voix et des chants', book 1: 'De la voix') and named Josquin as the composer. But whether he, like more recent scholars, supplied something that Glarean did not actually state or whether he had access to another source of information cannot now be determined. It may be well to mention, should Josquin one day prove to be the composer, that Clercx (1953) pointed out that Charlotte, the second wife of Louis XI, was the sister of Bona of Savoy, the wife of Duke Galeazzo Maria Sforza of Milan. Galeazzo Maria was in France when the death of his father Francesco in 1466 caused him to be recalled to Milan. It would have been possible for him to meet Josquin at the court of Louis XI (if Josquin were there) and to invite him to Milan. But at present this is wholly in the realm of conjecture.

The text of the motet *Omnium bonorum plena* by Loyset Compère, a prayer to the Virgin, includes a 'Despres' in the list of musicians on whose behalf she is asked to intercede. This seems likely to be a mention of Josquin and to have some bearing on his early life, since the motet can be dated before 1474. 'Despres', however, is given no first name, and Hamm (*RBM*, xiv, 1956, p. 48) has suggested that Pasquier Desprez, who served at the Burgundian court from 1464 to 1477, may be meant.

II Milan and Rome
It is not known just when Josquin went to Italy but he

clearly reached artistic maturity there. He remained
(with occasional short absences) at Milan Cathedral as a
singer from July 1459 to December 1472. His monthly
salary was five ducats, whereas other singers received
seven, eight, ten or twelve. He may have gone directly
from the cathedral to the chapel of Galeazzo Maria
Sforza. His presence there is first documented in a
register dated 15 July 1474 that lists him among 22
'cantori di capella' in the duke's service (others
included Johannes Martini and Loyset Compère, and
Gaspar van Weerbeke headed the list). Although he
received only 60 ducats a year directly as a singer in the
chapel, recognition of his superior talents is shown by
Galeazzo Maria's having provided for him amply
through a benefice conferred on him some time before
September 1473. This yielded him 100 florins a year
but with the right to engage a substitute at five ducats a
year in the event of his absence (100 florins = 82
ducats). Added to his yearly salary, it brought him an
annual income of some 142 ducats (see Lowinsky,
1971).

Galeazzo Maria, a lover of art but cruel and dis-
solute, was assassinated by three young Milanese
noblemen on 26 December 1476. Eventually Josquin
passed into the service of one of his brothers, Cardinal
Ascanio Sforza (1455–1505). Until recently only a few
facts were known regarding this service. Two frottolas
published by Petrucci (in 1504 and 1509) are attributed
to 'Josquin d'Ascanio'. The poet Serafino de' Ciminelli
dall'Aquila wrote a sonnet addressed to Josquin ('Ad
Giusquino suo compagno musico d'Ascanio'). Several
lines from this sonnet and an anecdote recounted by
Glarean (1547) concerning Josquin's *Missa 'La sol fa*

re mi' (the solmization syllables allegedly referring to Ascanio's putting off requests for payment with the words 'Lascia fare a me') are responsible for the belief that Ascanio was a miser; no contemporary documents, however, have been found to corroborate this opinion. On the contrary, histories of secular and papal politics of the period show that he was famous for his lavishness. It has generally been assumed, without documentary proof, that Serafino was in Ascanio's service between 1490 and 1493. Since Josquin is mentioned in the sonnet, it has been held that he served during those years as well. However, Lowinsky (1968) has presented much circumstantial evidence to suggest that he was in Ascanio's service from 1479 to 1486. Since Ascanio became a cardinal in 1484, this might explain why we find Josquin in Rome as a member of the papal chapel two years later. It should be noted, however, that he had by no means severed his connections with the north. In 1477, following Galeazzo Maria's assassination, he seems briefly to have entered the service of René of Anjou, titular king of Sicily and Jerusalem, in his Provençal retirement at Aix; documents from April of that year refer to him as a member of René's chapel (Esquieu, 1981). But in April 1479 we find him back at Milan, being issued, as a ducal singer, with the safe-conduct already mentioned for a visit to the shrine of St Anthony in Dauphiné. Still more revealing is Kellman's discovery of a payment-record (in the archives of the Herzog von Croy, Dülmen) for a 'vin d'honneur' presented to 'Gossequin des Pres' by the chapter of Notre-Dame at Condé in 1483 'on his first return after the French wars'. Since the wars in question had begun in 1477, the implication is clear that Josquin was already well known at Condé before that date.

Josquin's name first occurs in the list of members of the papal chapel in September 1486; he had already been granted the privileges attaching to this office the month before (Sherr, 1983). It is noteworthy that the benefices with which he was subsequently provided (whether or not he gained actual possession of any of them) were all in 'Burgundian' territory (Noble, 1971). Except for extended absences between February 1487 and May 1489, Josquin remained in the chapel until at least November 1494, probably until February 1495 (Noble), and possibly longer. The accounts of the papal chapel from 1495 to 1500 are lacking, but by 1501, when they again become available, his name is absent from the lists. Pietro Aaron, in his *Libri tres de institutione harmonica* (1516), remarked that he had friendly contact with Josquin in Florence (also with Obrecht, Isaac and Agricola) but gave no date.

III   Years in France

It is known that some time after his term of service at the papal chapel in Rome Josquin moved to France. He may also have gone north during one or other of his absences from the papal chapel, but the 'Josquin chantre' who in 1493 received a large payment at the court of René II of Lorraine (Pirro) has been shown by Kellman to be one Josquin Stellant.

A well-known anecdote related by Glarean in the *Dodecachordon* (referred to on p.3 above) indicates an association with King Louis XII; it is also reported by Petrus Opmeer in his *Opus chronographicum orbis universi* (1611) and by Claude Hémeré in his *Tabella chronologica ... S. Quintini* (1633). According to it, when the king had forgotten his promise to provide Josquin with a church benefice, he wrote a motet, for performance in the king's presence, based on the words from Psalm cxix 'Memor esto verbi tui servo tuo' (verses 49ff). The king quickly honoured his promise, for which it appears that Josquin thanked him with the motet *Bonitatem fecisti* (to verses 65ff of the same psalm). While *Memor esto verbi tui* is definitely by Josquin, however, *Bonitatem fecisti* has survived with a conflicting attribution to Carpentras. Two other pieces, *Adieu mes amours* and *Vive le roy*, also seem, at least on the surface, to link Josquin with the French court. Glarean named Josquin as the foremost of Louis XII's singers, while Hémeré referred to him as 'magister symphoniae regiae'.

Other evidence that places Josquin in France in the years 1501–3 comes from a letter written by Bartolomeo de Cavalieri, the Ferrarese ambassador to the French court. He wrote to his master, Duke Ercole I of Ferrara, on 13 December 1501 that at Blois he met 'a singer named Josquin, whom Your Excellency had sent to Flanders to find singers'. This communication suggests that Josquin had been in the service of the duke before 1501, but no corroborating evidence has been found. It seems possible that Ercole himself did not send Josquin on this recruiting mission but that the request for this service was made through an intermediary, perhaps Johannes Ghiselin, who at this time seems to have maintained a connection with both the French royal chapel and Ferrara. Cavalieri also mentioned the meeting between Louis XII and Philip the Fair, son of Maximilian I, at Blois. Philip requested that Josquin accompany him to Spain, but he is not mentioned in the 80 extant chapel registers from 1502–6 (Kellman). According to two other letters written by Cavalieri (on

13 and 17 April 1503), Josquin was at Lyons at this time for five or six days, as was Louis XII. From Josquin's journey to Flanders for the Ferrarese court it appears that he served the court of Louis XII only in an unofficial capacity. As a non-resident composer he probably provided the court chapel with new music but was free to offer his services to other courts. Finally, Osthoff (1962–5) claimed that Josquin composed the five-voice setting of *De profundis clamavi* for the funeral of Louis XII in January 1515, but he may have written it for a different funeral, possibly that of Philip the Fair (1507), Anne of Brittany (1514) or Maximilian I (1519).

IV Service at Ferrara

No record has been found of a formal relationship between Josquin and the court of Ferrara before 1503. Yet the close connections known to have existed between Ercole d'Este, the Duke of Ferrara from August 1491, and the Sforzas, particularly his association with Cardinal Ascanio, suggest that he may have had informal relations with Ferrara that are undocumented. An extended visit by Ascanio to Ferrara from spring 1480 to September 1481 is of special interest. According to Ugo Caleffini, an important chronicler, his retinue consisted of some 200 men. Josquin may have been among them and may have written his *Missa 'Hercules Dux Ferrarie'* at this period. The only documented connection between Josquin and Ferrara before 1502 is a reference in a letter to the availability of his music at the court. The writer of the letter, Joannes Vivaysius, a singer in the Ferrarese chapel, stated that he had been sent to Venice by the Duke of Ferrara to find suitable music for the Marquis of Mantua. Unable to discover

9

anything in Venice, 'even in the chapel of San Marco', he provided 'a song by Josquin also suitable for performance on instruments', which he considered appropriate and which he presumably found at Ferrara. It therefore seems that some of Josquin's music was known at the court before he arrived there.

Some recently discovered correspondence (in the Modena state archives; see Lockwood, 1971) not only shows how Josquin's services were secured for Ferrara but also provides information about talent-scouting in Italy in the late 15th and early 16th centuries. From these letters it transpires that 'Coglia', until recently identified only as Josquin's companion on his journey from France to Ferrara, played an important role in bringing him south again. His real name was Girolamo da Sestola, and he was a colourful figure at Ercole's court. Talented in many subjects, including music, he made a number of journeys to find musicians for the court chapel. Another courtier, 'Gian', whose full name was Gian de Artiganova or Gian Gascon, was also involved in talent-scouting. A rivalry developed between the two men; both were eager to continue in favour at court and to advise the duke on the selection of a major composer. In a letter dated 14 August 1502 Coglia urged Ercole to engage Josquin (trans. from Lockwood, 1971):

My Lord, I believe that there is neither Lord nor King who will now have a better chapel than yours if Your Lordship sends for Josquin. Don Alfonso [Ercole's son and heir] wishes to write this to Your Lordship and so does the entire company; and by having Josquin in our chapel I wish to place a crown upon this chapel of ours.

In a well-known letter to Ercole, Gian recommended that Isaac be brought to Ferrara (trans. from Lockwood, 1971):

To me he [Isaac] seems very well suited to serve Your Lordship, much more so than Josquin, because he is of a better nature among his companions and will compose new works more often. It is true that Josquin composes better, but he composes when he wants to, and not when one wants him to, and he is asking 200 ducats in salary while Isaac will come for 120 – but Your Lordship will decide what should be done.

This letter is dated simply 2 September. The year has been a matter of controversy for some time but in the light of new evidence can now be fixed as 1502; it was thus written less than three weeks after Coglia's. Some months later, Josquin rather than Isaac was chosen. As *maestro di cappella* at Ferrara from the end of April 1503 to April 1504 he received 200 ducats and was the highest-paid singer in the history of the Ferrarese chapel.

Josquin's activity at Ferrara is little documented: he is not, for instance, mentioned in family correspondence between the duke and his children. The available documentation suggests that he wrote primarily masses and motets there. *Miserere mei, Deus* and *Virgo salutiferi* were almost certainly two of the motets. According to Theophilo Folengo (*Opus . . . macaronicum*, 1521), *Miserere mei, Deus* was composed at the express request of Duke Ercole. Further evidence is provided by an added sixth voice written by the famous singer Bidon, who was a member of the chapel at Ferrara under Josquin. The text of the five-voice *Virgo salutiferi*, until a few years ago known only from a late 16th-century anthology of metrical prayers, is by the Ferrarese court poet Ercole Strozzi, who was working at Ferrara throughout Josquin's year of residence. Osthoff (1962–5) also assigned the *Missa 'Hercules Dux Ferrarie'* to Josquin's Ferrara period, which is certainly possible, even though its strict organization argues an earlier date.

Its publication in Josquin's second book of masses in 1505, the year of Ercole's death, brought it prominence as 'a tribute by a great composer to a famous patron' (Lockwood).

Josquin's departure from Ferrara may have been prompted by an outbreak of plague in July 1503. By September Ercole and his entire court, as well as two-thirds of the citizenry, had fled Ferrara. Josquin's place was taken by Obrecht, who fell victim to the plague early in 1505.

V Final return north

Further documents, discovered by Kellman, provide us with evidence of Josquin's presence at Condé as early as 1504. A cartulary for Notre Dame at Condé (Paris, Bibliothèque Nationale, lat.9917) lists both income and expenses in connection with a new spire, under the date 3 May 1504. One of the items is money received for admission into the chapter of four canons, including the provost 'Messire Josse Deprés'. In this year Josquin's predecessor had resigned in order to take up a post at Douai. Clearly Josquin went directly from Ferrara to Condé, where he may have become provost at the suggestion of his predecessor or of the chapter itself, rather than at the request of Margaret or Maximilian as previously supposed; at any rate the scant body of relevant documents does not suggest a close relationship with the Netherlands court. Three compositions, *Plus nulz regretz*, *Plaine de dueil* and *Parfons regretz*, and a letter from the chapter of Notre Dame, Condé-sur-Escaut, seemed to indicate some connection with the court of Margaret of Austria during the years 1508–11, but Kellman (1971) has shown that the association is at best only a possibility. Previous scholars (following Delporte) supposed the letter to have been written to Margaret in response to an inquiry from her concerning Josquin's health. Kellman has shown that it was intended only to inform Margaret that the post of provost at Condé was already occupied (by Josquin Desprez, who was 'in very good health') and was therefore not available to a candidate whom she had proposed. It would seem then that Margaret, who became regent in 1507, was not in particularly close contact with Josquin at the time of the correspondence (1508).

An entry in the disbursement ledger of Charles V for 1520 shows a generous payment to two singers from Condé, 'one of whom was called Joskin', for certain new songs which they had presented to him. However, Kellman (1971) has questioned whether so perfunctory a mention can refer to a famous and venerable composer who was also a senior dignitary of the church. Kellman's own study of Josquin's representation in the Netherlands court manuscripts, a complex of 49 books of polyphony, in comparison with that of Pierre de La Rue, the most prominent of the chapel composers, suggests that these sources do not 'give independent evidence of a close or consistent relationship of Josquin to the Netherlands court during the last decades of his life'. But that his works were known and admired there remains unquestioned.

Josquin died in Condé-sur-Escaut on 27 August 1521. A manuscript (in the Bibliothèque Municipale, Lille, MS 389), apparently dating from the 17th century, containing copies of inscriptions from tombstones in Flanders, Hainaut and Brabant, gives the following epitaph for him:

1. Josquin Desprez: woodcut from 'Opus chronographicum' (1611) by Petrus Opmeer

Chy gist Sire Josse despres
Preuost de cheens fut jadis:
Priez Dieu pour les trespasses
Qui leur donne son paradis.

Trepassa l'an 1521 le 27 d'aout:
Spes mea semper fuisti.

[Here lies Master Josse Despres. He was formerly the provost of Condé. Pray to God for the dead, that he grant them his paradise. He died on the 27th of August in the year 1521. Thou hast ever been my hope.]

The collegiate church at Condé-sur-Escaut, which contained Josquin's tombstone, was destroyed in 1793,

14

and the date of death reported above has been questioned by earlier scholars, but the newly discovered documents substantiate it. 'At his death, Josquin bequeathed his house and land to the church of Notre Dame in Condé, to endow regular commemorations for himself. These were to consist of the celebration of the *Salve* service every evening during Marian feasts and every Saturday of the year and the singing of his *Pater noster* and *Ave Maria*, in front of his house, during all general processions. Thus we learn that the choir of Notre Dame could sing polyphony, and even in six parts' (Kellman, 1971).

VI Iconography

In his volume entitled *Opus chronographicum orbis universi* Petrus Opmeer included (on p.440) a woodcut that he identified as a portrait of Josquin (see fig.1). This book was printed at Antwerp as late as 1611, however, and the woodcut was executed after an older portrait which was formerly in Ste Gudule, Brussels, but which was destroyed by fire in the 16th century. Opmeer described Josquin as having been depicted with 'truly distinguished countenance and attractive eyes'. The woodcut is evidently a feeble reproduction of the painting, but it is the only early picture definitely identified as portraying the composer. Efforts have been made to identify him as the subject of various other portraits. Special interest attaches to the recent attempt to see him as the unnamed subject of a fine painting of a musician (in the Biblioteca Ambrosiana, Milan) that has been attributed to Leonardo (it was formerly ascribed to Ambrogio de Predis) and has sometimes been thought to represent Gaffurius. Clercx-Lejeune (1972) offers some evidence that Josquin is the subject. Another portrait, one of eight figures in Jean Perréal's fresco of the Liberal Arts, has also been claimed to represent Josquin; it was discovered under the plaster in the chapter library of the cathedral at Le Puy, Auvergne. Yet another alleged portrait of Josquin, now at Condé, was painted by G. Housez in 1881. It is claimed that he restored an old portrait of the composer that had been in need of repair but substituted unauthentic elements (e.g. the costume) while retaining the features, which are close enough to those of the Opmeer woodcut to have been painted after it. (See Clercx-Lejeune, 1972, for further information on all the portraits.)

CHAPTER TWO

Reputation

Josquin's genius evidently met with wide-spread recognition during his lifetime, despite his own recorded complaints to the contrary. His works gradually spread throughout western Europe and were regarded as models of musical composition by many composers and theorists. Contemporary esteem for his masses in his later years is attested by Petrucci's devoting to them as many as three books, including his earliest mass publication (1502; the other two appeared in 1505 and 1514). No other composer was allotted more than one book by Petrucci, and publications were rarely devoted to the music of one composer in the first half of the 16th century. Printers continued to circulate Josquin's music for many years after his death – strong evidence of its continuing vitality. Thus in 1550 Attaingnant brought out a collection (Heartz no.162) which is devoted to chansons he believed to be by Josquin. Not only did reprinting of his compositions go on apace, especially in Germany, but printers often placed his name on works by other composers, apparently less through error than for the purpose of making them more salable, thus presenting modern scholars with some knotty problems of authenticity.

Several laments were written on Josquin's death. Jheronimus Vinders set the epitaph *O mors inevitabilis*, which, according to both Opmeer and Franciscus

Sweertius (*Athenae belgicae*, 1628) accompanied the portrait of Josquin at Ste Gudule, Brussels. (The same epitaph was later used for Palestrina.) Both Gombert and Appenzeller set an elegy, *Musae Jovis*, which Sweertius printed with an attribution to Gerardus Avidius of Nijmegen. Gombert drew on Josquin's favourite *Circumdederunt* tenor for his cantus, which is written down in the form of a puzzle, an archaic device no doubt used as a tribute to Josquin. An anonymous elegiac motet, *Absolve, quaesumus, Domine* (in the cathedral library in Piacenza), contains the name of the man who is being mourned – 'famuli tui Josquini'. Another motet (in the Archivo Capitular in Toledo, MS 21) has the same text, except that no deceased person is named, the letter 'N', however, reserving space for a three-syllable name. This work is ascribed in the manuscript to Josquin: he may thus have prepared a motet for his own obsequies, as Dufay had done (see Picker, 1971). A striking musical tribute to him from a somewhat later date is the motet *Dum vastos Adriae fluctus* by Jacquet of Mantua, first published in 1554 by Scotto in the fourth book of *Motetti del labirinto*. Its text includes a number of titles of motets by Josquin, *Praeter rerum seriem*, *Stabat mater*, *Inviolata*, *Salve, regina* and *Miserere mei*, and the music provided for them consists of freely varied versions of Josquin's own settings. Jacquet's unique act of homage suggests that Josquin's music was still known in Italy long after his death (see Dunning, 1969).

Josquin was praised by 16th-century literary figures such as Castiglione (*Libro del cortegiano*, 1528) and Rabelais (*Pantagruel*, 1533–5). He was the favourite composer of Luther, who said of him: 'Josquin is master of the notes, which must express what he desires; on the other hand, other choral composers must do what the notes dictate'. For Glarean, Josquin was first among all composers. Spataro and Lanfranco are among other theorists who specially praised him. Bartoli (1567; 35*v*), likened him to Michelangelo:

I know well that Ockeghem was, so to speak, the first who in these times rediscovered music, which had almost entirely died out – not in other wise than Donatello, who in his time rediscovered sculpture – and that Josquin, Ockeghem's pupil, may be said to have been, in music, a prodigy of nature, as our Michelangelo Buonarroti has been in architecture, painting and sculpture; for, as there has not thus far been anybody who in his compositions approaches Josquin, so Michelangelo, among all those who have been active in these his arts, is still alone and without a peer; both one and the other have opened the eyes of all those who delight in these arts or are to delight in them in the future.

Coclico (1552) paid tribute to Josquin as a teacher and gave what purports to be an account of his procedures. He stated that he was a pupil of Josquin, but he was given to making excessive claims, and his music provides little evidence of such distinguished training. His description rings true, however, and if he did not actually study with Josquin himself he may well have derived reliable information from someone who did. He wrote (trans. adapted from Smijers, 1926–7):

My teacher Josquin ... never gave a lecture on music or wrote a theoretical work, and yet he was able in a short time to form complete musicians, because he did not keep back his pupils with long and useless instructions but taught them the rules in a few words, through practical application in the course of singing. And as soon as he saw that his pupils were well grounded in singing, had a good enunciation and knew how to embellish melodies and fit the text to the music, then he taught them the perfect and imperfect intervals and the different methods of inventing counterpoints against plainsong. If he discovered, however, pupils with an ingenious mind and promising disposition, then he would teach these in a few words the rules of three-part and later of four-, five-, six-part, etc, writing, always providing them with examples to imitate. Josquin did not, however, consider all suited to learn composition; he judged that only those should be taught who were drawn to this delightful art by a special natural impulse.

Who may have been direct pupils of Josquin is open to question. Glarean (1547) referred to Févin as 'felix Jodoci aemulator' ('happy emulator of Josquin'). Although the only person testifying that Mouton was a pupil of Josquin is as late and peripheral a witness as Ronsard (in his *Meslanges des chansons*, 1560), there are resemblances between the two composers that might indicate such a relationship. Whether or not Févin and Mouton actually studied with Josquin, they were certainly much influenced by his style and helped to perpetuate it. Thus Willaert, according to Zarlino (in his *Dimostrationi harmoniche*, 1571), was a pupil of Mouton's, and Josquin's influence is clearly discernible in his writing. While, in the first half of the 16th century, the composers whose activities centred on Paris favoured a different style – decidedly more chordal and much less likely to incorporate canon – their contemporaries in the Low Countries continued to incline towards the earlier manner and to show the lasting effect of Josquin's influence. This is true not only of Gombert and Willaert but also of such composers as Clemens non Papa and Crecquillon. In the second half of the century, however, Josquin's influence declined, but even then Philippe de Monte wrote a parody mass based on his *Benedicta es, celorum regina*.

The rediscovery of Josquin may be said to have begun in the later 18th century with Burney, who scored various works by him, analysed the music and arrived at remarkably sound judgments. Similar in kind and at least as extraordinary in perception is the contribution of A. W. Ambros, which first appeared in 1868. The 20th century has seen the achievement of an edition of Josquin's works, largely by Albert Smijers (it was completed by Antonowycz and Elders). The list of Josquin scholars is large and distinguished and includes Charles van den Borren, Friedrich Blume and Helmuth Osthoff, whose two-volume study of the composer's life and works is a landmark in Josquin research. Another was the international Josquin festival and conference, whose moving spirit was Edward E. Lowinsky, held in New York in 1971 to mark the 450th anniversary of the composer's death. A new complete edition, incorporating the results of the most recent scholarship, is in course of preparation under the joint auspices of the Vereniging voor Nederlandse Muziekgeschiedenis (which published Smijers's edition), the American Musicological Society and the International Musicological Society.

CHAPTER THREE

Chronology of works

The evaluation of Josquin Desprez as by far the greatest composer of the high Renaissance, the most varied in invention and the most profound in expression, has become almost a commonplace of musical history, thanks to the work of scholars such as those mentioned above and of the performers who have helped to make his music known to modern audiences. And yet a total, organic picture of his creative development has been slow to appear, and it might be claimed with some justice that it has even now not come into sharp focus.

The reasons for this are not far to seek. Josquin's productive career was a long one, perhaps as much as 60 years, and the quantity of his music that survives is greater than that of any other composer of the period with the possible exception of Isaac. But the sources in which this music survives give relatively little help with its chronology. Music printing made its appearance only in the last two decades of Josquin's life; unlike later 16th-century publications, moreover, which almost always made a point of the novelty of their contents, Petrucci's earliest collections, both sacred and secular, are clearly anthologies drawn from the repertory of the previous 20 or even 30 years. For Josquin, the dates of Petrucci's publications provide only a *terminus ante quem*: how new or old a given composition may have been when it was published is something that has to be decided on other evidence. More surprising, perhaps, is the lack of information to be derived from manuscript sources. Time, war and enthusiasm (both religious and anti-religious) have wrought such destruction on the musical material of the later 15th century that very few manuscript copies of music by Josquin survive from before 1500. Yet the body of his surviving work is so large and so diverse that we cannot conveniently posit the loss of all his early music; some of it at least must be contained in these comparatively 'late' sources, though they themselves fail to provide an accurate date for its composition.

The works themselves also provide virtually no external historical evidence for dates of composition. The isorhythmic celebratory motets for specific and identifiable occasions, which provide such useful signposts in the generation of Dunstable and Dufay, had gone out of fashion by Josquin's time. Various topical references have been suggested by Osthoff, Lowinsky and others, and some of them may well be correct; but none has yet won universal acceptance, and even some of those that seemed most solidly documented (e.g. Osthoff's association of the chanson *Plus nulz regretz* with celebrations for the Treaty of Calais, New Year 1508) have been challenged by Kellman (1971). The elegy on the death of Ockeghem, *Nymphes des bois*, was presumably written soon after that event, now known to have taken place in February 1497, but Glarean's (1547) anecdotes associating particular works with particular patrons (Ascanio Sforza, Louis XII) could only be really useful if the facts of Josquin's life were more precisely known than they yet are. More definite, since it refers to a more restricted period, is Theophilo Folengo's information that the great psalm setting *Miserere mei, Deus* was composed at the request of Ercole d'Este, presumably, therefore, between April 1503 and April 1504, when Josquin was in his service at Ferrara, or at the latest by the following year, when Ercole died (see also pp.11–12).

The external evidence, then, is meagre, and yet for all its undoubted difficulty the question of chronology must be tackled, however speculatively, if the course of Josquin's development is to be understood. There is in fact little disagreement about its broad outlines. Commentators such as Ambros, Ursprung, Blume and Osthoff have all remarked on a move away from free-wheeling melisma towards motifs closely, often syllabically, related to the text; on the development of a technique of pervasive imitation between voices of equivalent importance that combines a rational and homogeneous integration of the musical space with a self-renewing rhythmic impetus; on a growing preoccupation with verbal texts, and on the development of a melodic and harmonic vocabulary capable of expressing their meaning in a totally new way. Through these developments Josquin's music, more than that of any other composer, represents the transition from the world of Dufay and Ockeghem to that of Willaert, Arcadelt and, eventually, Lassus and Palestrina.

Points of departure and arrival are clear enough; the stages of the journey have proved less easy to map convincingly. Ambros (1887–1911) recognized in Josquin's output the traditional three periods – early, middle and late – roughly corresponding to apprenticeship, maturity and the individual mastery that distinguishes only the last years of great composers. In dealing with the masses, in particular, Osthoff (1962–5) has attempted to give these periods more specific technical and temporal definition. For him the first period (lasting until about 1485, the year before Josquin's entry into the papal chapel) is characterized mainly by a rather abstract, melismatic counterpoint, deriving from Ockeghem, in which the relationship between verbal and musical phraseology is tenuous and inconsistent; the second period (ending about 1505, when Josquin had returned from Italy and settled at Condé-sur-Escaut) saw the development and perfection of the technique of pervasive imitation based on word-generated motifs; in the final period, lasting until Josquin's death, the relationship between word and note becomes closer than ever, and there is an increasing emphasis on declamation and rhetorical expression within a style of the utmost economy.

So far as it goes, this categorization is convincing, and only in one area has it been seriously challenged. Osthoff saw the mature, middle-period style as a synthesis of two traditions: the northern polyphony of Dufay, Busnois and Ockeghem in which Josquin presumably had his earliest training (a number of musical references suggest a closer relationship with Ockeghem than has yet been established biographically) and the more chordal, harmonically orientated practice of Italy, as exemplified in improvised *falsobordone* and *lauda*. He also accepted the traditional view that this process must have begun in the 1470s, when Josquin and several of his most talented contemporaries were gathered together in the lavish musical establishment of Galeazzo Maria Sforza at Milan. Against this Lowinsky (1963) has argued that our knowledge of the *laude* and their composers does not permit the assumption that

25

such an influence existed before the 1490s; thus it would follow that such pieces as the Elevation motet *Tu solus qui facis mirabilia* and the Passiontide cycle *O Domine Jesu Christe*, both almost entirely homophonic in texture, would belong not to the Milanese years but to the later Roman ones. The arguments for this theory have yet to be tested in detail, but it may be observed that other possible sources for a homophonic style exist (the chordal passages in northern music of the Dufay generation, for instance) or may have existed (a *lauda* tradition of which Petrucci's publications would represent only the later stages). A distinction should surely be drawn, too, between the concise rhetorical declamation of Josquin's later works and the slow-moving chords (with frequent melismas in the individual voice parts) of the Passiontide motet; such details as the sudden floridness of its final 'Amen' seem to place it altogether earlier than a flexible but homogeneous work such as *Ave Maria, gratia plena . . . virgo serena.*

CHAPTER FOUR

Motets

I Early and middle-period works

Ave Maria . . . virgo serena was chosen by Petrucci to stand
at the head of his first motet collection, *Motetti A* (1502),
and can hardly have been composed much more than 15
years earlier. (Thomas L. Noblitt's claim, in his study of
Munich, Bayerische Staatsbibliothek MS 3154 – published in *Die Musikforschung*, xxvii, 1974, p.36 – that it
was copied into that manuscript about 1476 rests on
questionable assumptions.) So well, in fact, does it typify
the motet style of Josquin's middle years that it seems
appropriate before embarking on a selective survey of
his work in this field (following, in the main, Osthoff's
periodization), to start with some account of it, if only to
suggest the distance he had already travelled by the mid-
1480s.

Its apparent simplicity conceals great subtlety and
technical mastery. The basic texture is imitative, yet
each section of the text is given a slightly different
treatment. For the opening words of the angelic salutation there is literal imitation at the octave or unison,
working (no doubt with symbolic intent) from the highest voice to the lowest; each phrase overlaps its
predecessor, but in such a way that all four voices are
heard together only in the three bars before the first
main cadence. For the first strophe of the rhyming
votive antiphon which follows, a duet of upper voices is

27

imitated by a trio of lower ones, leading more quickly this time into a longer full section whose denser texture is enlivened by sequence and close internal imitation; for the second strophe, duets of lower and upper voices, now imitating one another at the 5th, converge briefly to form a four-part texture, which then tapers away to the unrelieved duet of the third strophe. This is cunningly placed to enhance the effect of the crucial fourth strophe, 'Ave vera virginitas', whose four-part texture is given rhythmic life and a delicate pathos by the close canon between superius and tenor; then, after a fifth strophe in which this almost purely harmonic texture is resolved into melodic imitation once more, the motet ends, after a whole bar's pause, with a chordal invocation of almost stark simplicity. The musical form precisely mirrors that of the text, yet without any sense of constraint; articulation is achieved by subtle changes of procedure and texture, but with no loss of onward momentum in spite of the fact that every main cadence falls on C.

The frequent imitative duets that give this motet its characteristic transparency recur as a favourite device in Josquin's music, early and late. That they do not occur at all in the first section of the four-part setting of the Easter sequence *Victimae paschali laudes*, also published in *Motetti A*, suggests that this may be one of his earliest surviving motets. As Glarean (1547; iii, 24) pointed out, it is an ingenious piece in that it combines the plainsong melody (mostly in the tenor, but occasionally migrating to the two other lower voices) with the superius of two well-known chansons, first Ockeghem's *D'ung aultre amer* and then Hayne van Ghizeghem's *De tous biens playne*; yet the texture is uncharacteristically dense and is articulated by scarcely a trace of imitation until the lengthy duet that begins the second part. Patches of stagnant rhythm and a hole in the texture near the end which leaves the top voice momentarily isolated confirm the impression that this motet belongs to Josquin's prentice years.

Similar details of dissonance treatment and rhythm in some of its movements suggest that the motet cycle *Vultum tuum deprecabuntur* (clearly a set of *motetti missales*, to judge by both text and structure) must also be reckoned among Josquin's earliest surviving works; it is very likely to have been composed for Milan, where the liturgically dubious practice of systematically substituting motets for sections of the Ordinary of the Mass seems to have been most frequently indulged. A second Passiontide motet cycle, however, seems more advanced in style than *O Domine Jesu Christe*, mentioned above. *Qui velatus facie fuisti* (on a text attributed to St Bonaventure) has a swifter harmonic movement and a more varied texture; only one section, 'Honor et benedictio', is purely homophonic, and in this it presents an analogy (see p.42 below) with the Elevation motet *Tu solus qui facis mirabilia* – indeed, it reappears as an Elevation motet in the separately printed *Sanctus de Passione*. The association of chordal writing of this kind with moments of particular solemnity and devotion remains a feature of Josquin's style even in works that belong indisputably to his last years (cf the 'Et incarnatus est' of the *Missa 'Pange lingua'* and the words 'Et verbum caro factum est' in the motet *In principio*).

Earlier than any of these at first sight are two motets that both begin in the old-fashioned triple metre and with long melismatic duets of a kind that could almost have been written by Dufay. *Alma Redemptoris mater/*

Ave regina celorum combines paraphrases of both plainsong antiphons, *Ave regina* in the two equal middle voices, *Alma Redemptoris* in the outer ones; there is fairly consistent imitation between the pairs of voices based on the same material, but a rather heavy reliance on scalic note-spinning. Formally very similar, but musically more accomplished, is the five-part 'signed' motet *Illibata Dei virgo nutrix*, whose text presents Josquin's name as an acrostic. The structure is articulated, not only texturally, by the contrast between duets and full sections, whose alternation is gradually telescoped, but also by the presence of a transposing three-note *pes* or ostinato cantus firmus, sung in the tenor to a solmization of the word 'Maria'. Jejune as this phrase is in itself (it appears alternately as D–A–D and G–D–G), Josquin's use of it looks forward to preoc-cupations and procedures that recur in much later large-scale works: the gradual speeding-up of the statements, for instance, which can be seen as a last vestige of the old isorhythmic tradition but is here used to achieve a climactic integration, not only musical but also textual, with the other voices (cf *Ave nobilissima creatura* and *O virgo prudentissima*, both among Josquin's maturest masterpieces); the clearly articulated solo and full sec-tions; the concern for metrical variety, and not least the readiness to use straightforward musical repetition (here of a whole 12-bar clause) to build up the intensity of the final invocation to the Virgin. Though the range and abruptness of its stylistic contrasts make it probable that *Illibata* is a relatively early work, it already shows a mastery of at least one of the features in which Josquin is pre-eminent among his contemporaries: a control of large-scale musical architecture.

As a five-part work on a cantus firmus, however, *Illibata* stands slightly to one side of the main line of development leading to the homogeneous imitative texture displayed in *Ave Maria . . . virgo serena*. More relevant stages are marked by *Virgo prudentissima*, *Missus est Gabriel angelus* and the cycle of antiphons for the Circumcision, *O admirabile commercium*, which may betray a lack of complete maturity in its exclusive reliance on imitative texture (in this it is the counterpart of the almost exclusively homophonic *O Domine Jesu Christe*). *Gaude virgo, mater Christi*, on the other hand, with its climactic move into near-homophony and its relatively close matching of words and notes, seems like a small-scale study for *Ave Maria . . . virgo serena*.

Perhaps even more impressive are three motets (all published in *Motetti C*, 1504) which show Josquin's ability to set a long text in prose without recourse either to a cantus firmus scaffolding or to more than a bare minimum of plainsong reference; here the music derives its shape and its self-renewing impetus only from the free flow of original musical ideas. *Liber generationis* and *Factum est autem* may well be companion-pieces, perhaps composed for the papal chapel. They are settings of the genealogies of Christ taken from St Matthew's and St Luke's gospels and sung, before the Tridentine reforms, at Matins of Christmas and Epiphany respectively. In each, Josquin's only musical datum was a repetitive reciting-tone, and the variety with which he contrived to invest a singularly uninspiring text is astonishing. Even more striking, however, is the intensity he achieved in his setting of the lament of David for Saul and Jonathan, *Planxit autem David*; here the predominantly homophonic texture of the

2. Alto (top) and tenor parts of Josquin Desprez's motet 'Absalon, fili mi', from the MS copied by Alamire.

Passiontide motets is combined and varied with freely
imitative passages, out of which the Holy Week lamen-
tation tone emerges in long notes like a ritual keening.
Shorter, but even more expressive, is another lament of
David, *Absalon, fili mi*, which probably commemorates
the death either of Pope Alexander VI's son in 1497 or
of the Emperor Maximilian I's in 1506. Freely composed, it achieves its effect through a typically flexible
combination of textures; set at an unusually low pitch
(in the original notation the bass descends at the end to
B♭′) and in an unusually flat key, the concluding
sequence threatens to move the music still further
flatwards – a passage that may have been the starting-
point for more far-reaching tonal experiments by
Willaert and the later 16th-century exponents of *musica
reservata*.

II Later works

The motets that Josquin apparently composed, so far as
the external and internal evidence suggests, in the last
20 years of his life stand on a high plateau of mastery
where technical means are subordinated to formal and
expressive ends; so far as any continuing development
can be detected, it is in the direction of still further
motivic density and melodic succinctness (though extended melismas reappear at times), together with formal clarity. They fall into two main groups: settings of
biblical texts, mostly from the Psalms and freely composed in four parts, and large-scale five- or six-part
works based on cantus firmi, in which Josquin seems to
have discovered a renewed interest in his old age.

Whereas most of these cantus firmi are drawn from
the repertory of plainsong, in which Josquin's imagina-

tion was clearly steeped, *Stabat mater* is based on the tenor of Binchois' symbolically appropriate chanson *Comme femme desconfortée*, sung or played straight through in notes four times the length of the original. In contrast to this apparently archaic procedure, the remaining voices are in Josquin's most modern manner, their rhythms and phrasing declamatory, with the minim as the basic note value. This piece could only be by Josquin, but Lowinsky (MRM, iii, 223) is surely right to deny the authenticity of the only other motet attributed to him (and strongly) in which the cantus firmus has similar characteristics, a five-part setting of *Missus est Gabriel*; the tenor is borrowed from Busnois' *A une dame j'ay faict veu*, but the remaining voices are quite uncharacteristic of Josquin in their lack of imitative integration. Another exceptional cantus firmus is that of *Miserere mei, Deus*, composed, as has been mentioned above (pp.11 and 24), for Ercole d'Este. Here the two-pitch phrase to which the opening words are sung is shifted step by step – first downwards through an octave, then, in the second part of the motet, up again, and finally down a 5th to rest on A. Between its appearances, which usually coincide with a passage of full five-part texture, various smaller groups propound the verses of the long penitential psalm text; into these the phrase 'Miserere mei Deus' strikes like the refrain of a litany, though varied in both pitch and interval, since the modal structure ensures that it covers sometimes a tone, sometimes a semitone.

Two further motets, of very different character, provide something of a puzzle. These are *Ave nobilissima creatura*, a generalized salutation to the Virgin, and *Huc me sydereo*, a setting of elegiacs by the humanist

Maffeo Veggio in which Christ speaks from the cross of the divine love he represents and the love he demands in return. Their cantus firmi are identical in pitch and almost in rhythmic organization, though bearing different texts, respectively 'Benedicta tu in mulieribus' and 'Plangent eum quasi unigenitum' (cf Elders, 1971). One might imagine that Josquin had taken advantage of the musical identity of these two antiphons to compose a contrasting pair of motets, if the sixth voice missing in two important sources of *Huc* were not an obvious addition to the original texture, while *Ave nobilissima* was clearly conceived from the start in six parts. The explanation may be that *Huc* was composed first, for five voices, and that Josquin, later wishing to provide a companion-piece (perhaps for some dramatic performance representing both the Annunciation and the Crucifixion), both devised the text of *Ave nobilissima* (the words 'Ave Maria gratia plena, Dominus tecum' are placed precisely so that the tenor's entry with 'benedicta tu in mulieribus' will complete them) and also added a sixth voice to the earlier *Huc me sydereo* to increase the symmetry between the two motets. Placidly beautiful as the Annunciation motet is, that for the Crucifixion makes the deeper impression. The sophistication of the text is fully matched in Josquin's setting, which abounds in affective devices and word-painting: the melodic descent from the trebles' highest note to the basses' lowest to illustrate Christ's descent from 'Olympus'; the plangent fall of a 3rd to emphasize such words as 'crudeli' and 'durae' (a hallmark of Josquin's later style); the repeated phrase at 'verbera tanta pati' (singled out for its pathos by the publisher Hans Ott in the preface to the second part of his *Novum et insigne opus musicum*, 1538); and a

35

constant attention to clear and effective declamation.

In both these motets the cantus firmus is gradually speeded up to converge with the tempo of the surrounding voices, a feature already encountered in *Illibata*. The beautiful five-part *Salve, regina* takes up another feature of that seminal work, the controlled oscillation of a motif (this time the memorable four-note phrase that begins the relevant plainsong) between pitches a 4th apart. More commonly, though, Josquin achieved a similar effect by a canonic treatment of the cantus firmus, sometimes combined with a progressive reduction in note values. This may be rather freely handled, as in *Virgo salutiferi*, a work very probably written at Ferrara, since its text is by a Ferrarese court poet, Ercole Strozzi (see p.11 above). Here the superius and tenor at first present only the beginning of the angelic salutation 'Ave Maria gratia plena, Dominus tecum', in canon at the octave; in the second section the reduction of note values is nearly proportional, but in the course of the last the process is reversed and the salutation completed. In *Benedicta es, celorum regina* the canon is at the octave, but free in its time interval and in other details. More usually, though, the canon is at the 5th, as in *Inviolata, integra et casta* and in the transparently beautiful setting of Poliziano's Latin poem *O virgo prudentissima*; the superbly sonorous *Veni, Sancte Spiritus*, whose six voices contain two distinct canons at the 5th, may be by Forestier (see Blackburn, 1976).

In this last work, as in the texturally similar but in fact freely composed *Praeter rerum seriem*, plainsong melodies well known in Josquin's day are highlighted by the use of long note values, but in some of the very last motets the canons are dissolved, as it were, into the general texture, so that their structural function is hardly apparent to the listener. This is true, for instance, of the linked *Pater noster* and *Ave Maria* (a work not so much austere as sombre, which Kellman's research at Condé (1971) has shown to be Josquin's musical testament) and of the magnificent five-part *De profundis*, where the mourning of the three estates of the realm is symbolized by a canon at the 4th and the octave below. In all these works the canons perform a multiple function, partly symbolic, partly structural. As the strictest form of imitation they produce, on a larger scale, the same kind of textural integration as does the imitation between contrapuntal motifs. At the 5th, moreover, they help to ensure a certain alternation of tonal centre and thus to provide a controlled variety in the settings of large-scale texts (and not only large-scale ones, as can be seen in the late five- and six-part chansons, discussed on p.62 below).

Compared with a series of masterpieces such as these, it must be admitted that the other main category of apparently late works, the psalm settings, shows no such uniformity of excellence. The best of them – *Memor esto verbi tui*, for instance, or the setting for low voices of *Domine, ne in furore tuo* – are characterized by the same dense, and tense, motivic development, the same close attention to declamation and an even more vivid response to the meaning of the words. It may be noted that the two works mentioned both occur in sources printed in Josquin's lifetime, the first and third books of Petrucci's *Motetti de la corona* (1514, 1519) respectively. Many of the rest were first printed in Petreius's psalm collections (Nuremberg, 1538, 1539 and 1542) some 20 years after Josquin's death, and it is perhaps in order to view them with a certain scepticism. Works like *Usquequo, Domine* and *Celi enarrant* present some of the more obvious features of the 'Josquin style', notably his paired duets, but in comparison with the works already discussed their motivic development seems short-breathed and mechanical and their four-part writing often rhythmically congested and clumsy. Even a work such as *Benedicite omnia opera*, which has a far more consistent impetus than most and contains several distinctive features, such as the harmonic oscillation at 'glacies et nives', also commits a solecism of word-setting (at bar 131) which it is hard to imagine the mature Josquin permitting himself.

For a superb example of Josquin's late four-part style – as definitive in its way as the *Ave Maria* is for the middle period – we need look no further than *In principio erat verbum*, which stands first in an incomplete set of partbooks copied, evidently in the Netherlands, for Raimund Fugger (and containing two more, probably authentic, psalm settings). The texture is as transparent as ever, with its preponderance of duets, and characteristically it makes continuous reference to the underlying recitation tone, but with a variety of texture and an impetus informing the austerity that makes it possible to cover 14 verses of St John's gospel with no trace of monotony. Sparks (1971) has convincingly demonstrated the unauthenticity, on stylistic grounds, of a group of five- and six-part motets, three of which first appear in even later German publications; perhaps, with the touchstone of *In principio* to hand, it may be possible to subject the posthumously published psalms to a similar critical scrutiny. If so, it will perhaps have to be recognized that some at least are no more than a well-intentioned attempt to cater for the new Lutheran market with works supposedly by Luther's favourite composer. But fortunately a large enough body of authentic motets will remain to prove that he was indeed 'the master of the notes' that Luther called him.

CHAPTER FIVE

Masses

Josquin's motets, with their exceptionally wide-ranging choice of texts, show him at his most varied as a composer; yet taken as a whole the motets can be regarded as an appendix to the liturgy rather than as an essential part of it. Much work remains to be done on the liturgical practice of Josquin's day, but it seems likely that apart from the Mass itself polyphony was still generally confined (at least outside Germany) to the more peripheral parts of the services – hymns, *Magnificat* settings, antiphons for Vespers, for Compline or for votive Offices of the Virgin; the remainder of the prescribed texts would still be sung in plainsong, with or without the collaboration of the organ. But for some half a century the practice of singing the five main sections of the Ordinary of the Mass (Kyrie, Gloria, Credo, Sanctus and Agnus Dei) as a musically related cycle had been growing in the major collegiate churches and princely chapels. This development corresponded roughly with the lifetime of Dufay, in whose later masses the essential outlines of the form are fully developed and some of its characteristic procedures explored. It was confined at first to the greatest occasions of church and state, but it gained ground rapidly, and by the end of the century it had become a common, perhaps even daily, occurrence in churches that boasted a professional band of singers.

The demand was great, and so too was the challenge

to the composer: on the liturgical level, that of worthily adorning the Christian Church's central rite; musically, that of reconciling the claims of unity and diversity within a span of music lasting in all some half an hour or more. Thus stimulated, the best composers of Josquin's generation consciously vied with one another in following up the implications of mass settings by such acknowledged masters as Dufay and Ockeghem. If Josquin's own contribution to the form seems as a whole less forward-looking in style than his motets, this could be because the bulk of the masses were composed a little earlier in his career but also, even more probably, because of the inherent nature of the task, which places as much emphasis on structure as on expression. Although fewer of his masses survive than those of such younger contemporaries as Isaac, Obrecht and La Rue, the fact that Petrucci, in his series of mass publications, chose to devote three volumes to Josquin and no more than one to anyone else is some indication of his acknowledged supremacy in this field. This supremacy was based on his ability, at least in his mature masses, to combine an inexhaustible constructive power with a wealth of detailed invention that very rarely becomes completely abstract, even if it does not aim at the detailed expressiveness found in some of the motets.

I Individual mass sections

As well as full-scale masses, Josquin, like others, seems to have composed a number of isolated mass sections, perhaps for more modest occasions or establishments. Several are to be found in Petrucci's *Fragmenta missarum* (1505). Some of these, however, are found with conflicting attributions in manuscript sources, and it may be noted that only two are ascribed to Josquin in the body of Petrucci's text (superius volume); the remainder are given to him only in the index which precedes each partbook.

Of the individual mass sections that may, on stylistic grounds, be reasonably accepted as Josquin's, the *Gloria de beata virgine* (based on Gloria IX, including the tropes that were soon to be abolished by the Tridentine reforms) shows vigour and imagination in its range of rhythmic contrast and bold use of sequence, though the frequent use of incomplete triads points to an early date. The *Credo 'De tous biens'* is also attributed to Josquin in a Roman manuscript, but it is uncharacteristic both in its dissonance treatment and in its excessively bald use of the tenor of Hayne's chanson; however, the first of the Credos labelled 'Vilayge' (for the meaning of this term see Van den Borren, 1962), though exceedingly unvaried in texture for its length, could certainly be an early work by Josquin. The *Sanctus de Passione* incorporates (as has been noted on p.29) the chordal 'Honor et benedictio' section that also forms part of the motet *Qui velatus facie fuisti*; no plainsong reference has yet been identified in the Sanctus itself, but further research may clarify the liturgical connections between it and the motet. The *Sanctus 'D'ung aultre amer'* is also accompanied by a short homophonic motet, *Tu lumen, tu splendor Patris*, in this case apparently placed after the second 'Osanna'. The text of this motet is the second verse of the Christmas hymn *Christe redemptor omnium*, but since the setting makes no reference to the hymn melody it is likely that no close liturgical connection with Christmas is implied; Sanctus and Benedictus themselves each combine the superius of

Ockeghem's chanson with, it seems, a version of the plainsong for ferial days in Advent and Lent, which suggests that this too may be a setting 'de Passione'. The combination of *D'ung aultre amer* (principally the tenor of the chanson this time) and the Lenten plainsong is also found in the Sanctus and Agnus Dei of Josquin's *Missa 'D'ung aultre amer'*; this work, in common with some by Gaffurius explicitly labelled 'missae breves', is built on an exceptionally small scale with rapid parlando declamation in the Gloria and Credo; it too may have been designed for ferial use in penitential seasons. Like the above-mentioned Sanctus settings, it contains an Elevation motet (the first half of *Tu solus qui facis mirabilia*), this time not merely attached to the Benedictus but replacing it altogether. The mass is compositionally more sophisticated and presumably later in date than the separate Sanctus settings, though because of its exceptional character it is particularly difficult to place in relation to Josquin's other complete settings of the Ordinary.

II Introduction to the complete masses

The sources again give very little help to an attempt to trace the development of Josquin's complete mass settings in a roughly chronological order, and for the same reasons that have been stated in connection with the motets. Of the three Petrucci volumes which together contain all but one of Josquin's surviving masses, the first (1502) is the most homogeneous in style; the five works in it could all have been composed within the preceding 15 years (roughly speaking, Josquin's Roman period). The *Liber secundus* (1505) combines recent works such as *Ave maris stella* and perhaps *Hercules*

Dux Ferrarie with others (*L'ami Baudichon* and *Une musque de Biscaye*) which are clearly earlier than anything in the former volume. And when, after his removal to Fossombrone, Petrucci assembled yet a third collection of Josquin's masses, he was once again forced to include works from widely different periods: the *Missa de beata virgine* is, on both internal and external evidence (Glarean, iii, 24, again), a late work, but the *Missa di dadi* could only be an early one, and the remainder fall stylistically at various points in between (or, in the case of the *Missa 'Mater Patris'*, to one side).

A categorization by genre is no more helpful. As has been noted, Josquin came on the scene at a time when the field for stylistic experiment was wide open. The strict cantus firmus mass, drawing its musical unity primarily from a tenor part borrowed either from the Gregorian repertory or from that of secular song, was already beginning to show its limitations, while of the two techniques that were to become standardized in the 16th century – paraphrase of a plainsong melody, and so-called 'parody' (the transformation of a pre-existing polyphonic composition) – neither had yet become customary, let alone a matter of routine. Elements of all three types are mingled in many of Josquin's masses, and in various proportions. Sometimes Josquin restricted his borrowed material strictly to the tenor, in the old-fashioned manner (*L'ami Baudichon*, *L'homme armé super voces musicales*, *Hercules Dux Ferrarie*), sometimes the ostinato principle inherent in that technique was allowed to permeate the texture (*Faisant regretz*, *Gaudeamus*, *La sol fa re mi*); in other works he seems to be moving instinctively towards 'parody' of a complete composition (*Fortuna desperata*, *Malheur me bat*), while in two (*Ad fugam*, *Sine nomine*) and in the last three sections of *De beata virgine* he elevated strict canon to the governing principle for an entire work. (In *De beata virgine*, too, the technique of paraphrasing the appropriate plainsong, with which Josquin often played more or less consistently in his settings of the Credo, is employed throughout a mass.) But none of these groups can be assigned at all convincingly to a single period of Josquin's career. In general his instinct, at least in his mature works, seems to be to extract as much variety as possible from his given musical material, sacred or secular, by any appropriate means.

The relative poverty or wealth of resources that Josquin brought to his musical datum (of whatever kind) is therefore one of the criteria that have to be used in assessing the dates of his masses. Others are the extent to which that datum permeates the whole texture (a factor related to, but not identical with, the extent of imitative writing); the closeness or otherwise of the relationship between text and music, on both declamatory and expressive levels; the extent of agreement with the formal divisions that had become customary by the time of Josquin's death (separate sections for the 'Qui tollis' in the Gloria, the 'Et incarnatus', or 'Crucifixus', and 'Et in Spiritum Sanctum' in the Credo); and the extent to which he achieved a satisfactory musical climax in the final section or sections – though it should be borne in mind that these are particularly vulnerable to liturgically motivated pruning, to judge by the surviving sources.

III Early masses
None of the foregoing criteria for dating the masses is

alone sufficient to justify identification of a particular mass as early or late; they must be balanced against one another, and that is inevitably a subjective matter which can produce disagreement, as can be seen by comparing even the two most recent comprehensive accounts, those of Osthoff (1962–5) and Sparks (1963), let alone that of Ambros (1887–1911). Sparks and Osthoff are, however, in entire agreement in placing *L'ami Baudichon* as one of the very earliest of Josquin's surviving masses. It is a cantus firmus mass, based on an exceedingly simple dance formula (very like the first two phrases of *Three Blind Mice*); this is not quoted in any other voice than the tenor, except perhaps in inversion at the beginning of the 'Crucifixus'. As Sparks pointed out, the use of a virtually unchanging head-motif, the simplicity of melody and rhythm and the clarity of texture and harmony are strongly reminiscent of the later Dufay and must be taken as 'proof of a direct influence of the Burgundian style of the 1450s and 1460s'. It has been noted above (p.28) that among Josquin's early motets simplicity and clarity seem to be found side by side with a certain clumsiness, and it is only in the light of this that the *Missa 'Une musque de Biscaye'* can be accepted as being by Josquin at all, although the only known manuscript sources ascribe it unambiguously to him, and Petrucci included it in his *Liber secundus*. The basic tune (another secular melody, with a strongly marked popular character and a tonally anomalous ending) appears, or at least is referred to, in all voices, particularly superius and tenor, but with a lack of clarity and consistency that is quite uncharacteristic. Any attempt to regard this as mature richness of invention is contradicted by crudities of part-writing and dissonance treatment that are more frequent here than in any of Josquin's other masses. If this mass is by him, it must be early; and if it is early it reveals a quite different aspect of his character from *L'ami Baudichon*. The absence of any independent music at all for the Agnus Dei (it is directed to be sung to that of the Kyrie) also suggests a very early date, since Josquin soon learnt to invest the final section of the mass with a musically climactic character. This is apparent even in a work like the *Missa di dadi*, so called from the peculiarity that the proportions by which the tenor's notation is to be augmented in each section are indicated by dice faces, at least in the only known source, Petrucci's *Liber tertius*. The work is clearly early, to judge by its relative lack of imitation and general simplicity of style, but in the final Agnus the cantus firmus (the tenor of Morton's chanson *N'aray-je jamais mieulx*) is for the first time taken out of the tenor and stated, a 4th lower, in the bass; for the first time, moreover, it is allowed to penetrate the rest of the contrapuntal fabric. Here the use of ostinato suggests the influence of Busnois rather than Dufay.

Different features of the *Missa di dadi* are taken up and explored separately in two more masses which can hardly be very much later. In *Faisant regretz* the ostinato use of a single four-note catch-phrase (taken from the second half of a rondeau by Walter Frye) forms the guiding principle of the whole work; one begins to sense the power of an imagination that thrives on self-imposed limitations. In *Fortuna desperata*, on the other hand, Josquin made altogether freer use of the anonymous chanson that served as his model; all three of its voices are used separately as cantus firmi in different sections of the mass, but the relative looseness of musical con-

nection that this engenders is to some extent compen-
sated by brief quotations from the original three-part
complex – perhaps the first instances of the parody
principle in Josquin's music. (In the first of the two
sections of the Agnus Dei, the original superius is trans-
posed down, augmented and inverted, to form the bass
of Josquin's counterpoint, and Lowinsky (1943) has
seen in this a symbolic representation of the turn of
Fortune's wheel; it may be so, but in the second section
it is the chanson tenor's turn to be pushed to the bottom
of the texture, and it is not inverted, which seems to
weaken the force of the symbolism.) In *Mater Patris*
Josquin made a point of borrowing at least two voices at
a time from the three-part motet by Brumel on which
the mass is based; the Agnus Dei, indeed, consists of the
entire text of Brumel's motet, with two new voices added
to it – a technique for which there are analogues in
Josquin's secular music, but which it is surprising to
find him using so literal-mindedly in the climactic section of a mass. The rather stiff alternation of contrapuntal two-part and chordal four-part texture elsewhere in
the work can be seen, perhaps, as a deliberate exploita-
tion of a feature of the motet, but the structure of the
chords themselves – the upper voices often moving in
parallel 6-4s with a free bass beneath – is found nowhere else in Josquin's music; although the strictly
canonic duos which form the 'Pleni sunt coeli',
Benedictus and Agnus Dei point towards his later practice, they seem short of his usual rhythmic élan. *Mater
Patris* is an exceptional work – exceptional enough to
make Josquin's authorship questionable, but also
enough to make it very difficult to suggest anyone else
as its composer.

Canonic writing, which is a regular resource of Josquin's mature counterpoint, in both melodic and structural contexts, has been met with only sporadically in the masses so far discussed; further examples are the Benedictus of the *Missa di dadi* (where strictness is abandoned three-quarters of the way through) and the 'Osanna' of *Faisant regretz* (the tenor and bass of a four-part texture). In two masses, however, Josquin used it as his main principle of construction in almost every section. Of these the earlier is certainly the *Missa ad fugam*, unified not only by its canonic procedures but by a head-motif of no fewer than ten bars, repeated literally at the beginning of every section (Osthoff suggested that the different versions of Sanctus and Agnus Dei in one source, MS 31 in the Universitätsbibliothek in Jena, where the head-motif of the mass is much abbreviated, may represent Josquin's own second thoughts about this). In this mass, superius and tenor are in canon throughout all sections except the Benedictus (all but the 'Pleni' and 'Qui venit' in the Jena version); the alto quite often joins in the imitative game, but the bass remains aloof. In the *Missa sine nomine*, on the other hand, not only are the canons themselves distributed through all voices in turn; all voices including the bass share in the imitative texture. This mass, indeed, comes close in style to those of the very last period of Josquin's life, when technical mastery is simultaneously deployed and concealed and is subordinated to the claims of clarity and expression.

IV Mature masses

Before he reached that final stage of his musical development, however, Josquin seems first to have passed through a period of confident maturity in which every resource, both of compositional technique and of vocal virtuosity, is deployed with something like bravura. To this period belong some six or seven masterpieces which are difficult to set in any completely convincing chronological order precisely because they explore different paths and solve different problems with nearly equal accomplishment. Yet distinctions can be made. Of the two masses based on plainsong melodies, for instance, *Gaudeamus* is surely earlier than *Ave maris stella*, *Gaudeamus* combines cantus firmus techniques and those of ostinato with vigour and inventiveness, working to a magnificent climax in the final Agnus, where the memorable opening phrase of the introit melody is put through a vertiginous series of transpositions. Yet the sheer musical inventiveness of this work at times conflicts with the effective presentation of the text; in *Ave maris stella* the musical phraseology is more carefully matched to that of the words. Imitation is frequent in both works, but the texture of *Ave maris stella* is even more fully permeated by motifs drawn from the cantus firmus. Its use of canon also seems more structural: where *Gaudeamus* contains only a single extended canon (the second Agnus), *Ave maris stella* uses canon in all three of the Agnus sections. Comparing the two masses as a whole, one senses that in *Ave maris stella* the exuberance of *Gaudeamus* has begun to be tamed, even spiritualized.

The Janus-faced quality of Josquin's genius (and the difficulties this poses for historians) is well illustrated by the *Missa 'Malheur me bat'*. Like *Fortuna desperata* it is based on a chanson (variously attributed to Ockeghem, Martini and 'Malcort') and again makes very literal use of all three voice parts, separately and occasionally together, in an idiosyncratic linking of cantus firmus and incipient parody techniques. But various features indicate a later date for *Malheur me bat*: the calculated fantasy with which the Gloria's cantus firmus is laid out (two complete statements, but fragmented and shuffled), the considerable amount of imitative and strictly can-onic writing, and above all the concluding six-part Agnus. Here the original chanson's superius and tenor are sumptuously reclothed in a new texture woven from two close canons, a procedure which at once links this work with the probably later *L'homme armé sexti toni* and *Hercules Dux Ferrarie* masses. The second of these also illustrates the dangers of attempting to date Josquin's mature masses by a single criterion rather than by balancing several. It was composed as a tribute to Josquin's patron Ercole d'Este, and its cantus firmus is derived from a solmization of the title (*re, ut, re, ut, re, fa, mi, re* = D, C, D, C, D, F, E, D), a phrase as unpromising musically as it was complimentary to the duke. This may be one reason why Josquin con-spicuously confined it to the cantus firmus voice (usually the tenor, occasionally the superius), weaving around it a texture that is imitative within itself but melodically quite unrelated. If homogeneity of all four voices were the only criterion of Josquin's mature style one would have to place this mass among his earliest, but the declamation and imitation in the non-cantus firmus voices suggest that it belongs somewhere between *Gaudeamus* and *Ave maris stella*, and probably nearer the latter. The extensive use of canon also suggests a relatively late date: between alto and bass at the 5th in the 'Pleni'; between superius, alto and bass in the second

Agnus; and, in the last, a quasi-canonic antiphony between the upper three voices and the lower three of a
texture specially expanded to six, which at once recalls
such six-part motets as *Veni, Sancte Spiritus* and
Praeter rerum seriem. The systematic transposition of
the cantus firmus to the 5th and octave above, and the
proportionally controlled speed of its statements, also
relate this mass to the later motets.

Josquin's two masses on the famous *L'homme armé*
tune are both mature works yet extraordinarily contrasted in style. Of the two, that described as *super voces
musicales* is certainly the earlier, for all its ingenuity.
The title indicates that the melody is presented starting
in turn on every note of the natural hexachord – on C in
the Kyrie, D in the Gloria etc, up to A in the Agnus
Dei; since the music is in the D mode throughout, this
gives rise to some piquant shifts of tonal centre and
changes in the interval structure of the melody. The
element of compositional virtuosity is at once apparent
in the Kyrie, which presents the three sections of the
cantus firmus successively in mensuration canon between the tenor and each of the other voices in turn, but
it also enters into those sections of the work from which
the cantus firmus is absent: the Benedictus is a sequence
of three mensuration canons, each for two equal voices,
while the second Agnus is a mensuration canon for
three.

As with *Gaudeamus*, the work dazzles as much by
its intellectual energy as by its eloquence. It is possible
that the various processes through which Josquin put
his melody in the course of it may have suggested certain features which are exploited in his other *L'homme*

armé mass. This is described as 'sexti toni' (in the 6th mode) because the melody appears here with F as its final instead of the more usual G; this in practice gives it the major character that it has in Morton's chanson setting and in Ockeghem's mass, as against the minor character favoured by most other composers (including Dufay, Busnois, Tinctoris and Brumel). Apart from this transposition, the other features that may have been borrowed from the mass *super voces musicales* is that of retrograde statement of the theme: instead of presenting the two versions, direct and retrograde, successively, as he did in the Gloria and Credo of *super voces*, in the final Agnus Dei of *sexti toni* Josquin presented both versions in long notes simultaneously and then bedecked this severely intellectual scaffolding with two more close canons at the unison – a tour de force of musical skill that has few equals in the music of the period. Yet the hallmark of *L'homme armé sexti toni* is not strictness but freedom and variety. The melody appears in various speeds and rhythms in all voices, now complete, now with a single section repeated in ostinato or canon. And yet for all this wealth of contrapuntal fantasy, the expressive relationship with the words is never forgotten.

Josquin's ability to spin much out of little is even more strikingly shown in *La sol fa re mi*, whose basic material is no more than a solmization pun. Virtually the whole mass is derived from this single five-note phrase; even allowing for shifts between hexachords in interpreting the solmization syllables, it is a breathtaking feat of sheer inventiveness. Technically it is both a return to, and an extension of, the style of *Faisant regretz*: once again ostinato is much in evidence (inevitably), but the subtlety with which the basic figure is varied and the ease with which it permeates the entire texture show an enormous advance on the earlier work.

V Last masses

The masses of Josquin's high maturity already discussed establish securely his reputation in this genre as the supreme exponent of both the main trends of his time: free fantasy and rational organization. But in his old age he continued to develop. The exuberance, as has already been suggested, falls away – or at least is subsumed into a style that aims rather at inward communication of the essence of the sacred texts than at their outward adornment and expression. Together with this it is perhaps possible to detect a certain turning back to earlier preoccupations, a desire to rework old problems with new insight. It has been shown above how in the *Missa sine nomine* Josquin reinterpreted the canon mass derived from Ockeghem (which he had once explored in the *Missa ad fugam*), investing it with a new sweetness and expressivity. In the *Missa de beata virgine* he looked even further back, jettisoning much of the elaborate panoply of motivic unity deployed in the virtuoso middle-period masses in favour of a unity based solely on the appropriate Ordinary chants for feasts of the Virgin. Thematic and even tonal unity are sacrificed to liturgical propriety; the fact that from the Credo onwards the four-part texture is expanded to five by means of canon suggests that the work was not even conceived as a complete musical unity. As in the early mass sections, paraphrased plainsong is the main constructional principle, but it is handled now with a serene mastery that fully explains why this became (to judge by the number of sources in which it survives) the most popular of all Josquin's masses during the 16th century.

Whether or not the *Missa 'Pange lingua'* was composed by 1514, it was evidently not available to Petrucci for his third collection of Josquin's masses, published in that year. Though quite widely circulated in manuscripts, it was not printed until 1539, in Ott's *Missae tredecim*. But although one of the masses attributed to Josquin in this publication is by Pierre de La Rue and another (as Sparks, 1972, has convincingly demonstrated) by Noel Bauldeweyn, there can be no doubt about the authenticity of *Pange lingua*. The plainsong hymn melody impregnates every voice and every section of the mass, but except for the final Agnus Dei, where it at last emerges into the superius, it is not given the old-fashioned conspicuousness of a cantus firmus, but rather is digested into the counterpoint, which itself has a new austerity and economy. The vigour of the earlier masses can still be felt in the rhythms and the strong drive to cadences, perhaps more so than in the *Missa de beata virgine*, but essentially the two contrasting strains of Josquin's music – fantasy and intellectual control – are so blended and balanced in these two works that one can see in them the beginnings of a new style: one which reconciles the conflicting aims of the great 15th-century composers in a new synthesis that was in essence to remain valid for the whole of the 16th century.

It is the Corpus Christi version of Fortunatus's Easter hymn that Josquin had in mind in *Pange lingua*, as is shown both by the underlay of the final Agnus Dei in some sources and by the title (e.g. in Vienna, Österreichische Nationalbibliothek, MS 4809 and Jena, Universitätsbibliothek, MS 21): 'Missa de venerabili sacramento'. The two chief inspirations of Josquin's sacred music, to judge by the frequency with which they recur and the nature of the musical response they elicited from him, are the parallel ones of the virgin birth (more particularly its annunciation) and its re-enactment in the sacrament of the Mass. In this, of course, his piety was entirely typical of his time, but he transcended it in the intensity with which he expressed it. 'Le génie consiste . . . à concevoir son objet plus vivement et plus complètement que personne', observed Vauvenargues. It seems appropriate that in these two late masses Josquin should have given such profound expression to the twin concepts at the heart of his religious belief.

CHAPTER SIX

Secular works

The difficulties that prevent us from forming a clear picture of Josquin's development as a composer of masses and motets are if possible increased when we turn to his secular music, since the sources are fewer, more scattered and less reliable. Petrucci included some 20 three- and four-part pieces in his earliest collections of secular music, but in several cases the attribution to Josquin is questionable on grounds of style or the evidence of other sources, and in a few Petrucci himself withdrew it in subsequent printings. His first and third books of frottolas, first published in 1504 and 1505 respectively, contain one piece each attributed to 'Josquin d'Ascanio'; these two and the lively *Scaramella* seem to be Josquin's only surviving settings of Italian texts.

Individual as are these pieces and the two extracts from Virgil's *Aeneid* (perhaps composed for an Italian court), they hardly alter the fact that Josquin's main concern in secular composition was the chanson. Two double canons were included, anonymously, in Antico's collection of that specialized genre of chanson (*RISM* 1520³), and a further, very valuable, group of six three-part pieces in the same publisher's *La couronne et fleur des chansons à troys* (1536¹). A miscellaneous anthology published at Augsburg (1540⁷) was the first to make available a few of the five- and six-part chansons, but it was not until the appearance in 1545 of Susato's *Septiesme livre* (a memorial volume devoted entirely to Josquin, together with elegies on his death) that the bulk of these, some two dozen, were given the wider circulation of print. Susato's volume was reprinted four years later by his Parisian competitor Attaingnant, with the omission of the elegies by other hands and the addition of a few more pieces, mostly of dubious authenticity. This admittedly implies some degree of public response, but the fact remains that these two publications, together with a rather earlier set of manuscript partbooks written in Flanders (Vienna, Österreichische Nationalbibliothek, MS 18746), are almost the only surviving sources to transmit what seems, in retrospect, to have been the greatest of Josquin's achievements as a composer of chansons – a body of works that brings into this genre the pathos and constructive power, albeit on a smaller scale, that inform his later motets.

They provide a fairly clear idea of the last stage of Josquin's career as a chanson composer. Its beginnings, however, can only be deduced from the works printed by Petrucci and scattered, often anonymously, through various manuscripts, mostly Italian. The chronology of these works is still very much a matter of conjecture, but allowing for the possibility of false attributions it does seem safe to say that Josquin's starting-point as a secular composer was in the style developed during the 15th century at the Burgundian court above all and carried to its final flowering by Busnois and Ockeghem – a style in which directness of declamation and rhythmic repetition are deliberately suppressed in favour of a linear elegance matching the studied artificiality of the verse. This music further matches the poetry in its careful observance of the *formes fixes*, the system of smaller and larger repetitions which together go to make up the total shape of both poem and composition. In what are presumably Josquin's earliest surviving chansons these formalities are still observed: in *Cela sans plus*, for instance, the cadence that brings the music to a temporary halt at bar 33 clearly indicates that the original text (it has not survived) was a rondeau. What is already different from Ockeghem, however, is the emphasis on strict imitation (the two upper voices are in canon for the first 25 bars) and on rhythmic and melodic repetition; the fivefold rising sequence in the second half of the piece is as typical of the younger composer as it is untypical of the older. In *La plus des plus*, also printed in Petrucci's *Odhecaton*, continued movement in the bass prevents the median cadence from functioning as in a rondeau, nor does the only known poem with this incipit fit the music at all comfortably. The music seems, in any case, to have been composed almost autonomously and gives the impression that Josquin was here primarily concerned with the working out of purely musical problems: for instance, it explores the possibilities of imitation at three pitches a 5th and a 9th (instead of the usual octave) apart – a technical problem also handled in *Fortuna d'un gran tempo* (for which see Lowinsky, 1943 and Van Benthem, 1980).

The question arises as to how many of these early pieces were conceived to be sung at all and how many were from the start instrumental. Certainly Petrucci and most of the manuscript sources omit the words, so that the practice of purely instrumental performance must have been widespread. This is probably the origin of even more unambiguously instrumental pieces such as *La Bernardina* and *Ile fantazies de Joskin* (as it is called in its only source), where there seems to be no reference to any text or borrowed vocal material at all. These pieces give the impression of being completely free-composed and as such represent the earliest steps towards the specifically instrumental contrapuntal style that was to be explored by Willaert and his contemporaries in the next generation.

But as a general rule Josquin preferred to base a composition, whether or not voices were intended to take part in its performance, on pre-existing material, and for this purpose he drew on the 'popular' music of his time – not necessarily folksong in the accepted sense, but music in the popular consciousness – a rich but labyrinthine repertory which partly survives in monophonic chansonniers (notably Paris, Bibliothèque Nationale, fonds fr.9346 and 12744; for a discussion of this repertory see Brown, 1963). Josquin's practice in arranging such tunes naturally varies. One of the simplest examples is *Bergerette savoyenne* (or *savoisienne*); here an elaborated version of the pre-existing tune is given to the top voice, each line being anticipated in the lower, accompanying voices. In *Je sey bien dire* (from *Canti C*) a tune with a strongly marked dance character is put in the tenor, while a web of partly imitative counterpoint is spun above and below it. *L'homme armé*, a rather primitive four-part notational puzzle which seems originally to have been conceived as a three-part piece, also has its borrowed melody in the tenor.

Even in these relatively straightforward pieces there is a certain piquancy in the contrast between the simplicity of the basic material and the artfulness with which it is treated, but this is further heightened in the arrangements in which Josquin makes use of his favourite device of canon. In some, the type of strict imitation between the upper voices that we have already met in three-part pieces is transferred to the upper pair of four, as in the setting of *Une musque de Biscaye*, in which an elaborated version of the tune is presented in close canon at the 4th between the two upper voices. Even more ingenious are the four-part pieces which consist of two simultaneous canons: *En l'ombre d'un buissonet au matinet*, *Baisez moy* (spoilt in the possibly unauthentic six-part version by the addition of yet another canon) and *Recordans de my segnora* – if this latter, with its clumsy patch at bars 22–3, is really by Josquin. The canons in such pieces are too close to perform much more than a textural function; in others, though, Josquin can perhaps be seen to be working his way towards the concept of canon as an architectural scaffolding, articulating the melodic and tonal structure of an entire piece, which is so marked a feature of his later motets and masses. In *Adieu mes amours*, for instance, the very well-known tune is presented in turn, quasi-canonically, by the two lower voices, while the upper ones proceed more freely. (In one source the top voice is given a rondeau cinquain to sing, but the music takes no account of the requirements of the *forme fixe*.) The four-part setting of *Entré je suis* proceeds very similarly, but with more motivic integration of the free voices. The basic tune of this piece also appears with a German text beginning 'In meinem Sinn' and with cognate Flemish forms; no doubt this encouraged the dissemination of Josquin's arrangement. The same applies to *Comment peult haver joye*, in which the tune (also associated with the German text *Wohlauf, Gesell, von hinnen*) is presented in strict canon with great clarity; this piece was printed by Glarean as a motet (*O Jesu fili David*) – just one instance of the way in which Josquin's music, endorsed by Luther, was annexed for use in the German-speaking countries. The five-part arrangement of the basse danse melody *La Spagna* would be another, but the qualities of lucid structure and varied texture associated with Josquin (not to mention basic competence in the handling of dissonance) are so conspicuously absent from it that it is impossible to accept it as authentic on the shaky testimony of Ott, who published it as a motet (*Propter peccata*) in 1537.

The earliest stage in Josquin's development of the chanson for more than four voices is probably represented by his six-part setting of *Se congié prens*, another popular tune. Here the canonic voices clearly perform a structural function, with *dux* and *comes* ingeniously reversing roles during the central section, but the texture is by no means as integrated as in later works of this kind. This, in fact, is probably the earliest of the pieces included by Susato in his memorial volume, for they are on the whole conspicuous for the way in which the canonic voices (the great majority are constructed round a scaffolding of this kind) are blended into the surrounding texture. *Se congié prens* is not the only one to make use of a popular tune: *Faulte d'argent* (whose authenticity is questioned in Van Benthem, 1970), *Petite camusette*, *Vous ne l'aurez pas* and *Tenez-moy en voz bras* are further examples. Other chansons, most notably the famous setting of Jean Molinet's elegy on the death of Ockeghem, *Nymphes des bois*, make use of a plainsong cantus firmus. Occasionally Josquin reworked a voice part from some earlier composition: *Ma bouche rit* borrows the superius of Ockeghem's chanson and gives it a new, rich, and surely instrumental setting – a more elaborate development of the treatment Josquin had already accorded to Hayne's *De tous biens playne* in a piece published in the *Odhecaton*. Several of the most individual, however, seem to be completely free-composed, such as the profoundly pathetic *Regretz sans fin*. In these pieces, too, it is noteworthy that although the old *forme fixe* structure with its detachable cadence points had been completely abandoned in favour of through-composition, Josquin almost always takes care to mirror the rhyme structure of the poem with musical repetition, either strict or varied: this applies particularly to the opening lines or couplets, as in *Incessament livré*, *Plusieurs regretz*, *Je me complains* and *Douleur me bat*. The old relationship to the structure of the text has been replaced by a new one, more in keeping with the denser texture and slower movement of a new musical style.

In his later chansons for a smaller number of voices Josquin generally eschewed canon: *Plus nulz regretz* and *Mille regretz*, both for four, are freely composed, though with the same clear articulation of lines and melodic points of imitation, achieved by a carefully balanced hierarchy of cadences. Nor did Josquin confine himself to a mood of sombre pathos, though it certainly seems to have been the one most congenial to him in his later years. Of the three-part pieces transmitted by Antico, *Si j'avoys Marion*, *Si j'ay perdu mon amy* and the two different pieces beginning *En l'ombre d'un buissonet* all look forward in their elegant handling of lighthearted popular material to the 'Parisian' chanson of Janequin and his contemporaries. *Quant je vous voy* applies the same refined technique to more lyrical ideas (perhaps Josquin's own), while *La belle se siet* is an astonishingly original handling of an old ballad tune as the basis for what could almost be an instrumental fantasia if it were not for the patches of clearcut declamation; it is a unique and fascinating piece. In this collection Josquin rubs shoulders with a younger generation of French court composers, such as Févin. But there can be no doubt that the real influence of his later chanson style was felt farther north, above all by Willaert.

WORKS

Edition: *Josquin Desprez: Werken*, ed. A. Smijers and others (Amsterdam, 1921–): *Missen* [Missen deel: aflevering]; *Motetten* [Mot. deel: aflevering]; *Wereldlijke werken* [WW deel: aflevering]

FC 1971 – *Josquin des Prez: New York 1971*   Heartz no. – no. in Heartz (1969)

Only sources additional to 1st edn. of *Werken* are listed; those sources containing isolated sections for theoretical or instructional purposes are omitted. Intabulations have generally been disregarded, except when they provide a unique source or ascription; for printed intabulations see Kwee Him Yong (1971).

Numbers in the right-hand column denote references in the text.

Incipit/Title	No. of parts	Additional sources	Edition	Remarks	
MASSES					
Missa ad fugam	4	—	Missen iii: 28	canon mass	17, 40–56
Missa 'Ave maris stella'	4	*D-F* mus.fol.2; *E-Tc* 9; *I-Rvat* S Maria Maggiore 26	Missen ii: 15	on plainsong hymn	45, 49, 54 / 43, 50, 51
Missa de beata virgine	4–5	*CH-Bu* F.VI.26(h); *D-Dlb* Grimma 53 (Ky, Gl only), Ngm 83795; *E-Tc* 16, Res.23; *H-Bn* Bártfa Mus.20, 24, Mus.pr.6; *I-Bc* Q25, Bsp A xxxi (Cr only), Rvat C.S.160; *S-Uu* Vok mus i hs 76b, 76c	Missen ii: 30, 31	paraphrases appropriate Ordinary chants	44, 45, 54, 55
Missa di dadi ['N'aray-je jamais mieulx']	4	—	Missen iii: 29	on Morton's chanson	44, 47, 49
Missa 'D'ung aultre amer'	4	—	Missen ii: 23	on Ockeghem's chanson	43
Missa 'Faisant regretz'	4	*E-Tc* 9; *I-Rvat* Pal.Lat. 1980–81	Missen iii: 27	on 2p. of Frye's Tout a par moy	44, 47, 49, 53
Missa 'Fortuna desperata'	4	*E-Boc* 5; *S-Uu* Vok mus i hs 76b	Missen i: 13	on ?Busnois' chanson	44, 47, 50
Missa 'Gaudeamus'	4	*E-Tc* 27	Missen i: 12	on plainsong introit	44, 50, 51, 52
Missa 'Hercules Dux Ferrarie'	4	Tc 27, *I-Bsp* A xxxi	Missen ii: 17	on motto derived by solmization from title	9, 11, 43–4, 51
Missa 'L'ami Baudichon'	4	*D-Z* 119/1 (Ky, Gl, Cr only); *I-Sc* K.1.2 (Gl only)	Missen ii: 20	on popular song	44, 46, 47

Incipit/Title	No. of parts	Additional sources	Edition	Remarks	
Missa 'La sol fa re mi'	4	A-Wn 11883 (Ky and start of Gl only); D-Rp C100; E-Tc 19; I-Bsp A xxxi, Rvat SMM 26	Missen i: 11	on motto derived by solmization	5–6, 44, 53
Missa 'L'homme armé' sexti toni	4	D-Ju 31; E-SE; I-CMac M	Missen i: 14	on popular song	51, 52–3
Missa 'L'homme armé' super voces musicales	4	D-F mus.fol.2; E-Boc 5 (untexted Ky, Confiteor and Ag III only), Tc 9; I-Bsp A xxxi; S-Uu Vok mus i hs 76c	Missen i: 10	on popular song	44
Missa 'Malheur me bat'	4	E-Tc 9; I-Bsp A xxxi	Missen ii: 19	on ?Ockeghem's chanson	44–5, 50, 51
Missa 'Mater Patris'	4		Missen iii: 26	on Brumel's motet, 3vv	44, 48
Missa 'Pange lingua'	4	B-Br iv 922; D-Rp C100, ROu 71/3; H-Bn Bárfa 8; I-Rvat SMM 26, Rvat Pal.Lat. 1980–81, 1982	Missen iv: 33	on chant	29, 55–6
Missa sine nomine	4	CFm 59	Missen iii: 32	canon mass	44, 49, 54
Missa 'Une musque de Biscaye'	4	—	Missen ii: 22	on popular song	44, 46
INDEPENDENT MASS SECTIONS					
Gloria de beata virgine	4		Missen iv: 44	on plainsong Gloria IX, with tropes	42
Credo 'Ciascun me crie' [= De rouges nez]	4	D-Mbs Mus.Ms.53 (Brumel); I-Rvat SMM 26	Missen iv: 50		
Credo 'De tous biens'	4	—	Missen iv: 44	on T of Hayne's chanson, and plainsong Credo I	42
Credo 'Vilayge' (i)	4	—	Missen iv: 44	on plainsong Credo I	42
Sanctus de Passione	4	—	Missen iv: 50		29, 42
Sanctus 'D'ung aultre amer' (with Elevation motet Tu lumen, tu splendor Patris)	4	—	Missen ii: 23, appx	on Ockeghem's chanson	42, 43
MOTETS					
Absalon, fili mi	4	—	Suppl.		27–39
Absolve, quaesumus, Domine/Requiem aeternam	6	—	Mot.v: 49	authenticity questioned by M. Just, MJ, xviii (1965), 109; defended by M. Antonowycz, TVNM, xx/3 (1966), 154	32, 33

Incipit		Source	Mot.	Notes	Pages
Adjuro vos, o filiae Syon		I-Bc R142, BGc 1209, V Ecap		contrafactum of Plus nulz regretz	
Alma Redemptoris mater/Ave regina celorum	4	760	Mot.i: 7		29–30
Alma Redemptoris mater	4	I-Bc Q18	Mot.ii: 21		
Ave Christe immolate				see Ave caro Christi cara, 'Doubtful and misattributed works'	
Ave Maria, gratia plena … benedicta tu	4	Bc R142	Mot.i: 2		26, 27–8, 31, 38
Ave Maria, gratia plena … virgo serena	4	CS-HK II-A-7; D-Bds 40021, LEu 1494, Ngm 83795; E-Bc 454, Boc 5, SE; GB-Lcm 1070; I-MOd 9, Md 2266; PL-Wu Rps. Mus.58 (formerly WRu Mf.2016)	Mot.i: 2		
Ave Maria	6	E-Zs 17; NL-Uu (Lerma)	—	2p. of Pater noster	15, 37
Ave maris stella (see Monstra te esse matrem)			Suppl.		
Ave mundi spes Maria	4	E-Tc 13	Mot.ii: 18		30, 34–6
Ave nobilissima creatura/Benedicta tu	6	—			
Ave sanctissima virgo	5	—		see Osthoff (1962–5), ii, 133, 268	
Ave verum corpus	2–3	D-Z 81, 82	Mot.i: 4		
Benedicite omnia opera Domini Domino	4	DK-Kk Gl.Kgl.Sml.1872; E-TAc 8, Tc Res.23; F-Pn Rés.Vma 851; GB-Eu 64; NL-Uu (Lerma); S-Uu Vok mus i hs 76c	Mot.iii: 37		38
Benedicta es, celorum regina	6		Mot.iii: 35		20, 36, 114
Celi enarrant gloriam Dei	4	—	Mot.iii: 39		
Christum ducem	4	CS-HK II-A-6, 7; I-Pc A 17	Mot.i: 2	6p. of Qui velatus	
Christus mortuus est pro nobis/ Circumdederunt me	6	D-Z 73	Mot.v: 51	companion-piece of Sic Deus dilexit mundum; authenticity of both questionable on stylistic grounds	
Da(te) siceram moerentibus		CS-RO A 22; D-Mu 326, Rp B211–15, B1018; H-Bn Bártfa Mus. 23; PL-WRol 12		contrafactum of Je ne me puis tenir d'aimer	
Delevi ut nubem		D-LEu 49			38
De profundis clamavi (low vv)	4	A-Wn 15941 (Champion); D-ERu 473/4	Mot.iii: 35	contrafactum of Faulte d'argent I-VEcap 760 listed by Osthoff (1962–5) in error	

Incipit/Title	No. of parts	Additional sources	Edition	Remarks	
De profundis clamavi	5	1521*; discantus ptbk in private possession	Mot.v: 51	source described by Elders (1982), 47	9, 37
Domine, Dominus noster	5	D-Hau 1147, Dlb Grimma 59a	Mot.v: 51		
Domine, exaudi orationem meam	4	discantus ptbk in private possession	Mot.v: 52	source described by Elders (1982), 47	
Domine, ne in furore tuo (Ps xxxvii)	4	CS-HK II-A-21; D-HB 93/3, ROu 71/1, Rp C120, Z 81, 2	Mot.ii: 2		37
Domine, ne in furore tuo (Ps vi)	4	D-Dl Mus.1/D/6; I-Bc Q20	Mot.iii: 39		
Domine, ne projicias me	4		Mot.iv: 40		
Domine, non secundum peccata	4	D-Ngm 83795; E-Boc 5	Mot.i: 4		
Dominus regnavit	4		Mot.iv: 41		
Ecce Maria genuit	4	Sc 1	Mot.i: 2	5p. of O admirabile commercium	
Ecce, tu pulchra es, amica mea	4		Mot.ii: 16	contrafactum of Tenez-moy en voz bras	
Ego sum ipse	6	D-Dlb Grimma 55, LEu 49, Ngm 83795			
Factum est autem	4		Mot.i: 6		31
Gaude virgo, mater Christi	4	D-Usch 237	Mot.i: 7		31
Germinavit radix Jesse	4		Mot.i: 2	4p. of O admirabile commercium	
Haec dicit Dominus	6	1537*; 1558*; D-Bds 40013, GOl A 98, Ju Weimar B, Ngm 83795, Rp B 211, Z 74, 1; DK-Kk Gl.Kgl.Sml.1872, 1873; H-Bn Bártfa 2		contrafactum, ? by Conrad Rupsch (to whom it is attrib. in 1537*), of Nymphes, nappés	
Homo quidam fecit cenam magnam	5	D-Z 73	Mot.i: 9		
Honor, decus, imperium [Nardi Maria pistici]	4	D-Rp A.R.893; DK-Kk Gl.Kgl.Sml.1872 4*; H-Bn Bártfa Mus.pr.6	Suppl.		
Huc me sydereo descender/Plangent eum	6		Mot.iii: 16	v.2 of hymn	34–6
Illibata Dei virgo nutrix/La mi la	5	PL-WRu 428	Mot.i: 9		
In amara crucis ara	4		Mot.i: 4	4p. of Qui velatus	
In exitu Israel	4	D-Dl Mus.1/D/6; E-Tc Res.23	Mot.iii: 36		
In illo tempore assumpsit Jesus	4		Mot.v: 48	formerly Königsberg 1740 (?lost), 1 ptbk in D-Ga ?	
Iniquos odio habui/Verbum tuum	4		Suppl.		2, 30–31, 36
In pace in idipsum (see Que vous madame)					

Title	Voices	Source	Mot.	Remarks	
In principio erat verbum	4	D-Rp A.R.840, A.R.940; E-Tc Res.23; I-MOd9	Mot.iii:38		29,38
In te Domine speravi: non confundar (see In te ... per trovar pietà under 'Secular')					
Inviolata est Maria, Jesu Christi mater	5	D-ROu 71/2 c1521²; D-Mu 326; E-Bc 681, Sc 1, Tc 10; I-Fl Acq. e Doni 666	Mot.ii:25	contrafactum of Inviolata, integra	18,36
Inviolata, integra et casta es, Maria	5	A-Wn S.m.15500; D-Dl Mus.1/ D/501	—		
Jubilate Deo omnis terra	4	1554²¹	Mot.iv:41		
Lauda Syon	(5)		—	intabulation of Je ne me puis tenir d'aimer, here attrib. Gombert; see Blackburn (1976)	
Laudate, pueri, Dominum	4	I-VEcap 760	Mot.iv:42		
Levavi oculos meos in montes	4	D-Dl Mus.1/D/505 (formerly ABGa 1248); E-Tc Res.23; S-Uu Vok mus i hs 76c	Mot.v:42		
Liber generationis Jesu Christi	4		Mot.i:6		31
Magnificat tertii toni	4	D-LEu Thomaskirche 49 (Brumel); I-MOd3 (La Rue), IV (Agricola)	Mot.v:47		
Magnificat quarti toni	4		Mot.v:47	Maas, 1966, supported Josquin's authorship, but of an original setting of even verses only, adapted in I-Rvat C.S.44 to all verses by repetition	
Magnus es tu, Domine	4	A-Wn S.m.15500	Mot.i:6	anon. in 1504¹, attrib. Josquin in Glarean and related sources, attrib. Finck in 1538³; possibly by neither	
Memor esto verbi tui	4	I-MOd4	Mot.ii:16		4,7-8,37
Mente tota	4	PL-Wu Rps.Mus.58 (formerly WRu Mf.2016)		5p. of Vultum Tuum	
Mirabilia testimonia tua, Domine	4		Mot.iv:42	contrafactum of Se congié prens	
Miserator et misericors Dominus	6	D-Dlb Grimma 59a; I-Fl Acq. e Doni 666	Mot.ii:21		
Miserere mei, Deus	5				11, 18, 34
Misericordias Domini	4	E-Tc 10; S-Uu Vok mus i hs 76c	Mot.i:25		
Missus est Gabriel angelus	4	GB-Lcm 1070	Mot.i:6		31, 34
Mittit ad virginem	4		Mot.i:2		
Monstra te esse matrem [Ave maris stella] (see Ave maris stella)	4		Suppl.	vv.4, 6, 7 of hymn	
Nardi Maria pistici (see Honor, decus, imperium)					

Incipit/Title	No. of parts	Additional sources	Edition	Remarks	
O admirabile commercium	4	Cmc Pepys 1760; I-Fl Acq. e Doni 666	Mot.i: 2		31
O bone et dulcis Domine Jesu/Pater noster/Ave Maria	4	VEcap 758	Mot.i: 6	attrib. Josquin only in Fn Magl.XIX. 58; Osthoff (1962–5), ii, 296, questioned possibility of confusion with O bone et dulcissime Jesu	
O bone et dulcissime Jesu	4	Bsp A xxxi, Rvat C.S.45	Mot.v: 52	contrafactum of Comment peult haver joye	26, 29, 31
O Domine Jesu Christe	4		Mot.i: 4	contrafactum of Se congié prens	62
O Jesu fili David	4	I-Bc R 142	Cw, xxx		
O Maria, virgo sanctissima	6	1508²; US-Wc M2.1. M.6	K. Jeppesen: Die mehrstimmige italienische Laude (1935)	Marian adaptation of Tu solus qui facis mirabilia	
O mater Dei et hominis	4				
O virgo genitrix	5	—	Mot.iii: 35	contrafactum of Plusieurs regretz	30
O virgo prudentissima/Beata mater	6	I-Rvat C.S.46	Mot.v: 49		
O virgo virginum	6	—	Mot.iv: 41		
Paratum cor meum, Deus	4				
Pater noster, qui es in celis (2p. Ave Maria)	6	CS-HK II-A-22a; D-Bds 40043, Ngm 83795; DK-Kk Gl.Kgl.Sml. 1872 4°, E-Tc Res.23	Mot.iii: 36		15, 37
Pauper sum ego (see Ce povre mendiant)					
Petite et accipietis	6	D-Dlb Grimma 55	Mot.i: 6		
Planxit autem David	4	D-Dl Mus.1/D/505 (formerly ABGa 1248); I-Fn Magl. XIX.58 ('Ninot' in index)		contrafactum of Petite camusette	31–3
Praeter rerum seriem	6	CS-RO A.V.22a, b; D-Dlb Grimma 57; DK-Kk Gl.Kgl.Sml.1872 4°; E-Sc 1, T Ac 8, T c Res.23; H-Bn Bartfa 2; I-Fd 11, Rv S.Bor.E.II.55–60, Rvat Lat.11953; S-Uu Vok mus i hs 76b	Mot.ii: 18		18, 36–7, 52, 171

Quando natus es	4	—	Mot.i:2	2p. of O admirabile commercium	
Qui habitat in adjutorio Altissimi	4	CS-HK II-A-21; D-Dlb Grimma 57, Rp A.R. 940–41, Z xli, 73; E-Tc Res.23	Mot.iii:37		29, 42
Qui habitat in adjutorio Altissimi	24	1542⁴, 1568⁷; D-HB iv, 2–v, 2, Kl4⁹ Mus.24	see Stam (1971)		
Qui velatus facie fuisti	4	D-Ga 7 (olim Königsberg 1740) 1546³⁴	Mot.i:4		
Regina celi	4		Suppl.	intabulation of Je ne me puis tenir d'aimer, here attrib. Gombert; see Blackburn (1976)	
Respice in me Deus	(5)				
Responde mihi	4	NL-Lml 423 ('incertus auctor')	Mot.v:46		
Rubum quem viderat Moyses	4		Mot.i:2	3p. of O admirabile commercium	
Salve, regina	4	D-Dl Mus.1/D/505 (formerly ABGa 1248)	Mot.v:52		
Salve, regina	5	E-Boc 7, Bc 681, Zs 17; P-C M.M.48	Mot.iii:35		36
Salve, sancta facies	4	I-Md 2267	Suppl.		
Sana me, Domine	5				
Sic Deus dilexit mundum/Circumdederunt me	6	D-Z 73	Mot.v:51	contrafactum of Pluisieurs regretz companion-piece of Christus mortuus est pro nobis; authenticity of both questionable on stylistic grounds	
Stabat mater dolorosa/Comme femme desconfortée	5	CS-HK II-A-26, 41; D-Rp A.R.892; DK-Kk Gl.Kgl.Sml.1872 4°, 1873 4°; E-Tc 10, V 16, 17; I-Rvat Lat.11953; S-Uu Vok mus i hs 76c	Mot.ii:21		18, 34
Stetit autem Salomon	4	D-Rp A.R.888	Mot.iii:39		42
Tu lumen, tu splendor Patris (see Sanctus 'D'ung aultre amer')					
Tu solus qui facis mirabilia	4	I-MOd 4, S Maria della Neve, Rocca di Mezzo	Mot.i:4	see A. Ziino, Documenti di polifonia in Abruzzo (Rome, 1974)	26, 29, 43
Usquequo, Domine, oblivisceris me in finem	4	D-Dl Mus.1/D/501, ROu 71/1	Mot.iii:39		38
Ut Phoebi radiis	4		Mot.i:7		
Veni, Sancte Spiritus	6	CS-HK II-A-22a, 29; D-Bds 40013, Dlb Grimma 55, Ngm 83795, Rp A.R.879; S-Uu Vok mus i hs 76b (Forestier)	Mot.iii:36	probably by Forestier (see Blackburn, 1976)	36, 52

Incipit/Title	No. of parts	Additional sources	Edition	Remarks	
Venite ad me	5	D-LEu 49		contrafactum of En non saichant	28–9
Victimae paschali laudes/D'ung aultre amer	4	—	Mot.i: 9		
Videte omnes populi	6	I-Bc R142		contrafactum of Nymphes, nappés	
Vidi speciosam	6	I-Bc R142		contrafactum of Tenez-moy en voz bras	
Virgo prudentissima	4	CS-HK II-A-7; D-Dl Mus.1/D/6	Mot.i: 9	attrib. Isaac in 1537[b] and derivative sources, probably through confusion with Isaac's 6-voice setting	31
Virgo salutiferi/Ave Maria	5	I-Fl Acq, e Doni 666	Mot.ii: 18		11, 36
Vultum tuum deprecabuntur	4	D-Usch 237 (2p.–6p.); I-Md 2266 (3p.–6p.), Pc A17 (1p.–3p., 5p., 7p.)	Mot.i: 7		29
SECULAR					
Ach unfal, was zichstu mich	4	CH-Bu F.X.21	WW iii: 53	contrafactum of Qui belles amours	57–64
Adieu mes amours	4	c1535[a]			
Adieu mes amours	6	I-Bc R142; PCd	—	only 3vv survive, with text Ave Maria; see 'Doubtful and misattributed works'; 3 extant voices in Picker, FC 1971, 247	8, 61
A la mort/Monstra te esse matrem	3	I-Fc Basevi 2439	WW iii: 53		
A l'eure que ie vous p.x.	4		WW i: 5		
Allégez moy	6	D-Hs Hans.III, 12–16; DK-Kk Gl.Kgl.Sml.1872; 1520[b]; B-Br IV.90, Tv 94	WW i: 5	also attrib. Le Brung, Barbé, Willaert; Van Benthem (1970) accepted it as authentic for 6-voice version see 'Doubtful and misattributed works'	61
Baisez moy, ma doulce amye	4				
Belle, pour l'amour de vous	4	Br 11239; I-Fn Magl.XIX.178	Picker (1965)		60
Bergerette savoyenne [savoisienne]	4		WW ii: 53		59
Cela sans plus	3		WW i: 53		
Ce povre mendiant/Pauper sum ego	3		WW i: 53		
Comment peult haver joye	4		WW ii: 54	also with text Fortune d'estrange plummaige; for full text see edn. in MRM, ii (1967), no.19; see also O Jesu fili David	61–2
Cueur langoreux	5		WW i: 3		
Cueurs desolez par toute nation/Plorans ploravit	5		WW i: 8		

De tous biens playne	3	1502[1]	Osthoff (1962–5), ii, 395f		
De tous biens playne	4	—	WW ii: 53		63
Douleur me bat	5	—	WW i: 5		
Dulces exuviae	4	—	WW iii: 54		
Du mien amant	5	—	WW i: 5		
El grillo	4	—	WW iii: 54		
En [A] l'ombre d'un buissonet au matinet	3	Fc Basevi 2442	WW iii: 54		61, 63
En l'ombre d'un buissonet au matinet	4	B-Br IV.90, Tr 94	WW iii: 54		63
En l'ombre d'un buissonet tout au loing d'une rivière	3		WW iii: 54		
En non saichant	5	—	WW i: 33	D-Usch 237a–d, listed in WW, does not contain this piece; authenticity questioned by Van Benthem (1970); see also Venite ad me	
Entré je suis en grant pensée	4	S-Uu Vok mus i hs 76a	WW iii: 54	see also In meinem Sinn, Par vous je suis	61
Entré je suis en grant pensée	3	—	WW iii: 54		
Fama, malum	4	—	WW iii: 54		
Faulte d'argent	5	DK-Kk Gl.Kgl.Sml.1853; S-Uu Vok mus i hs 76c	WW i: 5	authenticity questioned by Van Benthem (1970); see also Delevi ut nubem	62
Fortuna d'un gran tempo	3	—	Suppl.		59
Fortune d'estrange plummaige	3	—	WW i: 53	also with text Ce povre mendiant original 3-voice version in E-Sco 5-1-43, I-Fn Magl.XIX.178; other sources, all anon, add. altus part	
Helas, madame	3	—	Suppl.		
Ile fantazies de Joskin	3	—	WW ii: 53		60
Incessament livré suis à martire	5	—	WW i: 53		63
In meinem Sinn	4	D-WGl S.403/1048		contrafactum of Entré je suis, 4vv	
In te Domine speravi, per trovar pietà	4	1504*; CH-Sk Tir.87-4; E-E 2-1-5; F-Pn Rés. Vm⁷ 676; GB-Lbm Eg.3051; I-Bc Q18, Fc Basevi 2441, Fn Banco rari 337, P27	ed. R. Schwartz in Publikationen älterer Musik, viii (Leipzig, 1935/R1967)	1538* and subsequent MSS have complete Lat. text in place of macaronic one	
J'ay bien cause de lamenter	6	—	WW i: 8		

Incipit/Title	No. of parts	Additional sources	Edition	Remarks	
Je me	3	Fn Magl.XIX.178	—	no more text given in source	63
Je me complains	5	—	WW i: 3		
Je ne me puis tenir d'aimer	5	D-Mbs 1508	WW i: 8	see also Da(te) siceram moerentibus, Lauda Syon, Respice in me	
Je n'ose plus	3	I-Fn Magl.XIX.178	Osthoff (1962–5), ii, 189		
Je sey bien dire	4	—	WW ii: 53		60
La belle se siet	3	—	WW ii: 54		64
La Bernardina	3	—	WW ii: 53		60
La déploration de Johan. Ockeghem (see Nymphes des bois/Requiem)					
L'amye a tous/Je ne viz oncques la pareille	5	—	WW i: 8		59
La plus des plus	3	—	WW ii: 53		
Le villain	4	D-As 2° Cod.142a	WW ii: 54		60
L'homme armé	4	—	WW i: 5		63
Ma bouche rit	6	S-Uu Vok mus i hs 76b	WW i: 8		
Mi lares vous tousjours languir	5	—	WW i: 8	authenticity questioned by Van Benthem (1970)	
Mille regretz	4	Heartz no.41 ('J. Lemaire'); CH-Bu F.IX.59–62, Tv 94; D-Bds 40194; PL-GD 4003	WW i: 8	attrib. to Lemaire carries more weight in that chanson is attrib. Josquin only in 1538²² and 1549³⁰ but it may rest on a confusion; see Heartz (1969), 97	63
Mon mari m'a diffamée	3	1578¹⁵; B-Br IV.90, Tv 94; GB-Lbm Add.35087; S-Uu Vok mus i hs 76a	Van Benthem, FC 1971, 443		
N'esse point ung grant desplaisir	5	DK-Kk Gl.Kgl.Sml.1872, 1873 1508¹; I-Fl Acq. e Doni 666	WW i: 3		
Nymphes des bois/Requiem (La déploration de Johan. Ockeghem)	5	—	WW i: 5; MRM, iv (1968), 338		23
Nymphes, nappés/Circumdederunt me	6	—	WW i: 3	see also Haec dicit Dominus, Videte omnes populi; in spite of Osthoff (1962–5), ii, 276, and Van Crevel (1940), 103ff, this is probably the original form	

Title	No.	Sources	WW	Remarks	Pages
Parfons regretz	5	—	WW i: 3	Entré je suis has this incipit in *I-Fc* 2439	12
Par vous je suis	6	*DK-Kk* Ny Kgl.Sml.1873; *I-Rvat* Pal.Lat.1980–81	WW i: 5	see also Petite et accipietis	62
Petite camusette					12
Plaine de dueil	5	—	WW i: 3		
Plusieurs regretz	5	*DK-Kk* Ny Kgl.Sml.1848 2°; *S-Uu* Vok mus i hs 76b	WW i: 3	see also O virgo genitrix, Sana me, Domine	63
Plus n'estes ma maistresse	4		WW i: 8		
Plus nulz regretz	4	*B-Br* IV.90, *T.* 94; *D-Rp* C120 (pp.14–15); *GB-Lbm* Roy.App.41–4; *I-Fn* Magl.XIX.117 (inc.), *Rvat* Lat.11953; *S-Uu* Vok mus i hs 76c	WW i: 8	see also Adjuro vos	12, 23, 63
Pour souhaiter	6	*DK-Kk* Gl.Kgl.Sml.1873	WW i: 3	Osthoff (1962–5), ii, 225, questioned authenticity	64
Quant je vous voy	3	—	WW ii: 54		
Que vous madame/In pace in idipsum	3	*PL-Wu* Rps.Mus.58 (formerly *WRu* Mf.2016); *A-Wn* 18810; *D-Mu* 328–31	WW ii: 53	most sources have only Lat. text	
Qui belles amours	4	—	WW ii: 53	see also Ach unfal, was zichstu mich	61
Recordans de my segnora	4	—	WW i: 3		63
Regretz sans fin	4	—	WW iii: 54		57
Scaramella va alla guerra		—			
Se congié prens	6	*I-Bc* A.71, *Rvat* Pal.Lat.1980–81	WW i: 3	see also Miserator et misericors Dominus, O Maria virgo	62
Si j'avoys [j'eusse] Marion	3	—	WW iii: 54		63
Si j'ay perdu mon amy	3	—	WW iii: 54		63
Tenez-moy en voz bras	6	—	WW i: 5	see also Ego sum ipse, Vidi speciosam	62
Une musque de Biscaye	4	*E-Sco* 5-1-43	WW iii: 53		61
Vive le roy		—	WW iii: 53		8
Vous l'arez, s'il vous plaist	6	—	WW i: 5	Osthoff (1962–5), ii, 223f, questioned authenticity	
Vous ne l'aurez pas	6	—	WW i: 3	Osthoff (1962–5), ii, 223f, questioned authenticity	62

DOUBTFUL AND MISATTRIBUTED WORKS

The works listed below range from those very probably by Josquin, though not attributed to him in any source, to those which, though attributed to him in a source before 1600, are certainly not by him; for fuller information on conflicting attributions and stylistic considerations, see Osthoff (1962–5).

Incipit	No. of parts	Edition	Source of attribution to Josquin	Remarks
			(masses)	
Missa 'Allez regretz'	4	Missen iv: 43	D-Ju 21	stylistically doubtful, though accepted with some reservations as authentic by Smijers and Osthoff; ? same as work attrib. 'Nicolaus Scomtianus' in Bds 40634
Missa 'Allez regretz'	4	CMM, xv/1 (1958)	LEu 51	by Compère, to whom it is attrib. in A-Wn 15495, D-Ju 3
Missa 'Da pacem'	4	Missen iv: 34	1539³, Sl 46, E-Tc 19	probably by Bauldeweyn, to whom it is attrib. in D-Mbs Mus.Ms.7; see Sparks (1972)
Missa 'Dirige'	4	—	I-Ma E46	by La Rue, to whom it is attrib. in A-Wn 1783 and elsewhere
Missa ferialis	4	—	1505⁵	very probably by Martini, to whom it is attrib. in I-MOe α.M.1.13
Missa 'L'homme armé' (Phrygian mode)	4	CMM, xv/1 (1958)	D-Mbs Mus.Ms.3154, LEu Thomaskirche 51	by Compère, to whom it is attrib. in I-Rvat C.S.35 and Chigiana C.VIII.234
Missa 'Missus est angelus'	4	—	D-ROu Mus.40	by Moulu, to whom it is attrib. in I-Rvat C.S.55; ed. J. G. Chapman (diss., New York U., 1964)
Missa 'Mon seul plaisir'	?4	—	D-LEu Thomaskirche 51	only T and B extant; attrib. to Josquin improbable on stylistic grounds; see Osthoff (1962–5), i, 200
Missa 'Quem dicunt homines'	4	—	I-Ma E46	improbable on stylistic grounds; Fox (IMSCR, viii New York 1961, ii, 66) suggested it might be by Richafort
Missa 'Rosina'	4	—	D-HO Paed. 3713 (Cr only) and printed copy of this treatise	anon. in earliest source (CH-Bu F.IX 55) and stylistically very improbable; see Ward (1984)
Missa 'Sub tuum praesidium'	4	—	1539³	by La Rue, to whom it is attrib. in B-Br 9126 and elsewhere
Missa 'Veni Sancte Spiritus'	5	—	D-ROu Mus.49	doubtful on stylistic grounds; anon. in Mbs Mus.Ms.6, an earlier source containing works by Divitis and Richafort
Requiem	6	—	NL-Lml 423	probably by Richafort, to whom it is attrib. in 1532⁴, D-Mbs Mus.Ms.46 and I-MOd 10

		(independent mass sections)		
Gloria de beata virgine	3	—	CH-SGs 463	doubtful on stylistic grounds; Glarean quotes a section in 1548¹ without attrib.; ed. D. G. Loach (diss., U. of California, Berkeley, 1969)
Credo	4	Missen iv: 50	F-CA 18	doubtful on stylistic grounds
Credo 'La belle se siet'	4	—	1505¹	probably by R. de Févin, to whom it is attrib. in I-Rvat C.S.41
Credo 'Vilayge' (ii)	4	Missen iv: 50	1505¹ (index only), A-Wn 11778	probably by Brumel, to whom it is attrib. in D-Mbs Mus. Ms.53

		(motets)		
Alleluia, Laudate Dominum	4	—	—	attrib. 'Jus.' when source complete as Königsberg 1740; 1 ptbk in D-Ga 7 without attrib.
Ave Christe immolate	4	Mot.v: 46	1564³	attrib. (with orig. text Ave caro Christi cara) Bauldeweyn in A-Wn 1941 and E-Tc Res.23
Ave festiva ferculis	4	—	TZ 2	Ave festiva corporis in index; unique attrib. and peripheral source
Ave Jesu Christe	6	CMM, xxviii/2	Breslau, Stadtbibliothek 2 and 5 (lost)	by Verdelot, a contrafactum found in several German sources of his Sancta Maria virgo virginum
Ave Maria, gratia plena [= Adieu mes amours]	?6	Suppl.	I-Bc R142	probably contrafactum; 3 extant voices printed in Picker, FC 1971, 247
Ave Maria, gratia plena . . . virgo serena	8	—	V Eaf 218	only Sup by Josquin, borrowed from his 4-voice setting
Ave maris stella	4	Mot.v: 52	Bc Q20 (in altus only)	doubtful on stylistic grounds
Ave sanctissima virgo	5	—	1540⁷	doubtful on stylistic grounds; source unreliable
Ave verum/Ecce panis/Bone pastor/O salutaris	4	—	CH-Bu X.22-4	doubtful on stylistic grounds
Ave verum corpus	.5	Mot.v: 48	1545⁵, 1568⁷	doubtful on stylistic grounds; see Sparks, FC 1971, 352
Beati omnes qui timent	4	EDM, 1st ser., xiii (1939)	D-LEu 49 (B only)	by Senfl, to whom it is attrib. in 1520⁴
Beati omnes qui timent Dominum	6	CMM, lx (1973)	Kl 4° Mus.24	probably by Nicolas Champion, to whom it is attrib. in 1542⁸ and 1569¹
Beati quorum remissae sunt	5	Mot.iv: 40	1538⁶, 1553⁴	doubtful on stylistic grounds
Benedicta sit Sancta Trinitas	4	—	Rtt FK76/II	unique attrib. in peripheral source
Bonitatem fecisti	4	CMM, lviii/5	CH-SGs 463, D-Kl 4° Mus.24	probably by Carpentras, to whom it is attrib. in 1514¹ and elsewhere
Caelorum decus Maria	9	—	I-V Eaf 218 (index only)	doubtful on stylistic grounds

Incipit	No. of parts	Edition	Source of attribution to Josquin	Remarks
Cantate Domino canticum novum	5	Mot.v: 45	1553[3]	doubtful on stylistic grounds; see L. Finscher, *IMSCR*, viii *New York 1961*, ii, 64
Christus resurgens	6	CMM, xxviii/2	Breslau, Stadtbibliothek 2 and 5 (lost)	by Verdelot, a contrafactum of his *Sancta Maria virgo virginum* apparently found only in the lost Breslau MS
Clamavi: Ad Dominum cum tribularer	4	—	*D-Kl* 4° Mus.24, *Rp* B211	doubtful on stylistic grounds
Confitemini Domino/Per singulos dies	6	—	*I-Rv* S.Borr.E.II.55-60	attrib. Mouton in *Rvat* C.S.38
Congratulamini mihi omnes	4	R. van Maldeghem: *Trésor musical*, 1st ser., xvii (Brussels, 1881)	1537[1] (index only) and derivative MSS	attrib. Le Brung in *A-Wn* 18825, Richafort in *I-Bc* Q19; either is more probable than Josquin
Conserva me, Domine	4	—	1538[4], 1553[3] (both discantus only), *D-LEu* 49	apparent attrib. to H. F[inck] in *Kl* 4° Mus.24, but main attrib. to Martin Wolff in 1538[6] and 1553[4] is more probable
De profundis clamavi (high vv)	4	Mot.v: 52	1539[5], *Kl* 4° Mus.24	doubtful on stylistic grounds
De profundis	5	EDM, 1st ser., xiii (1939)	*Dl* Mus.1/D/3 (discantus I and II only)	by Senfl, to whom it is attrib. in *Mbs* Mus.10, 1537[7] and elsewhere
Descendi in ortum meum	4	Suppl.	*A-Wn* 15941	doubtful on stylistic grounds
Deus in adjutorium	4	DTB, v, Jg.iii/2 (1903)	*D-Kl* 4° Mus.24	attrib. Senfl in 1538[6], Champion in *A-Wn* 15941; perhaps more probably by Champion
Deus, in nomine tuo	4	Mot.ii: 25; CMM, lviii/5	1553[3]	probably by Carpentras, to whom it is attrib. in *I-Rvat* C.S.46
Deus pacis reduxit	4	Mot.iii: 38	1538[3]	probably by Stolzer, to whom it is attrib. in *D-Z* 81, 2
Dilectus Deo	4	—	1538[6]	attrib. A. de Févin in 1538[6], but both this and attrib. to Josquin may result from misreading of 1514[1], where it is anon.; ed. E. Clinkscale (diss., New York U., 1965)
Dixi Dominus domino meo	4	—	*D-ROu* 71/1	late source
Domine ne in furore (Ps vi)	4	—	*Kl* 4° Mus.24	possibly by Verdelot, to whom it is attrib. in 1544[4] and *I-Bc* Q20; also attrib. Josquin Baston (*B-LVu* 163) and Stolzer (in private possession; see Elders, 1982)
Domine, quis habitabit	4	—	*D-Kl* 4° Mus.24	doubtful on stylistic grounds
Domini est terra	4	—	*Kl* 4° Mus.24	attrib. Benedictus [?Appenzeller] in *GRu* BW 640-41, Jheronimus Vinders in 1542[3] and *F-CA* 125-8; ed. G. K. Diehl (diss., U. of Pennsylvania, 1974)

Title	No.	Edition	Source	Notes
Ecce Dominus veniet	5	—	D-Z 74, 1	? by Senfl, to whom it is attrib. in *Ela* Cantionale tablature only
Fecit potentiam	2	CMM, v/5	1554[22]	probably by Brumel, to whom it is attrib. in 1505[2]; see Antonowycz (1961), i, 62
Gloria laus et honor	4		1538[3]	doubtful on stylistic grounds
Illumina oculos meos	4	Mot.v: 45	Kl 4° Mus.24	doubtful on stylistic grounds; anon. in 1538[6]
In Domino confido	4	—	1553[4]	by Mouton, to whom it is attrib. in 1521[3] and many other sources; ed. J. M. Shine (diss. New York U., 1953)
In illo tempore Maria Magdalena	4	—	I-VEcap 760	doubtful on stylistic grounds; see Sparks, FC 1971, 354
In illo tempore stetit Jesus in medio/Et ecce terrae motus	6	Mot.iii: 38	Bc R142, 1538[8] and later sources	probably by Mouton, to whom it is attrib. in I-Bc R142
In nomine Jesu omne genu flectatur	6	PÄMw, vi (1877/R)	1558[4], 1564[3], D-Mbs Mus.Ms.1536	doubtful on stylistic grounds
In pace in idipsum	4		I-Fn Magl.XIX.107bis	doubtful on stylistic grounds; see Sparks, FC 1971, 356
Inter natos mulierum	6	Mot.v: 49	Bc R142, Rv S.Borr.E. II.55–60	doubtful on stylistic grounds; source unreliable
Inviolata, integra et casta es, Maria	12	Suppl.	D-Kl 4° Mus.38	attribs. in source generally unreliable
Ite in mundum	4	—	D-Ga 7 (olim Königsberg 1740)	by A. Caen, to whom it is attrib. in 1519[4]; ed. D. M. Gehrenbeck (diss. Union Theological Seminary, 1971)
Judica me, Deus	4	—	1538[4], 1553[4]	by A. de Silva, to whom it is attrib. in 1532[10] and elsewhere
Laetare nova Syon	4	CMM, xlix/1	1546[23], 1546[24]	probably by Maistre Jhan, to whom it is attrib. in I-Fl Acq. e Doni 666; attrib. Heugel in 1537[3]
Lauda Jerusalem	4	MRM, iii (1968)	D-Kl 4° Mus.24	attrib. Mathias Eckel in DK-Kk Gl.Kgl.Sml.1872 and D-Dlb Grimma 49; attrib. W. Heintz in Kl4° Mus.24
Laudate Dominum	16	—	D-LEu Thomaskirche 49	probably by Jo. Viardot, to whom it is attrib., without initial phrase, in I-Rvat C.S.42; see Sherr (1977)
Lectio actuum apostolorum: Dum complerentur	5	Mot.ii 24	1519[3], Mu 401	1p. probably by Gombert, to whom it is attrib. in GB-Lbm Roy.App.49–54 (as Je prens congié), I-VEaf 218 (as Sustinuimus pacem) and 1552[35] (as Tulerunt Dominum); 2p. is also found separately with text Tu sola es virgo pulcherrima (anon.) in VEaf 218; see also Tulerunt Dominum, below
Lugebat David Absalon	8	—	1564[1] and derivative MSS	
Magnificat septimi toni	4	—	D-LEu Thomaskirche 49 (A only); H-Bn Bártfa Mus.22	doubtful on stylistic grounds; 'incerti auctoris' in D-ROu 49
Magnificat	4	—	E-SE	doubtful on stylistic grounds; contains no reference to Magnificat tones

62

Incipit	No. of parts	Edition	Source of attribution to Josquin	Remarks
Mirabilia testimonia tua	4		ptbk in private possession	see Elders (1982); attrib. possibly due to confusion with Josquin's authentic setting
Miseremini mei	4	A. Smijers: *Treize livres*, i (Paris, 1934)	1520[2]	attrib. Richafort in 1519[1] and *A-Wn* 15941, Mouton in *CH-SGs* 463, 1547[1] and *D-Mbs* Mus.Ms.16; probably by Richafort
Missus est Gabriel angelus	5	MRM, iv	1519[3], 1526[4], *D-Mu* Cim.44i, *I-Rvat* C.S.19, C.G.XII.4	Lowinsky (MRM, iii, 1968, pp.222f) argued strongly in favour of ascription to Mouton in *Fl* Acq. e Doni 666 and elsewhere
Nesciens mater	5	Mot.v: 45	1545[3], 1546[3], *CS-HK* II-A-22, II-A-26	doubtful on stylistic grounds; see Sparks, FC 1971, 350
Nunc dimittis	4	Mot.v: 52	*I-Bc* Q20	doubtful on stylistic grounds; attribs. in source unreliable
O admirabile commercium	5	CMM, ix/2	*NL-Lml* 422 (index only)	by Regis, to whom it is attrib. in *I-Rvat* Chigiana C.VIII. 234
O dulcis amica	6	—	1540[7]	doubtful on stylistic grounds; source unreliable
Obsecro te, domina	?	—	1547[23]	tablature only
Pange lingua	4	EDM, 1st ser., xxi (1942/R)	*D-Rp* A.R.847, A.R.866	doubtful on stylistic grounds
Petre, tu pastor ovium	—	—		attrib. 'Jus.' when source complete as Königsberg 1740; 1 ptbk in *Ga* 7 without attrib.
Propter peccata (see La Spagna)				
Puer natus est nobis	4	H. Albrecht (Kassel, 1959)	*Dlb* Grimma 51	attrib. to Mouton in 1538[4] (except bassus) is probably due to confusion with Mouton's much better-authenticated setting; attrib. Mahu in bassus is more probable
Quam delecta tabernacula	5	—	1553[3] (A only)	main attrib. to Certon is correct
Quam pulchra es	4	—	1537[1] (index only), 1559[2]	attrib. Mouton in 1519[1] etc, Moulu in *CH-SGs* 463 etc; probably by Moulu; ed. J. G. Chapman (diss., New York U., 1964)
Queramus cum pastoribus	4	A. Smijers: *Van Ockeghem tot Sweelinck*, vii (Amsterdam, 1956)	1546[25], 1546[26]	by Mouton

Qui regis Israel, intende	5	Mot.iv. 40	1538[3], 1553[3] and derivative MSS	doubtful on stylistic grounds
Recordare virgo mater	4	Suppl. MT, cxii (1971), 749		doubtful on stylistic grounds
Regina celi	6		1520[1] (index) —	anon. in only source, I-Rvat C.S.46, but attrib. Josquin in inventory; see Noble (1971)
Responsum acceperat Simeon	6	Mot.v: 49	1543[1], 1546[3]	doubtful on stylistic grounds; see Sparks, FC 1971, 356f
Salva nos, Domine	6	CMM, iii/4 (1952); MRM, iv (1968)	Bc R142	attrib. Willaert in 1542[10], but certainly by Mouton to whom it is attrib. in 1521[6] and many other sources; see Lowinsky, MRM, iii (1968), 178f
Salve regina	6	CMM, xxviii/2 (1973)	Bc R142 (2nd index only)	attrib. Jacquet in body of Bc R142 and in Rvat C.S.24; attrib. Verdelot in Rv S.Borr.E.II.55–60
Sancta mater, istud agas	4	Suppl.	E-Bc M.454	by Peñalosa, to whom it is attrib. in E-Sco 5-5-20 and elsewhere; see Stevenson, FC 1971, 219f
Sancta Trinitas unus Deus	6	DTÖ, xcix (1961)	D-ELa Cantionale	orig. 4-part motet is by Févin; in 1555[11] the 2 added vv are attrib. Arnoldus de Brouck
Sancti Dei omnes	4	Mot.v: 46	E-Tc 13	by Mouton, to whom it is attrib. in I-Rvat C.S.42 and elsewhere
Scimus quoniam diligentibus	4	—	D-Dl Mus.1/D/505	probably contrafactum of a setting of De tous bien plaine; see Osthoff (1962–5), ii, 102f
Te Deum laudamus (i)	4	—	ROu Mus.49; contemporary MS attribs. in Bds and Ju copies of 1537[11]	also attrib. De Silva and Mouton; ? by De Silva
Te Deum laudamus (ii)	4	—	ROu Mus.49	doubtful on stylistic grounds
Tribulatio et angustia	4	Mot.iii: 37	1537[1], 1559[1], LEu Thomaskirche 49 etc	? by Verdelot, to whom it is attrib. in c1526[8]
Tulerunt Dominum meum	4	—	CH-SGs 463; D-Mu Cim.44a	probably by Pre Michael de Ver[ona], to whom it is attrib. in 1519[6]; ed. D. M. Gehrenbeck (diss., Union Theological Seminary, 1971)
Tulerunt Dominum meum	8	Cw. xxiii (1933/R)	1554[10] and derivative MSS	attrib. Gombert in GB-Lbm Roy.App.49–54 (as Je prens congié), I-VEaf 218 (as Sustinuimus pacem) and 1552[28], and probably by him; see Lugebat David above
Verbum bonum et suave	5		D-Mu Cim.44i (T only)	anon. in 1519[6] etc; doubtful on stylistic grounds; ed. D. M. Gehrenbeck (diss., Union Theological Seminary, 1971)
Verbum caro factum est	5	Mot.v: 51	Z 73	probably by Benedictus [Appenzeller], to whom it is attrib. in 1546[7]
Victimae paschali laudes	6	Mot.v: 48	E-Tc 10, I-Rv S.Borr.E.II. 55–60	doubtful on stylistic grounds; probably by Brunet, to whom it is attrib. in Rvat C.S.24; see Sparks, FC 1971, 374f

Incipit	No. of parts	Edition	Source of attribution to Josquin *(secular)*	Remarks
Ach hülf mich leid	4	SMd, v (1967)	CH-SGs 530 (later hand)	attrib. Pierson [= La Rue] in Bu F.X.1-4, Bauldeweyn in A-Wn 18810
Baisez-moy, ma doulce amye	6	WW i: 5	1545¹¹, Heartz no.162	no conflicting attribs. but see Blume (1930), 68, and MRM, ii (1967), pp.ix f, 71f
Cela ne plus	3	—	I-Fn 178	not Josquin's setting
Cent mille regrets	5	WW i: 8	Heartz no.162	attrib. La Rue in Rvat Pal.Lat.1982 and probably by him
Considerés mes incessantes plaintes/Fortuna desperata	5	—	—	anon. in sole source, A-Wn 18746; attrib. Josquin by Van Benthem (1971) on stylistic grounds
Cueurs desolez par toutes nations	4	WW i: 8	c1528⁴ (= Heartz no.29)	also printed in Chansons a quattre parties (Antwerp, 1542), as by Benedictus [Appenzeller], certainly the composer
Dame donner [d'honneur]	5	Van Benthem (1971), suppl.	—	anon. in sole source, Wn 18746; attrib. Josquin by Van Benthem (1971) on stylistic grounds
Duo [textless]	2	—	D-As 2° Cod.142a	unidentified
Et trop penser	3	—	—	attrib. in I-Rc 2856 to 'Bosfrin'; ? a scribal error for 'Josquin'; ed. A. S. Wolff (diss., North Texas State U., 1970)
Fors seulement	?6	—	Bc R142	only 1v survives in sole source, and contains only the voice borrowed from Ockeghem
Fors seulement	3	—	MS attribs. in D-Ju copy of 1538⁶ and Bds copy of 1541²	attrib. A. de Févin in GB-Cmc Pepys 1760 and later sources, and certainly by him; ed. E. Clinkscale (diss., New York U., 1965)
Fors seulement	4	F. J. Giesbert: Ein altes Spielbuch (Mainz, 1936)	CH-SGs 461	attrib. Ghiselin in I-Fc Basevi 2439: anon. in 1504³
Fors seulement	4	—	—	anon. in only known sources, I-Fn Magl.XIX.164 and D-As 2° Cod.142a, but in the latter forms part of a 'Josquin gathering'; see M. Staehelin, TVNM, xxiii/2 (1973), 79
Fortuna disperata	3	WW ii: 53	E-SE	doubtful on stylistic grounds
Guillaume se va chaufer	4	SMd, v (1967)	—	attrib. to Josquin stems from misreading of Glarean (1547)
Incessament non povre cueur	5	WW i: 8	Heartz no.162	attrib. La Rue in CH-SGs 463 and elsewhere, and probably by him
J'ay bien nourri sept ans	3	A. W. Atlas: The Cappella Giulia Chansonnier (1976)	I-Fn Magl.XIX.178	attrib. Japart in Fn Banco rari 229, 'Johannes Joye' in E-SE

La Spagna	5	WW ii: 54	—	anon. in *DK-Kk* Gl.Kgl.Sml.1872, the only source that preserves the probably orig. inst version; contrafactum *Propter peccata* attrib. Josquin in 1537¹ and 1559¹ and derivative MSS, but most unlikely to be by him
Lourdault, lourdault	4	MRM, ii (1967), 108	*CH-Bu* F.X.1-4	attrib. Compère in 1502² and *D-Rp* C120, Ninot le Petit in *I-Bc* Q17; probably by Compère; see MRM, ii (1967), 28ff, and Finscher (1964)
Ma dame, helas	3	H. Hewitt, ed.: [O. Petrucci:] *Harmonice musices odhecaton A* (Cambridge, Mass., 1946)	1501¹, *D-Z* 78, 3	no conflicting attribs. but anon. in later edns. of *Odhecaton*; called (? or attrib.) 'Dux Carlus' in *I-Bc* Q16
Mala se nea	?	—	*Brown1* 1548³ and 1548³	cf Lebrun's *N'avons point veu mal assenée* in Le Roy & Ballard's *Livre de meslanges* (1560) and 1572²
Mon seul plaisir	4	Picker (1965)	*CH-Bu* F.X.1-4	attrib. Ninot le Petit in *I-Fc* Basevi 2439 and probably by him; see Picker (1965), 158
O venus bant	3	Hewitt, op cit	1501¹, *CH-SGs* 463	attrib. Weerbeke in *E-Sco* 5-1-43
Petite camusette	3		1578¹⁴	by A. de Févin, to whom it is attrib. in *GB-Cmc* Pepys 1760; ed. E. Clinkscale (diss., New York U., 1965)
Saillies avant	5		—	anon. in sole source, *A-Wn* 18746; attrib. Josquin by Van Benthem (1971) on stylistic grounds
Sans vous veoir	5		—	anon. in sole source, *Wn* 18746; attrib. Josquin by Van Benthem (1971) on stylistic grounds
Si j'ay perdu mon amy	4	F. J. Giesbert: *Ein altes Spielbuch* (Mainz, 1936)	*I-Fc* Basevi 2442	some doubts on grounds of style, and anonymity of other sources (*Fn* Magl.XIX.164-7, *CH-SGs* 461) may outweigh this ascription
Soubz ce tumbel	4	Picker (1965)	—	anon. in *B-Br* 228, the only source, but Droz and Thibault suggested Josquin as composer (1924) and are supported by Picker (1965)
Tant vous aime, bergeronette	4		*I-Fc* Basevi 2442	attrib. in sole source may be result of confusion with *Bergerette savoyenne*
Tous les regretz	4	MRM, ii (1967), 153	*D-Rp* C120	many attribs. to La Rue and undoubtedly by him; see MRM, ii (1967), 50
Vivrai-je tousjours en telle paine	4	R. van Maldeghem: *Trésor musical*, 2nd ser., xiv (1878), 12	*F-CA* 125-8	attrib. to Josquin in sole source questioned by Osthoff (1962-5), ii, 179f, and piece is rejected by eds. of complete edn.
Vrai dieu d'amours	?	*Brown1* 1549¹	—	anon. in *GB-Lbm* Add.35087 and Harl.5242

BIBLIOGRAPHY

GENERAL AND BACKGROUND STUDIES

BurneyH

H. Glarean: *Dodecachordon* (Basle, 1547; Eng. trans., MSD, vi, 1965)

A. P. Coclico: *Compendium musices* (Nuremberg, 1552/*R*1954)

C. Bartoli: *Ragionamenti accademici . . . sopra alcuni luoghi difficili di Dante* (Venice, 1567)

J. N. Forkel: *Allgemeine Geschichte der Musik*, ii (Leipzig, 1801)

R. G. Kiesewetter: *Die Verdienste der Niederländer um die Tonkunst* (Amsterdam, 1829)

E. vander Straeten: *La musique aux Pays-Bas avant le XIXe siècle* (Brussels, 1867–88/*R*1969)

A. W. Ambros: *Geschichte der Musik*, iii (Leipzig, rev. 2/1893 by O. Kade); v (Leipzig, rev. 3/1911 by O. Kade)

H. Besseler: *Die Musik des Mittelalters und der Renaissance*, HMw, ii (1931)

M. van Crevel: *Adrianus Petit Coclico: Leben und Beziehungen eines nach Deutschland emigrierten Josquinschülers* (The Hague, 1940)

A. Pirro: *Histoire de la musique de la fin du XIVe siècle à la fin du XVIe* (Paris, 1940)

C. van den Borren: *Geschiedenis van de muziek in de Nederlanden*, i (Antwerp, 1948)

G. Reese: *Music in the Renaissance* (New York, 1954, rev. 2/1959)

H. C. Wolff: *Die Musik der alten Niederländer* (Leipzig, 1956)

H. M. Brown: *Music in the French Secular Theater, 1400–1550* (Cambridge, Mass., 1963)

E. E. Lowinsky: 'Scholarship in the Renaissance: Music', *RN*, xvi (1963), 255

E. H. Sparks: *Cantus Firmus in Mass and Motet, 1420–1520* (Berkeley and Los Angeles, 1963)

L. Finscher: *Loyset Compère: Life and Works*, MSD, xii (1964)

M. Picker: *The Chanson Albums of Marguerite of Austria* (Berkeley and Los Angeles, 1965)

H. L. Clarke: 'Musicians of the Northern Renaissance', *Aspects of Medieval and Renaissance Music: a Birthday Offering to Gustave Reese* (New York, 1966, rev. 2/1978)

D. Kämper: *Studien zur instrumentalen Ensemblemusik des 16. Jahrhunderts in Italien*, AnMc, no.10 (1970) [whole vol.]

F. A. D'Accone: 'The Performance of Sacred Music in Italy during Josquin's Time, c. 1475–1525', *Josquin des Prez: New York 1971*, 601

M. L. Gatti Perer: 'Art and Architecture in Lombardy at the Time of Josquin des Prez', *Josquin des Prez: New York 1971*, 138

E. H. Sparks: *The Music of Noel Bauldeweyn* (New York, 1972)

Bibliography

E. E. Lowinsky, ed.: *Josquin des Prez: Proceedings of the International Josquin Festival–Conference* (London, New York and Toronto, 1976) [*Josquin des Prez: New York 1971*]

H.-K. Metzger and R. Riehn, eds.: *Josquin des Prés*, Musik-Konzepte, no.26–7 (Munich, 1982) [incl. critical discography and worklist]

S. R. Charles: *Josquin des Prez, a Guide to Research* (New York, 1983)

WORKS AND STYLE

A. Smijers: 'Een kleine bijdrage over Josquin en Isaac', *Gedenkboek aangeboden aan Dr. D. F. Scheurleer* (The Hague, 1925), 313

——: 'Josquin des Prez', *PMA*, liii (1926–7), 95

Y. Rokseth: 'Notes sur Josquin des Prés comme pédagogue musical', *RdM*, viii (1927), 202

O. Ursprung: 'Josquin des Prés', *Bulletin de la Société 'Union musicologique'*, vi (1928), 11–50

F. Blume: 'Josquin des Prés', *Der Drachentöter* (1930), 52

E. E. Lowinsky: 'The Goddess Fortuna in Music', *MQ*, xxix (1943), 45–77

M. Antonowycz: *Die Motette 'Benedicta es' von Josquin des Prez und die Messen super Benedicta von Willaert, Palestrina, de la Hêle und de Monte* (Utrecht, 1951)

H. Osthoff: 'Besetzung und Klangstruktur in den Werken von Josquin des Prez', *AMw*, ix (1952), 177

S. Clercx: 'Lumières sur la formation de Josquin et d'Obrecht', *RBM*, xi (1953), 158

M. Antonowycz: 'Renaissance-Tendenzen in den Fortuna-desperata Messen von Josquin und Obrecht', *Mf*, ix (1956), 1

H. Osthoff: 'Die Psalm-Motetten von Josquin Desprez', *Kongressbericht: Wien Mozartjahr 1956*, 452

——: 'Das Magnificat bei Josquin Desprez', *AMw*, xvi (1959), 220

E. Stam: 'Eine "Fuga trium vocum" von Josquin Desprez', *Mf*, xiii (1960), 28

M. Antonowycz: 'Die Josquin-Ausgabe', *TVNM*, xix/1–2 (1960), 6

——: 'The Present State of Josquin Research', *IMSCR, viii New York 1961*, i, 53

J. Mattfeld: 'Some Relationships between Texts and Cantus Firmi in the Liturgical Motets of Josquin des Prés', *JAMS*, xiv (1961), 159

H. Osthoff: *Josquin Desprez* (Tutzing, 1962–5)

C. Titcomb: 'The Josquin Acrostic Re-examined', *JAMS*, xvi (1963), 47

M. Antonowycz: 'Zur Autorschaftsfrage der Motetten *Absolve, quaesumus, Domine* und *Inter natos mulierum*', *TVNM*, xx/3 (1966), 154

E. Clinkscale: 'Josquin and Louis XI', *AcM*, xxxviii (1966), 67

C. Maas: 'Josquin–Agricola–Brumel–De La Rue: een authenticiteitsprobleem', *TVNM*, xx/3 (1966), 120

M. Antonowycz: 'Die *Missa Mater Patris* von Josquin des Prez', *TVNM*, xx/4 (1967), 206

E. E. Lowinsky: 'Josquin des Prez and Ascanio Sforza', *Il duomo di Milano: congresso internazionale: Milano 1968*, 17

A. Dunning: 'Josquini antiquos, Musae, memoremus amores: a Mantuan Motet from 1554 in Homage to Josquin', *AcM*, xli (1969), 108

W. Elders: 'Das Symbol in der Musik von Josquin des Prez', *AcM*, xli (1969), 164

J. van Benthem: 'Zur Struktur und Authentizität der Chansons à 5 & 6 von Josquin des Prez', *TVNM*, xxi/3 (1970), 170

M. Antonowycz: ' "Illibata Dei Virgo": a Melodic Self-portrait of Josquin des Prez', *Josquin des Prez: New York 1971*, 545

J. van Benthem: 'Josquin's Three-part "Chansons rustiques": a Critique of the Readings in Manuscripts and Prints', *Josquin des Prez: New York 1971*, 421

F. Blume: 'Josquin des Prez: the Man and the Music', *Josquin des Prez: New York 1971*, 18

N. Bridgman: 'On the Discography of Josquin and the Interpretation of his Music in Recordings', *Josquin des Prez: New York 1971*, 633

H. M. Brown: 'Accidentals and Ornamentation in Sixteenth-century Intabulations of Josquin's Motets', *Josquin des Prez: New York 1971*, 475

V. W. Callahan: ' "Ut Phoebi radiis": the Riddle of the Text Resolved', *Josquin des Prez: New York 1971*, 560

C. Dahlhaus: 'On the Treatment of Dissonance in the Motets of Josquin des Prez', *Josquin des Prez: New York 1971*, 334

W. Elders: 'Plainchant in the Motets, Hymns, and Magnificat of Josquin des Prez', *Josquin des Prez: New York 1971*, 523

——: 'Zusammenhänge zwischen den Motetten *Ave nobilissima creatura* und *Huc me sydereo* von Josquin des Prez', *TVNM*, xxii/1 (1971), 67

L. Finscher: 'Historical Reconstruction versus Structural Interpretation in the Performance of Josquin's Motets', *Josquin des Prez: New York 1971*, 627

C. Gallico: 'Josquin's Compositions on Italian Texts and the Frottola', *Josquin des Prez: New York 1971*, 446

J. Haar: 'Some Remarks on the "Missa La sol fa re mi" ', *Josquin des Prez: New York 1971*, 564

D. Harrán: 'Burney and Ambros as Editors of Josquin's Music', *Josquin des Prez: New York 1971*, 148

B. Jeffery: 'The Literary Texts of Josquin's Chansons', *Josquin des Prez: New York 1971*, 401

Bibliography

R. B. Lenaerts: 'Musical Structure and Performance Practice in Masses and Motets of Josquin and Obrecht', *Josquin des Prez: New York 1971*, 619

E. E. Lowinsky: 'Ascanio Sforza's Life: a Key to Josquin's Biography and an Aid to the Chronology of his Works', *Josquin des Prez: New York 1971*, 31

J. A. Mattfeld: 'An Unsolved Riddle: the Absence of Ambrosian Melodies in Josquin's Sacred Music', *Josquin des Prez: New York 1971*, 360

A. Mendel: 'Towards Objective Criteria for Establishing Chronology and Authenticity: what Help can the Computer give?', *Josquin des Prez: New York 1971*, 297

J. Noble: 'A New Motet by Josquin?', *MT*, cxii (1971), 749, suppl.

S. Novack: 'Tonal Tendencies in Josquin's Use of Harmony', *Josquin des Prez: New York 1971*, 317

G. Reese: 'The Polyphonic "Missa de Beata Virgine" as a Genre: the Background of Josquin's Lady Mass', *Josquin des Prez: New York 1971*, 589

W. H. Rubsamen: 'Unifying Techniques in Selected Masses of Josquin and La Rue: a Stylistic Comparison', *Josquin des Prez: New York 1971*, 369

E. H. Sparks: 'Problems of Authenticity in Josquin's Motets', *Josquin des Prez: New York 1971*, 345

E. Stam: 'Die vierundzwanzigstimmige kanonische Psalmmotette *Qui habitat in adiutorio altissimi* von Josquin des Prez', *TVNM*, xxii/1 (1971), 1

G. Thibault: 'Instrumental Transcriptions of Josquin's French Chansons', *Josquin des Prez: New York 1971*, 455

W. Wiora: 'The Structure of Wide-spanned Melodic Lines in Earlier and Later Works of Josquin', *Josquin des Prez: New York 1971*, 309

S. Clercx-Lejeune: 'Fortuna Josquini: a proposito di un ritratto di Josquin des Prez', *NRMI*, iii (1972), 315

M. Picker: 'A Josquin Parody by Marco Antonio Cavazzoni', *TVNM*, xxii/3 (1972), 157

L. L. Perkins: 'Mode and Structure in the Masses of Josquin', *JAMS*, xxvi (1973), 189

J. van Benthem: 'Einige Musikintarsien des frühen 16. Jahrhunderts in Piacenza und Josquins Proportionskanon "Agnus Dei" ', *TVNM*, xxiv/1 (1974), 97

W. Elders: 'Report of the First Josquin Meeting, Utrecht 1973', *TVNM*, xxiv/1 (1974), 20

L. Lockwood: ' "Messer Gossino" and Josquin Desprez', *Studies in Renaissance and Baroque Music in Honor of Arthur Mendel* (Kassel and Hackensack, 1974), 15

A. Ghislanzoni: *Josquin Des Prez (Joducus Pratensis)* (Frosinone, 1976)

I. Godt: 'Motivic Integration in Josquin's Motets', *JMT*, xxi/2 (1977), 264

L. Finscher: 'Zum Verhältnis von Imitationstechnik und Textbehandlung im Zeitalter Josquins', *Renaissance-Studien: Helmuth Osthoff zum 80. Geburtstag* (Tutzing, 1979), 57

J. van Benthem: '*Fortuna* in Focus: concerning "Conflicting" Progressions in Josquin's *Fortuna dun gran tempo*', *TVNM*, xxx/1 (1980), 1

B. Meier: 'Josquins Motette *Dominus regnavit*: ein Sonderfall des Tonartwechsels', *TVNM*, xxxii/1 (1982), 45

J. Milsom: '*Circumdederunt*: "A Favourite Cantus Firmus of Josquin's"?', *Soundings*, no.9 (1982), 2

ARCHIVAL AND SOURCE STUDIES

E. Motta: 'Musici alla corte degli Sforza', *Archivio storico lombardo*, 2nd ser., iv (1887), 29–64

H. Osthoff: 'Zur Echtheitsfrage und Chronologie bei Josquins Werken', *IMSCR, v Utrecht 1952*, 303

C. Sartori: 'Josquin des Prés, cantore del duomo di Milano (1459–1472)', *AnM*, iv (1956), 55

C. van den Borren: 'Un hypothèse concernant le lieu de naissance de Josquin des Prez', *Festschrift Joseph Schmidt-Görg zum 60. Geburtstag* (Bonn, 1957), 21

——: 'L'énigme des *Credo de Village*', *Hans Albrecht in memoriam* (Kassel, 1962), 48

W. Kirsch: *Die Quellen der mehrstimmigen Magnificat- und Te Deum-Vertonungen bis zur Mitte des 16. Jahrhunderts* (Tutzing, 1966)

E. E. Lowinsky, ed.: *The Medici Codex of 1518*, MRM, iii–iv (1968)

N. Böker-Heil: 'Zu einem frühvenezianischen Motettenrepertoire', *Helmuth Osthoff zu seinem siebzigsten Geburtstag* (Tutzing, 1969), 59

D. Heartz: *Pierre Attaingnant, Royal Printer of Music* (Berkeley and Los Angeles, 1969)

A. W. Atlas: *Rome, Biblioteca Apostolica Vaticana, Cappella Giulia XIII 27, and the Dissemination of the Franco-Netherlandish Chanson in Italy, c. 1460–c. 1530* (diss., New York U., 1971)

J. van Benthem: 'Einige wiedererkannte Josquin-Chansons im Codex 18746 der Österreichischen Nationalbibliothek', *TVNM*, xxii/1 (1971), 18

L. Hoffmann-Erbrecht: 'Problems in the Interdependence of Josquin Sources', *Josquin des Prez: New York 1971*, 285

W. Kirsch: 'Josquin's Motets in the German Tradition', *Josquin des*

Bibliography

Prez: New York 1971, 261

H. Kellman: 'Josquin and the Courts of the Netherlands and France: the Evidence of the Sources', *Josquin des Prez: New York 1971*, 181

Kwee Him Yong: 'Sixteenth-century Printed Instrumental Arrangements of Works by Josquin des Prez: an Inventory', *TVNM*, xxii/1 (1971), 43

L. Lockwood: 'Josquin at Ferrara: New Documents and Letters', *Josquin des Prez: New York 1971*, 103

J. Noble: 'New Light on Josquin's Benefices', *Josquin des Prez: New York 1971*, 76

M. Picker: 'Josquiniana in some Manuscripts at Piacenza', *Josquin des Prez: New York 1971*, 247

J. Snížková: 'Josquin in Czech Sources of the Second Half of the Sixteenth Century', *Josquin des Prez: New York 1971*, 279

R. Stevenson: 'Josquin in the Music of Spain and Portugal', *Josquin des Prez: New York 1971*, 217

M. Honegger: 'La tablature de D. Pisador et le problème des altérations au XVIe s.', *RdM*, lix (1973), 38, 191; lx (1974), 3

B. J. Blackburn: 'Josquin's Chansons: Ignored and Lost Sources', *JAMS*, xxix (1976), 30–76

I. Godt: 'The Restoration of Josquin's *Ave mundi spes, Maria*, and some Observations on Restoration', *TVNM*, xxvi/2 (1976), 53

E. Stam: 'Josquins Proportionskanon *Agnus Dei* und dessen Piacentiner Überlieferung', *TVNM*, xxvi/1 (1976), 1 [with reply by Van Benthem]

R. Sherr: 'Notes on Two Roman Manuscripts of the Early Sixteenth Century', *MQ*, lxiii (1977), 48

Y. Esquieu: 'La musique à la cour provençale du roi René', *Provence historique*, xxxi (1981), 299

H. M. Brown: 'Words and Music in Early 16th Century Chansons: Text Underlay in Florence, Biblioteca del Conservatorio, Ms Basevi 2442', *Formen und Probleme der Überlieferung mehrstimmiger Musik im Zeitalter Josquins Desprez*, ed. L. Finscher (Munich, 1982), 97–142

W. Elders: 'Ein handschriftlicher "Liber Psalmorum" aus deutscher Überlieferung', *Formen und Probleme der Überlieferung mehrstimmiger Musik im Zeitalter Josquins Desprez*, ed. L. Finscher (Munich, 1982), 47

H. Kellman: 'Music in the Renaissance *collégiale*: Josquin des Prez and Notre-Dame at Condé-sur-Escaut', *IMS: Strasbourg 1982*

T. Noblitt: 'Textual Criticism of Selected Works published by Petrucci', *Formen und Probleme der Überlieferung mehrstimmiger Musik im Zeitalter Josquins Desprez*, ed. L. Finscher (Munich, 1982), 201–44

R. Sherr: 'Notes on some papal documents in Paris', *Studi musicali*, xii (1983), 5

T. Ward: 'A Newly-discovered Josquin Attribution', *TVNM*, xxxiv (1984)

GIOVANNI PIERLUIGI
DA
PALESTRINA

Lewis Lockwood

Jessie Ann Owens

Life

I Origins and early years

Giovanni Pierluigi da Palestrina was probably born in the town of Palestrina (known in antiquity as Praeneste), in the Sabine Hills near Rome, in 1525 or 1526. Throughout his life he was known by the surname Palestrina or Prenestino, sometimes by the nickname 'Giannetto'; in his own letters he normally signed himself as 'Giovanni Petraloysio', only once as 'il Palestrina'.

The dates between which Palestrina is presumed to have been born – 3 February 1525 and 2 February 1526 – derive from an important eulogy by a younger contemporary, a certain Melchiorre Major (see Mercati, 1924), entered into the tenor partbook of a printed volume of motets by Claudin de Sermisy that is still part of the library of the Cappella Sistina in Rome. It states that at his death on 2 February 1594 Palestrina was 68 years old, and the eulogy then concludes with a verse epitaph beginning 'O mors inevitabilis', a text strikingly similar to the epitaph for Josquin that had been set to music by Jheronimus Vinders and published in 1545. As for Palestrina's birthplace, it has long been assumed, plausibly enough, that he was born in the town from which his name is taken and in which his family had settled some years before he was born. Yet although this is indeed likely, Jeppesen observed that the earliest known document in which he is named (a will made by his grandmother Jacobella in October 1527) originated in Rome (see Cametti, 1903). Jeppesen further noted (in *MGG*, x, col.658) that a Roman census of 1525 listed a certain 'Santo de Prenestino' as the head of a household of 12, then living in a Roman quarter near St John Lateran; he suggested that if this Santo were Palestrina's father, whose name was given elsewhere as Sante or Santo (see Casimiri, *NA*, i, 1924, pp.24ff), the composer might actually have been born in Rome. In any event there is no doubt that his early training took place there and that a subsequent period of employment at Palestrina was an interlude in an essentially Roman career. Indeed his entire later life was deeply rooted in the papal Rome of the ascendant Counter-Reformation and was steeped in the musical and liturgical traditions of three of the oldest and most celebrated of Roman churches, in which he held successive appointments – S Maria Maggiore, St John Lateran and St Peter's.

Palestrina seems to have been first trained in music at S Maria Maggiore; a document of October 1537 (first published in Casimiri, 1918–22) lists a 'Giovanni da Palestrina' among the choirboys there. Although Baini (1828) and others after him have claimed that the choirmaster at S Maria Maggiore then was Giacomo Coppola, Casimiri (*NA*, i, 1924, p.64) asserted that Coppola was merely a singer there and that Palestrina's probable teachers at this time were the successive *maestri* of these years: Robin Mallapert in 1538–9, a certain 'Robert' in 1540 and Firmin Lebel from the end of 1540. An early but unfounded legend had it that Palestrina's teacher was one 'Gaudio Mell'. Baini took this to be Goudimel, but his theory was later disproved by Michel Brenet (in *Claude Goudimel*, Besançon,

1898) on the grounds that he was never in Rome. It is important, on the other hand, to note that among these presumed early teachers two at least (Mallapert and Lebel) were French.

How long Palestrina remained at S Maria Maggiore as a choirboy is not definitely known, but it could not have been beyond 28 October 1544, when a document shows his engagement as organist at the cathedral of S Agapito in the town of Palestrina (text given by Casimiri, *NA*, i, 1924, pp.43f). Here he was obliged to play the organ and also to teach music to the canons or alternatively to some of the boys. He remained in this familiar but relatively provincial setting until 1551, a period of his life for which there is little or no documentation apart from a notice of his marriage on 12 June 1547 to Lucrezia Gori, daughter of a local citizen of evidently modest means (see *NA*, i, 1924, pp.51f). Their children were Rodolfo (1549–72), Angelo (1551–75) and Iginio (1558–1610). Although Palestrina's activity as a composer is wholly undocumented before his first publication in 1554, it can be assumed that during his years in Palestrina he must have begun to develop that broad knowledge of earlier and contemporary motet and mass traditions and that remarkable technical control manifest in his own works. Although very few of his masses can be dated exactly (a problem rarely discussed by scholars) he may have written a number of them at this period.

II Cappella Giulia and St John Lateran

During the years 1542 to 1550 the Bishop of Palestrina was Cardinal Giovanni Maria del Monte, who in February 1550 was elected pope, assuming the name of

3. Title-page of Palestrina's 'Missarum liber primus' (Rome: Dorico, 1554) showing the composer presenting his work to Pope Julius III

Julius III. He was evidently Palestrina's first and most powerful patron: he was responsible for the young composer's permanent return to Rome in 1551 for his first important appointments and for the publication in 1554 of his first book of masses which is dedicated to him.

On 1 September 1551 Palestrina was unexpectedly appointed *maestro* of the Cappella Giulia, the musical establishment of St Peter's that had been named after Pope Julius II, who had reorganized it and given it increased importance in 1513 as a kind of training centre for native musicians, in contrast to the foreign-dominated Cappella Sistina (see Rostirolla, 1975). In this post Palestrina, now 25 or 26, succeeded Mallapert. By 1554 his first works were appearing: a madrigal came out at Venice in an anthology (*RISM* 1554[28]), and his first book of masses was issued at Rome in a handsome volume containing a large woodcut showing the composer kneeling bare-headed before the pope, presenting his work (fig.3). Similar woodcuts had adorned earlier musical publications dedicated to popes, including Antico's anthology of masses of 1516 for Leo X (see illustration in *MGG*, i, col.549) and Morales's *Liber secundus missarum* (1544), dedicated to Pope Paul III. Indeed it appears that Palestrina's volume is modelled on that of Morales in several respects: for instance, it opens with a tenor mass with separate text celebrating the reigning pope (Palestrina's mass is his *Ecce sacerdos magnus*), and it contains a letter of dedication to the pope. Moreover, the woodcut used for Palestrina's print is the very one that had been employed for Morales's. While the faces of both pope and composer have been altered, along with the papal arms, the music in both illustrations is the same, though with the words deleted;

97

thus Palestrina is inadvertently depicted presenting Morales's mass. Except for the volume of masses by Gasparo Alberti published in 1549, Palestrina's 1554 book is in fact the first single publication of masses by a native Italian composer, and it is the very first issued in Rome. It must have made a powerful impression.

A year later Palestrina's career advanced another step, again with the aid of Julius III. On 13 January 1555 he was admitted to the Cappella Sistina, the pope's official musical chapel. This was in spite of his being married and 'on the orders of His Holiness Pope Julius, without any examination . . . and without the consent of the singers' (see the *Diarii Sistini* in *NA*, xiii, 1936, p.209). Three months later Julius III died and was succeeded by Cardinal Marcello Cervini, who took the name of Marcellus II. In turn Marcellus's reign was cut short by death; it lasted scarcely three weeks. He was succeeded by that intransigent defender of the Counter-Reformation, Paul IV. From this point to the end of Palestrina's life there is no indication that he directly enjoyed the favour of any pope as he had that of Julius III; the only possible exception is Gregory XIII, to whom he offered a later dedication and with whose family he seems to have been connected in some way. The title of the famous *Missa Papae Marcelli* (published in 1567) quite possibly reflects a particular event in Marcellus's short reign, when he called his singers together on Good Friday 1555, the third day of his reign, to inform them that the music for Holy Week should be more in keeping with the character of the occasion and that as far as possible the words should be clearly understood (see Weinmann, 1919, p.148). In September 1555 a rigorous enforcement of the chapel's rule on celibacy brought about the dismissal of Palestrina and two other married singers, though they were given modest pensions.

On 1 October 1555 Palestrina became *maestro di cappella* of the great church of St John Lateran, a position that Lassus had briefly held a short while previously. A musical *cappella* had been installed as late as 1535 and it had never been furnished with sufficient funds to ensure more than minimal proficiency. In 1560 Palestrina found himself opposed to the chapter over funds for the musicians, and at the end of that July he abruptly left his post, taking with him his son Rodolfo, who had been a choirboy. From then until March 1561 his exact employment is unknown.

III   S Maria Maggiore and private service

After five unsuccessful years at St John Lateran, Palestrina returned to S Maria Maggiore, where he had been trained. His employment there seems to have lasted until 1566. It was evidently less demanding than his earlier posts, since in 1564 he was able to accept an offer from the wealthy Cardinal Ippolito II d'Este to take charge of music during the summer months at his sumptuous country estate, the Villa d'Este, which he had built at Tivoli, outside Rome. He was again in Ippolito's service, now apparently on a full-time basis, from 1 August 1567 to March 1571. As a way of ensuring the education of his sons he also taught music at the Seminario Romano during the years 1566–71 (see Casimiri, *NA*, xii, 1935, pp.17ff).

The remarkable spreading of Palestrina's reputation during the 1560s is indicated by a flattering offer made to him in 1568, on behalf of the Emperor Maximilian II, to transfer to Vienna as imperial choirmaster, a post left vacant by Jacobus Vaet's death in 1567. But the negotiations broke down when the emperor's ambassador found Palestrina's terms too high, and subsequently the post went to Philippe de Monte. Additional and important testimony to his growing circle of influential acquaintances is afforded by his correspondence with Duke Guglielmo Gonzaga of Mantua, which began in 1568 and continued until 1587, the year of Guglielmo's death (the texts are published in Bertolotti, 1890, pp.47ff). No other correspondence by Palestrina is known to exist, and these 12 letters are valuable for what they reveal of his character and his thoughts on various aspects of music, including his opinion of two compositions written by the duke and sent to Palestrina for his judgment (see Jeppesen, 1926, pp.100ff; Eng. trans. in Lockwood, 1975, p.25). In addition Palestrina wrote a series of masses for the special use of the ducal chapel of S Barbara at Mantua, based on plainsongs peculiar to the Mantuan liturgy, selected by the duke and even 'revised' according to late 16th-century views on the proper declamation of a text (see Strunk, 1947 and Jeppesen, 1950 and 1953).

These same years witnessed the publication of important collections: his second book of masses (containing the *Missa Papae Marcelli*) in 1567 and the third in 1570, as well as his first book of motets for four voices in 1563 and his first book of motets for five voices in 1569. That he also maintained at least an occasional connection with the papal chapel is known from an entry in the Sistine records of 1565, indicating an increase in his pension 'owing to certain compositions that he has written already and is to write for the use of the chapel' (see Jeppesen in *MGG*, x, col.685).

IV Last years
Palestrina's last 23 years afforded relative security of employment. In April 1571, on the death of Animuccia, he returned to the post of choirmaster of the Cappella Giulia, and he remained at St Peter's until his death. Yet once again there were signs of his latent dissatisfaction with the terms of his employment; in 1575 an increase in his salary at St Peter's prevented his transferring once again to S Maria Maggiore, which was anxious to have him back; and in 1583 there was serious discussion with his northern patron Duke Guglielmo Gonzaga about the possibility of his going to Mantua as choirmaster. But again the terms he proposed were too high, and the inducement to leave Rome was insufficient.

The 1570s were, however, also years of personal hardship for Palestrina. Between 1572 and 1581 plague caused the deaths of his brother Silla (in 1573), his sons Rodolfo and Angelo (in 1572 and 1575) and his wife Lucrezia (in 1580). In 1580, after her death, he seriously considered joining the priesthood. He initiated preliminary arrangements, receiving the tonsure in December of that year and a benefice a month later. Yet before this step could be consummated he had turned back to the world of practical affairs. On 28 February 1581, just eight months after the death of his first wife, he married again. This marriage, to the well-to-do Virginia Dormoli, widow of a Roman fur merchant, seems to have freed him at last from the financial strains imposed by many years as a poorly paid choirmaster.

He combined his last productive years as a composer with a lively interest in his wife's business, investing both in it and in land and houses on the city outskirts. He died in Rome on 2 February 1594.

At the very end of his life, in 1593, Palestrina was actually planning to return to the post of choirmaster of Palestrina Cathedral that he had held in the 1540s (see Casimiri, *NA*, i, 1924, pp.15, 47). Jeppesen rightly interpreted this as evidence of a characteristically conservative and retrospective tendency in his personality, a last indication of his strongly rooted attachment to his native place. Yet it is equally clear that throughout his career he was well able to look after the practical side of affairs, to demand his due unflinchingly from often niggardly church authorities and to improve his status through dedications to well-placed luminaries of church and state. His career exhibits not only enormous artistic power and fecundity, exercised with great restraint, but also a strong religious feeling coupled with a sense of worldly purpose. It is difficult to know how to interpret the famous dedication of his settings of the Song of Songs (1584), addressed to Pope Gregory XIII, in which he confessed his shame at having set worldly poems to music in former times, that is, in his madrigals: it may be taken as a sincere expression of pious regret or, as Einstein (1949, p. 312) interpreted it, as 'pure hypocrisy'.

It is evident that in his later years Palestrina was held in awe by musicians, both theorists and composers. As early as 1575 the agent of the Duke of Ferrara had written of him that he was 'now considered the very first musician in the world', and in the early 17th century many theorists, especially Cerone, lauded him above all others. The most unusual testimony is the special tribute paid him in 1592, two years before his death, in an anthology of vesper psalms for five voices edited by G. M. Asola (*RISM* 1592[3]) and dedicated to him with an eloquent letter of praise; the composers who contributed to it include Asola himself, Ippolito Baccusi, Giovanni Croce, Giovanni Giacomo Gastoldi, Pietro Pontio and Costanzo Porta. Thus the legend of Palestrina, which was to grow with unceasing vigour during the 17th and 18th centuries and to wax even further in the 19th century (see pp.129–133), had actually begun before he died.

CHAPTER TWO

Palestrina and the Counter-Reformation

That Palestrina's life and music were influenced by
the Counter-Reformation is beyond doubt, but it is
equally beyond doubt that the legends surrounding his
role in these developments, particularly those concerning the *Missa Papae Marcelli*, have distorted the known
reliable evidence beyond the limits of credibility.

The first important phase of the papal Counter-
Reformation took place during Palestrina's early maturity. When the Council of Trent was convoked in 1545
he was a young organist at Palestrina; when it ended in
1563 and the reform movement began in earnest, he was
an established figure in Rome and *maestro* at S Maria
Maggiore and had already been directly connected with
the Cappella Giulia and the papal chapel. He had also
benefited from the patronage of Julius III and was
known to the prelates who were most concerned with
post-Tridentine reform in all its phases, notably
Cardinal Carlo Borromeo. The Council of Trent did
not itself devise legislation dealing with the reform of
church music but simply adopted a broad policy and left
its implementation to local councils. There was discussion of plainsong and polyphony when the subject of
sacred music came up at Trent in 1562 and 1563, but it
is not at all clear that the idea of a specific ban on
polyphony went beyond the stage of preliminary con-

sideration. Some of the delegates at Trent were strongly opposed to the intrusion of secular elements into sacred music and were anxious to ensure the intelligibility of sacred texts when these were set to music. A group of proposals drawn up in 1563 by two papal legates, cardinals Bernardo Navagero and Giovanni Morone, contained a prohibition of 'musica troppo molle', and it is surely relevant that Morone as Bishop of Modena had in 1538 actually abolished polyphony at his cathedral in favour of plainsong, at least for a time, 'because', as a local chronicler put it, 'when they sang plainsong everyone understood [the words]' (see L. Lockwood, *Quadrivium*, vi, 1966, p.44).

The central point of controversy regarding Palestrina and the Counter-Reformation concerns the *Missa Papae Marcelli* and the post-Tridentine Commission of Cardinals established in 1564–5, of which the principal members were cardinals Vitellozzo Vitelli and Carlo Borromeo. According to Baini (1828) this commission was primarily concerned with the encouragement of intelligible polyphony. Baini found an entry in the Sistine Diary showing that on 28 April 1565 the singers of the papal chapel 'were assembled in the home of Cardinal Vitellozzi to sing some masses and test whether the words could be understood, as their Eminences desire'. It was for this occasion that Baini believed the *Missa Papae Marcelli* to have been composed. To buttress this contention he developed an elaborate pseudo-historical narrative, based on sparse evidence, and this became the basis for many later versions of the origins of this mass which have since been repeated in popular accounts up to the present time.

In 1892 Haberl rejected Baini's thesis on the basis

of a close re-examination of the documentary and manuscript evidence for the mass, concluding that the commission's activity was 'purely disciplinary' and that the
Missa Papae Marcelli was probably written as early as
1555 – some ten years before the commission was set
up – perhaps as a celebratory mass for Marcellus II at
the time of his election. This theory receives some slight
confirmation from a recently discovered letter written
by Bishop Cirillo Franco in which he recalled that
Marcellus II, shortly before his election as pope, had
discussed the problem of intelligible sacred music with
him at Loreto, had promised to write to him from Rome
on the matter and had later actually sent him a mass
embodying these principles (see Jeppesen in *MGG*, x,
col.683). On the other hand, Jeppesen's re-examination
of the manuscript evidence for the *Missa Papae
Marcelli* argues for a date closer to 1562 than to 1555
and thus speaks for a closer connection with the
Tridentine discussions on sacred music.

Still other documents show that between January and
March 1565, preceding the trial at the home of Vitelli,
Cardinal Borromeo expressly ordered his vicar in
Milan, Nicolo Ormaneto, 'to reform the singing so that
the words may be as intelligible as possible', and on 10
March 1565 he specifically sent an order to Vincenzo
Ruffo, his choirmaster at Milan Cathedral, to write a
mass 'that should be as clear as possible and send it to
me here'. That Ruffo did indeed write such a mass is
confirmed in the preface to his own mass collection of
1570 (see Lockwood, 1970). It now seems entirely
plausible that Palestrina's *Missa Papae Marcelli*,
whatever its title at the time or its precise date of composition, could have been performed at the trial of 28

April 1565, while at the same time there is no concrete evidence that it was indeed performed then. Masses by Palestrina had certainly been known to cardinals Vitelli and Borromeo as much as three years earlier, for they had been among works exchanged between Rome and Munich in 1562 with Cardinal Truchsess von Waldburg as intermediary. But at that time the exchange of music did not explicitly turn on questions of textual clarity or the idea of reform. (For a substantial selection of the known documents bearing on the date and origin of the *Missa Papae Marcelli* see Lockwood, 1975, pp.6–36.)

That the *Missa Papae Marcelli* was indeed designed for intelligibility, however, has been shown by Jeppesen (1923) through a statistical comparison of its Gloria and Credo sections with those of other masses. The connection between this work and the intelligible style was noticed as early as 1607 by Agostino Agazzari, the first to claim in print that its clarity of declamation had prevented the Council of Trent from abolishing polyphony in church. But the *Missa Papae Marcelli* is not Palestrina's only contribution to this special type of mass. On 2 February 1568 he fulfilled his first commission from Duke Guglielmo Gonzaga by sending him a mass for the private use of his chapel, and he wrote in an accompanying letter that if this work were not satisfactory 'I beg you to let me know how you prefer it: whether long or short or composed so that the words may be understood'. Among the Mantuan masses discovered by Jeppesen is an untitled one for four *voci mutati* that is even more fully declaimed in chordal style in its Gloria and Credo than anything in the Marcellus mass (see Jeppesen in the introduction to G. P. da Palestrina: *Le opere complete*, xviii). Yet this style was too limited artistically for Palestrina. It is realized in these works and in certain masses by his contemporaries, especially Ruffo, but is otherwise bypassed in favour of contrapuntal artifice joined with supple treatment of the melodic lines and with a rich interplay of the voices in polyphonic textures.

It has also been claimed recently (Powers, 1982) that in Palestrina's collection of offertories (1593) the combination of the cycle of texts according to the liturgical calendar and the eight-mode system as a principle of musical organization reaffirms the 'timeless validity' of these properties of Catholic church music, so that the collection is closely allied to the spirit of the Counter-Reformation.

Another important aspect of Palestrina's role in the Counter-Reformation lay in his work on the revision of the plainsongs of the Roman Gradual and Antiphoner. In 1577 he and Annibale Zoilo were entrusted by Gregory XIII with this project, the purpose of which, as stated in Gregory's letter, was to rid these books of their 'superfluities ... barbarisms and obscurities' (trans. from O. Strunk: *Source Readings in Music History*, New York, 1950, p.358). In 1578 Palestrina was much engaged in this work, as is clear from his correspondence with Duke Guglielmo Gonzaga, but he subsequently set it aside and never completed it. The revision was eventually made by others, and the *Editio Medicaea* of 1614 doubtless resembles the kind of revisions that Palestrina would have made, to judge from his correspondence over the revision of plainsongs sent from Mantua (see p.100).

CHAPTER THREE

Works

I Scope, publications and dedications

The scope of Palestrina's work is enormous even by the standards of such prodigious contemporaries as Lassus and Monte, and it is centrally devoted to sacred music. His output of 104 securely attributed masses (not 105 as given by some writers because of the misattribution to him of the *Missa 'Christus resurgens'*, for four voices, by Pierre Colin) is greater in quantity alone than that of any composer of his age. To this fundamental domain of sacred music can be added a large number of motets – about 250 that are securely attributed to Palestrina and over 100 more that are so ascribed though their authenticity may be open to question. Determining the authenticity of the latter group is a major task of future research. Definitely by Palestrina, however, are 68 offertories, at least 65 hymns, 35 *Magnificat* settings and four or five settings of the Lamentations. But he also composed more than 140 madrigals (including some very famous pieces) if his spiritual madrigals are counted alongside his settings of secular poetry. Although he was the first 16th-century composer whose works were produced in a complete edition as early as the 19th century and for whom a second one has been achieved in the 20th, a number of works attributed to him in manuscript sources remain of doubtful authenticity, and the first truly comprehensive *catalogue raisonné* of the sources for all his works was published as late as 1962 by Jeppesen (in *MGG*, x, cols.663ff).

Within Palestrina's own lifetime the publication of his works followed a pattern of increasing frequency after relatively slow beginnings. His first book of masses in 1554 was followed in 1555 by the extremely successful first book of madrigals, which was reprinted eight times before 1600. But between 1555 and 1563, during his difficult period at St John Lateran, there were no new publications apart from madrigals in anthologies, while in contrast his prominent Roman contemporary Giovanni Animuccia brought out two books of madrigals and a book of motets during the 1550s, using Roman publishers who can also be presumed to have been at Palestrina's disposal. In the 1560s the pace quickened. His first book of motets for four voices came out in 1563 and the first book for five voices in 1569; these were again both Roman prints, as was the second book of masses (1567). The 1563 motet volume went through as many as seven reprints before his death in 1594 and four more by 1622; significantly, most of these came from Venetian presses (see below).

Major collections by Palestrina followed steadily in the 1570s and 80s: his second and third books of motets for five or more voices in 1572 and 1575; the second book of motets for four voices in 1581 and the fourth and fifth for five voices in 1584; also the third and fourth books of masses in 1570 and 1582. In 1581 he turned to the newly developing sphere of the *madrigale spirituale*, a favoured genre in the post-Tridentine years, and in 1586 he issued a second set of secular madrigals as well. The last phase of his publishing career began in 1588 with the issuing of single volumes, each devoted to sets of compositions in a single liturgical sector apart from the broad field of the motet: the Lamentations (1588), hymns (1589), *Magnificat* settings (1591), offertories (1593) and litanies (1593 according to Baini, but the only surviving print dates from 1600). There were still more books of masses between 1590 and 1594, bringing the total published during his lifetime to six collections, while a seventh appeared a month after his death – a remarkable total, though still comprising less than half of his entire output.

The rapid diffusion of Palestrina's works was evidently based on quick recognition of their value by Venetian as well as Roman publishers and possibly on direct transmission from Rome to Venice through channels that scholars have not yet traced but that seem to involve the activities of the publisher Alessandro Gardane at Rome and his brother Angelo at Venice, as well as other publishers in both cities. In the 1560s and 1570s Venice became at least as important as Rome for the publication of his new works, and in many cases new volumes issued at Rome were reprinted at Venice the next year (e.g. the motets of 1563 and the fourth book of motets for five voices of 1584). In other cases Roman and Venetian editions appeared in the same year (e.g. the fifth book of motets for five voices of 1584, the hymns, the *Magnificat* settings and the offertories). It is not at all unlikely that Palestrina himself had some connections with Venetian publishers; witness the isolated eight-part mass '*Confitebor tibi*' published as a separate work (with a mass by Bartolomeo Roy in a Venetian edition (*RISM* 1585[5]) that advertised it as a work 'a due cori'. The traditional assumption that the Roman school of Palestrina and the Venetian school of the Gabrielis were entirely separate developments needs to be partly revised in the light of publishing trends. Furthermore, there is still considerable uncertainty about the dating and precise location of a number of Palestrina editions mentioned by Baini (1828) and other 19th-century writers (see Jeppesen in *MGG*, x, cols.663ff). Despite the very large number of publications and reprints of his work during his lifetime, his productivity greatly outran them. This helps to explain the dissatisfaction voiced in the preface to the Lamentations of 1588, addressed to Pope Sixtus V, in which he complained that he had 'composed a great many works and published many, but many more are still in my possession'.

Palestrina's dedications reflect both his worldly ambitions and something of his attitudes as a composer. He dedicated the first five books of masses either to reigning popes or to foreign rulers of great stature (two were dedicated to King Philip II of Spain and one to Duke Wilhelm of Bavaria). Until 1581, on the other hand, the motets were addressed to actual or potential Italian patrons: cardinals Rodolfo Pio de Carpi (1563) and Ippolito d'Este (1569), Duke Guglielmo Gonzaga (1572) and Ippolito's nephew, Duke Alfonso II d'Este (1575). Most of the last works of the late 1580s and 1590s, when the aging composer was in the twilight of his career at St Peter's, bear dedications to popes.

II Masses

Of Palestrina's 104 settings of the mass, 43 were published during his lifetime, all but two of them in the six books that span the 40 years from 1554 until his death. His seventh book was presumably then ready for the press, since it appeared only a month later with a preface by his son Iginio. Between 1599 and 1601 Iginio succeeded in having six more books of masses published in rapid succession at Venice. Altogether some 38 masses were issued for the first time between 1594 and 1601, from which one can easily infer how many settings Palestrina had left unpublished at his death; still more were subsequently discovered in manuscript sources. Elements of style and derivation in some of his masses, as well as remarks in certain of his prefatory letters, suggest that he may have written many of them long before they appeared in print. Thus, in the dedication of his fourth book (1582), he wrote: 'since I have composed a great many works in this genre, I have sent forth these few'. Although some masses were copied into manuscripts that can be dated, the dates are rarely much earlier than the prints: for example, the *Missa 'Ut re mi fa sol la'* was first printed in 1570 but was copied in 1563. However, the *Missa 'Illumina oculos meos'*, first published in 1595, was copied as early as 1565. In general few of the masses can be dated, and the problem of their chronology remains almost entirely unexplored.

The tendency of earlier biographers and historians to deal with Palestrina as a great but solitary figure is nowhere more misleading than in a discussion of his masses. While his entire output spans every type of mass cultivated during the century, the largest group (54 works) is made up of works derived from pre-existing polyphonic compositions; of these, 27 are based on works by others, 24 on his own compositions. They thus correspond to the familiar 16th-century type of mass commonly called 'parody mass' but more accurately termed 'imitation mass'.

The masses based on works by other composers provide substantial insight into Palestrina's knowledge of
earlier repertories, his predilection for particular groups
of composers and types of models, and his specific techniques of composition. At least three of his imitation
masses are based on as yet unidentified models (Reese,
1954, pp.470–72, nos.46, 56 and 93; no.40 is claimed
in L. L. Perkins: *The Motets of Jean l'Héritier*, diss.,
Yale U., 1965, to be based on a motet by Lhéritier, but
the identification is not wholly convincing). For the
works whose models are definitely identified he drew
chiefly on motets of the period after Josquin and principally on the French, Flemish and Spanish composers
who had been assimilated into papal and other Roman
circles during and after the reign of Leo X (1513–21);
these include especially Andreas de Silva, Lhéritier,
Hilaire Penet and Morales. Of these 27, at least 21 are
based on motets, five on madrigals and one on a chanson, while to judge from their titles the three derived
from still unidentified works are also drawn from
motets. In addition to the identifications given in the list
in Reese, valuable new identifications of models were
given by Jeppesen (in *MGG*); these include the observa-
tion that the Mass no.26 (*Missa secunda* of 1582) is
based on the *Veni Sancte Spiritus* published in the
Palestrina *Werke*, xxxii, as a work of doubtful authenticity; that the Mass no.36 is based on the motet
Cantabo domine for six voices in a manuscript in Rome
(Conservatorio di Musica S Cecilia, G.792–5); and that
the *Missa 'Dilexi quoniam'* (no.43), is based on a motet
by Hieronymo Maffoni.

Among motets used by Palestrina as models only one
was published as early as 1520 (Josquin's *Benedicta es*)

while no fewer than 11 had been published in Moderne's *Motetti del fiore* collections of 1532 and 1538. It is particularly suggestive that of the six masses definitely based on motets derived from Moderne's 1532 volume (which is for four voices) three appear consecutively in Palestrina's first book of masses (nos.2, 3 and 4) and are based on motets by Silva, Mathieu Lasson and Philippe Verdelot. This suggests that he used models from that book at a relatively early stage of his development. Other prominent choices of models include – for masses nos.10, 11, 13 and 18 – his selection of four works by Jacquet of Mantua, an outstanding figure at the Gonzaga court, with which he himself had close connections. The absence, so far as is known, of any masses on works by Adrian Willaert, Nicolas Gombert or Clemens non Papa is striking. That only one motet is by an Italian (the obscure Maffoni) emphasizes the primacy of Flemish and French composers in this field and shows Palestrina's absorption of this tradition into his own work. Of his madrigal models (for masses nos.14, 35, 70, 76 and 94) one each is by Cipriano de Rore and Giovan Leonardo Primavera, two are by Domenico Ferrabosco, and one (for no.70) is ascribed to Rore and Morales but is anonymous in its earliest printed source and may be by neither. The lone chanson model (for mass no.41) is by Johannes Lupi or Pierre Cadéac.

On present evidence it would appear that, except for the madrigal used in mass no.35, all the published works by other composers that Palestrina used as models were circulating in print by 1563. They were thus available for his use before the publication in that year of his own first book of motets, the first of his own collections from which he drew models for masses. This evidence offers

Palestrina

Ex.1
(a) Dies sanctificatus

(b) Missa 'Dies sanctificatus', Kyrie I

116

some general support to the speculative assumption that his works on models by others may generally be earlier works, while those based on his own motets may generally be later and have been written fairly close in time to the motets themselves.

While much remains to be understood about the techniques of derivation used in these masses, it appears that in their means of larger distribution of material the imitation masses generally follow the procedures outlined by Pontio (1588) and Pietro Cerone (1613) in their chapters on the mass. The beginnings of the main movements of the mass normally elaborate their counterparts in the model and end with a version of its final cadence. If the motet has a second section this is used for subordinate sections of the mass. The internal distribution of material is, however, highly variable; it seems to be in part cyclic, following the order of the model but reworking it, and in part independent of the model. Particular motifs of the original are often shifted from their original position in order to let them correspond to words that they fit well or to establish verbal parallels between model and mass text. Motifs of symbolic importance in the original, such as those mentioning Jesus Christ, are sometimes taken out of order to reinforce certain phrases of the mass text.

Valuable studies of Palestrina's procedures of polyphonic derivation have recently been published by Quereau (1978, 1982). To illustrate the transformation of the opening of a Palestrina model in an imitation mass, ex.1 shows the opening of his own four-part motet *Dies sanctificatus* and the beginning of the Kyrie of his mass based on it. The entire Kyrie I is based on the first segment of the motet and replicates, with delicate variation, its primary motivic content and organization. This even includes the way in which, in the motet, the opening interval of a 5th between superius and altus is repeated in tenor and bass but with a full realization of the harmonic implications of the interval through a V–I cadence. The Kyrie I contracts the spacing of the opening imitative pairing, and then condenses and simplifies the motivic material of the highest voice throughout the movement. It makes even clearer than does the model the close relationship of motives in this voice-part (e.g., Kyrie I, bars 5–6, 14–15, 17–19).

The other broad classes of Palestrina's output of masses may be divided into several categories: paraphrase, tenor mass, freely composed masses and, as a partly overlapping category, canonic masses. No fewer than 35 works are paraphrase masses based on pre-existing plainsong or, less frequently, secular melodies. These in turn can be subdivided into several groups. 16 masses are based on plainsong mass cycles, including the Requiem (which is always a paraphrase), the *Missa De beata virgine* and the *Missa De feria*, as well as the masses for Mantua (nos.38 and 95–104). Others are based on single melodies, whether longer plainsongs such as the antiphons *Alma Redemptoris mater* (mass no.72) and *Ave regina coelorum* (mass no.57) or short melodies, such as hymns (as in nos. 29 and 30), whose use gives rise to much cyclic repetition in the mass. The tenor mass is a relatively outmoded type in this period and is exemplified by only seven works (nos.1, 17, 20, 50, 71, 87 and 89), including the *Missa 'Ecce sacerdos'* for Julius III, one of the two *L'homme armé* masses (no.17) and the rigidly structured *Missa 'Ave Maria'* published in 1596. The free masses include such works as the *Missa brevis* of 1570 (a special type by virtue of its proportions), the *Missa Papae Marcelli* and several others whose movements do not exhibit the thematic correspondences characteristic of the masses based on polyphonic models.

III Motets and other liturgical works

In sharp contrast to his masses, more of Palestrina's motets were published during his lifetime than were published posthumously or even discovered later as attributed works and added to the supplements of the 19th-century edition of his works. The seven books of motets issued between 1563 and 1584 contain no fewer than 177 motets (as well as two by his brother Silla and one each by his sons Rodolfo and Angelo), while 72 were published posthumously. The largest number of his published motets is for five voices, indicating a predilection for the diversity of imitative and voice-grouping techniques available in this texture; if one takes the full range of his motets together, however, the number in each voice group is as follows: 138 for four voices; 124 for five voices; 41 for six voices; two for seven voices; 60 for eight voices; and ten for 12 voices.

It seems at least a plausible supposition that a number of the motets may have been written later than many of the masses, and closer to their actual dates of publication than was the case with the masses. This is suggested by the generally greater ease of publication of motets, the absence of first publication of motets in contemporary anthologies, the drop in his production of motet volumes after 1584 while other types of work by him were appearing increasingly frequently, and the tightly organized contents of his books of motets of 1563 and 1569 and of the Song of Songs.

An approach to the classification of Palestrina's

motets by means of their liturgical antecedents, both in text and musical characteristics, has been made by Strunk (*PAMS 1939*) but has not yet been followed up. Despite a pronounced tendency towards the neutralization in late 16th-century polyphony of earlier liturgical distinctions, it is clear that the main motet types that he cultivated are those based on antiphon and responsory texts; lesser categories include motets based on sequences, *orationes*, an occasional hymn or devotional text, and psalms.

The four-part motets of the first book display in full perfection that equilibrium in every phase of composition that is the hallmark of Palestrina's art. Throughout a given motet each voice formulates successive melodic segments containing normally complete phrases of text in correct declamation, shaped with maximum care to create well-balanced melodic motion even in inner voices. The balance of leaps and stepwise motion is so precisely conceived that one virtually never finds a wide leap that is not followed by a leap or stepwise motion in the opposite direction, occasionally by a step or smaller leap in the same direction (Jeppesen, 1923; Eng. trans., 1946). At the same time Palestrina's extraordinary control of dissonance creates a texture of unparalleled purity and consistency of sonority. Ex.2, the opening of *In diebus illis* from the motets of 1563, provides in the opening bars of a single voice a sample of the fine balance of linear motion coupled with careful control of durational units that progress gradually from longer to shorter note values. After the opening of a typical motet each successive motivic segment is grafted on to the preceding one with remarkable subtlety; each phrase is well adapted to the phrase of text around which it is

Ex.2 *In diebus illis*

formed, yet the phrases often exhibit subtle hints of interrelationship. Compared with the highly contrasting and vividly dramatic style of Lassus, Palestrina's motets convey an emphasis on the gradual unfolding of motivic segments that are subtly related to one another and thus provide a strong sense of organic unity. While in the first book the opening imitation is often given only to two voices, later motets display widely varied ways of beginning and a tendency towards increased richness of sonority throughout the work.

This latter point was evidently a matter of conscious

attention on Palestrina's part, as is suggested by his letter to Duke Guglielmo Gonzaga of 3 March 1570 in which he gave his opinion of a motet by the duke that had been sent to Rome for his appraisal (Eng. trans. of the entire letter in Lockwood, 1975, p.25). He said that he had scored it to be able to judge it better, then praised the work for its ingenuity and for its 'imparting a living spirit to the words'; but considered it less effective than it should be in that its imitations involve too many unisons. As Jeppesen pointed out in his study of this letter (1926, pp.100ff), the saturation of the texture by full harmonies wherever possible was a cardinal tendency in Palestrina's work as a whole.

Of the four great collections of liturgical compositions that Palestrina issued in the period 1588–93, all except the Offertories had been anticipated by settings he had written in earlier years in each genre, and all of them are powerful contributions to the vast late 16th-century Italian repertories of liturgical polyphony which implicitly replaced their plainsong antecedents that had long been in use.

The Lamentations of 1588 are presumably the last of his settings of these important texts for Holy Week. Haberl knew of four sets of Lamentations in all (the print of 1588 for four and five voices as well as other sets in Roman manuscripts), while Jeppesen (*MGG*, x, col.699) reported a newly found fifth set at Spoleto (Duomo, MS 9). The dating of the earlier sets is unclear. A set for four voices (St John Lateran, MS 59; see fig.4) has been accepted as a holograph of Palestrina's since Casimiri's monograph on it (1919); in his edition of these works (*Opera omnia*, xiii) Casimiri gave improved

4. *Autograph of part of a set of Lamentations for four voices by Palestrina; the names of the singers Thomas, Petrus and Nicolaus are given against the upper three parts*

readings based on the versions in this manuscript. A letter of 17 April 1574 mentions that Palestrina was just then writing Lamentations for use in the papal chapel, and on 14 April 1575 a payment shows that Lamentations by him were copied for the Cappella Giulia (see Cascioli, 1923, p.28, and illustration). Contemporary writers such as Pontio and Cerone described the proper style of writing Lamentations as being appropriately grave, with little animation in any voice and with much use of 'dissonances, suspensions, and harsh passages' (Cerone; trans. from Strunk: *Source Readings*, 273). In the 1588 settings the writing is often dense and shows substantial conformity to Cerone's description in its use of suspension dissonances, though always within the austere boundaries of Palestrina's style and with dissonances prepared by consonances.

The hymns of 1589 form a cycle for the liturgical year and were written not later than the early 1580s, or even before, if a set of hymns copied in 1582 is identical to the published volume, as it is taken to be by Jeppesen and others. The 45 hymns of the 1589 collection are for four voices, and a large number of them are found in the St John Lateran manuscript 59. Jeppesen (in *MGG*, x, col.699) pointed out the existence of three more hitherto unknown hymns attributed to Palestrina in a manuscript at Bologna (Civico Museo Bibliografico Musicale, MS Q 31), which he considered to be authentic. They belong to the venerable traditions of polyphonic hymns, always based on their plainsong melodies, that had begun in the 15th century with Dufay (who in writing them was particularly closely connected with the papal chapel) and been continued in the 16th century by many composers but especially – among those who served the papal chapel – Carpentras, Costanzo Festa and Morales.

The book of *Magnificat* settings for four voices published in 1591 is similarly related to a vast tradition and
to earlier works by Palestrina. It consists of two series
of works in the eight tones. Following precedent they
adhere closely to the psalmodic formulae associated
with the *Magnificat* tones and follow the traditional plan
of setting alternate verses – the odd verses in the first
eight settings, the even ones in the second. Two other
sets probably earlier than the published ones are found
in manuscripts in Rome (one in the Biblioteca Apostolica
Vaticana, C.G. XV, 22, the other in XV, 2, and also in St
John Lateran, MS 59).

In the view of many scholars the last in this series of
cycles is also the greatest – the offertories for the entire
year, published in 1593. These settings, for five voices,
are virtually unprecedented at this period; their only
possible rival is the shorter set by Lassus. For this
collection Palestrina assembled no fewer than 68 settings, of which 40 are for the major festivals from
Advent to the ninth Sunday after Pentecost and the
remaining 28 for the additional Sundays after that.
There is no evidence in these works of chant paraphrase,
and they are superficially much like the shorter single-
section motets of the 1584 collection (the fifth book for
five voices). But in contrapuntal refinement and
prodigality of invention in a short span they may well
surpass the motets or any other of his later works, while
they also show a tendency towards sectional repetition
that is rare in the motets (e.g. the offertory *De
profundis*). A lengthy assessment of them, their liturgical function and their place in the history of the Mass
Proper of the period is given by Lipphardt (1950,

pp.55ff); on their liturgical and modal organization see Powers (1982) and p.108 above.

IV Madrigals

As a composer of madrigals Palestrina is often characterized as a conservative musician who stood wholly apart from the more experimental and text-expressive tendencies of the late 16th century; one writer has said of the Roman madrigalists of his time that they were 'living in another world' from that of the progressives such as Marenzio and Gesualdo. This may be true with regard to harmonic content and chromatic exploration, but in their time Palestrina's madrigals were considered to be perfectly valid and accomplished works; indeed there is ample evidence of their success and of the lasting fame of some of them. Biographers have not always sufficiently stressed that he maintained his close interest in the madrigal: he began as a madrigal composer in 1554, his first book for four voices of 1555 had an extraordinary success and was frequently reprinted, and he may have had many more occasions for the writing of madrigals in later years than is often realized, particularly in the period of his association with Cardinal Ippolito d'Este at Tivoli in the 1560s. Einstein (1949, p.314) interpreted the first book as showing no sign of interest in the newer developments in the madrigal during the 1550s but rather as a continuation of the classic early madrigal style of Costanzo Festa and Jacques Arcadelt, both, significantly, Romans. This book is still for four voices despite the general trend towards five at this time, and there is no trace in it of notational or harmonic experiments. In later madrigals Palestrina did show a considerable capacity for growth of imagination in this genre, however, and two pieces in particular became as celebrated as any in the entire period: *Io son ferito* (*RISM* 1561[10]) and *Vestiva i colli* (1566[3]). Both were quoted by other composers and widely used as the basis of imitation masses (the former even by Lassus); and both were later paid the supreme compliment of being parodied in madrigal comedies by Orazio Vecchi and Adriano Banchieri – a sure sign of their fame.

In later life, while apologizing for his early indiscretions as a madrigalist in the preface to the Song of Songs (1584), Palestrina nevertheless maintained a foothold in secular music and also turned to the profitable genre of the spiritual madrigal. His second book of secular madrigals for four voices appeared in 1586, but its contents may well be of much earlier vintage; he said in the preface that 'these fruits ... are mature'. The madrigals are as a class appropriately lighter in texture and more flexible in rhythmic motion than the motets, and they make sharper use of contrasts. Yet they share the general lucidity of texture common in his music, and this quality may well have contributed to the popularity of the most famous among them. These pieces may also have made Palestrina a more distinctive figure as a madrigalist than many modern historians have been disposed to admit. It is no doubt indicative of his musical outlook that in a letter to Mantua in 1583 he should have described Marenzio as being 'not greater than Soriano, either in knowledge or in managing musicians', but it should be remembered too that Soriano was his pupil, the Duke of Mantua his revered patron, and Marenzio a newcomer to Rome as well as an outsider. The position of Palestrina in relation to a man like Marenzio need not be considered substantially different from that of any great conservative composer in relation to a contemporary innovator of genius; it bears comparison with the relationship of Brahms to Wagner.

CHAPTER FOUR

Pupils, contemporaries and reputation

Palestrina's role as the leader of the so-called Roman school in the late 16th century and early 17th has been widely accepted as historical fact, yet no survey should leave his specific relationship to the Roman milieu entirely unexamined. There can be no doubt that, by virtue of his positions in various Roman musical establishments, including both the papal chapel and St Peter's, as well as the other major churches of Rome, and also through his private service with Ippolito d'Este, he must have exerted a strong influence on the younger musicians of his time; nor can it be doubted that he was accepted by many of them as a musical mentor in a general sense. Yet evidence of his role as teacher of the next generation of Roman composers is not as plentiful as might be casually supposed. Of those who were ten to 15 years younger than he, only Annibale Stabile (*b* *c*1535) and G. A. Dragoni (*b* *c*1540) specifically claimed in printed dedications that they had been his pupils (see Casimiri, 1931, p.235). Among other prominent Roman musicians of this generation, Annibale Zoilo (*b* *c*1537) may be counted as a close younger contemporary and was his would-be collaborator in the project of plainsong revision, but there is no concrete evidence that he was his pupil. Francesco Soriano (*b* *c*1549), on the other hand, was certainly a pupil, as Palestrina himself stated in a letter of 1583 (see p.127); yet Soriano had also studied with the little-known G. B. Montanari. In the next generation stand two pairs of brothers: the Nanino brothers (Giovanni Maria, *b* c1543, and Giovanni Bernardino, *b* c1560), the first of whom is said by Giovanni d'Alessi (in *MGG*, ix, col.1256) to have been a Palestrina pupil, though the evidence is unclear; and the Anerio brothers (Felice, *b* c1560, and Giovanni Francesco, *b* c1567), who were both choirboys in the Cappella Giulia during the 1570s and thus under Palestrina's general charge as *maestro*, though it remains uncertain whether they were pupils in the personal sense.

An important contribution to a sense of unity among late 16th-century Roman musicians was undoubtedly provided by the rising tide of the Counter-Reformation, particularly among the musicians working in churches located in the seat of the papacy. A telling symptom of this is the formation in 1584 of the 'Vertuosa Compagnia de i Musici di Roma', founded under papal auspices for the purpose of fraternal association as well as the performance of music and dedicated to St Cecilia as patron saint of musicians. Works by members of the group, one of the first of all professional musical guilds, were brought together by Felice Anerio in the madrigal collection *Le gioie* (*RISM* 1589[7]). Its members, who included Palestrina, also collaborated in the composition of a mass for 12 voices on the Cecilian text *Cantantibus organis*, with separate movements written by Stabile, Soriano, Dragoni, Palestrina, Ruggiero Giovannelli, Prospero Santini and Curzio Mancini (see Casimiri, 1931, pp.233ff).

Palestrina's historical reputation resembles that of

no other composer in musical history. While Josquin had remained a celebrated figure in the 16th century, his star then waned in the light of changing tastes and styles and has only been revived in the 20th century. With Palestrina, however, a concatenation of historical developments combined to maintain his prestige at an ever higher level for 200 years after his death, while most of his predecessors and contemporaries were virtually lost to view. One of these factors was the legend of Palestrina as the 'saviour of church music' because of the alleged effects of the *Missa Papae Marcelli*. This tale was propagated as early as 1607 by Agazzari, was picked up by countless later writers up to the 18th and 19th centuries and, despite the leaven of more objective investigation carried out since the 1890s, remains in broad circulation as popular history.

Another essential strand has been Palestrina's place in musical pedagogy, where from the early 17th century on his name became indelibly associated with the ideal of the *stile antico* – the strict style of diatonic counterpoint that became a widely accepted model for teaching. Long after the real style of Palestrina's music had ceased to be a norm of composition in the wake of the broad stylistic developments of the 17th century, it continued to be used as a pedagogical model, which, however, inevitably derived from a limited perception of the full range of his music. Among the 17th-century writers who assigned him this posthumous role one of the earliest was Cerone in his *El melopeo y maestro* (1613); subsequent admirers included Angelo Berardi, who in 1689 called him 'the prince and father of music' (see Hucke, 1968). How firmly contrapuntal theory remained bound to this image of Palestrina is evident in Fux's

Gradus ad Parnassum (1725), the most influential reformulation of contrapuntal theory in the period of incipient classical tonality. Fux gave the master in his dialogue the name Aloysius, denoting Palestrina, and named the pupil Joseph, meaning himself; he described Palestrina as 'the celebrated light of music . . . to whom I owe everything that I know of this art and whose memory I shall never cease to cherish'. Through this powerfully influential treatise and other works the image of Palestrina remained vivid during the 18th century and into the 19th, when for the first time a more objective historical view became possible. In contrapuntal pedagogy he continued to be revered in works such as Bellermann's treatise (1862); this sought a more accurate representation of his style than that of Fux, which was felt to have been too much influenced by 18th-century idioms. In turn Bellermann's formulation has been wholly displaced in modern times by that of Jeppesen (*Kontrapunkt,* 1930), whose work was in turn based on exhaustive scholarly study of Palestrina's music. A parallel approach to contrapuntal technique through the work of Palestrina is provided by Andrews (1958).

In earlier historical writings Palestrina also remained the centre of attention while his contemporaries faded, and for generations a larger understanding of 16th-century music was impeded by the assumption that he was its fundamental culmination. Burney and Hawkins preserved an image that had already been established by such Roman epigones as Adami da Bolsena (in 1711) and Fornari (in 1749); as Hawkins put it, 'to enumerate the testimonies of authors in favour of Palestrina would be an endless task'. The first attempt at a truly comprehensive biography was that of Giuseppe Baini

(1775–1844), whose monograph of 1828 is a vast mixture of erudition and hero-worship. It was immediately translated by Kandler, and the image created thus spread far and wide, eventually culminating in the wholly romanticized portrait of Palestrina painted by Pfitzner in his allegorical opera *Palestrina*, completed in 1915. A more objective trend was exhibited in the discussion of Palestrina by Ambros, whose knowledge of the 16th century was as comprehensive as the available monuments of his time permitted, and the anti-romantic tendency was also greatly fostered by Haberl's research and his editing of Palestrina's works. The great product of his leadership was the first truly complete edition of the music, based on the original sources and published in 33 volumes between 1862 and 1907 under his general editorship, with the collaboration of Theodor de Witt, Franz Espagne and Franz Commer. This edition, using original clefs and note values, is still a vital representation of Palestrina's works, even though a second fully complete edition, the *Opera omnia*, has sought to displace it. This latter edition was begun under Casimiri's editorship in 1938; since his death, volumes have been edited by Lavinio Virgili, Jeppesen (the Mantuan masses) and Lino Bianchi. It makes use of modern clefs and reduced note values and is based on a somewhat wider array of sources than had been known to Haberl. Nevertheless it too is likely to require addenda and revision as the advance of modern scholarship continues to facilitate a balanced understanding not only of Palestrina's achievement but of his complex role in the vast surrounding developments of his time as it increasingly becomes divested of the myths and legends that have distorted his reputation for too long.

133

WORKS

Editions: *G. P. da Palestrina: Werke*, ed. F. X. Haberl and others (Leipzig, 1862–1907) [H]
G. P. da Palestrina: *Le opere complete*, ed. R. Casimiri and others (Rome, 1939–) [C]
For MS sources beyond those cited here, see modern editions and Jeppesen (*MGG*), who also deals with problems of authenticity.
Numbers in right-hand margins denote references in the text.

MASSES

Missarum liber primus, 4–6vv (Rome, 1554) [1554] — 112–19
Missarum liber secundus, 4–6vv (Rome, 1567) [1567] — 96, 97, 98, 100, 115
Missarum liber tertius, 4–6vv (Rome, 1570) [1570] — 100, 110
Missarum liber quartus, 5vv (Venice, 1582) [1582] — 100, 110
Missarum liber quintus, 4–6vv (Rome, 1590) [1590] — 110, 113
Missarum liber primus, 4–6vv (Rome, 1591; as 1554 with 2 add. masses) [1591]
Missae quinque, liber sextus, 4, 5vv (Rome, 1594) [ded. dated 1593] [1593/4] — 112
Missae quinque, liber septimus, 4, 5vv (Rome, 1594) [1594] — 112–13
Missarum liber sextus, 4–6vv (Venice, 1596; as 1593/4 with 1 add. mass) [1596]
Missarum liber octavus, 4–6vv (Venice, 1599) [1599] — 113
Missarum liber nonus, 4–6vv (Venice, 1599) [1599a] — 113
Missarum liber decimus, 4–6vv (Venice, 1600) [1600] — 113
Missarum liber undecimus, 4–6vv (Venice, 1600) [1600a] — 113
Missarum liber duodecimus, 4–6vv (Venice, 1601) [1601] — 113
Missae quatuor, 8vv (Venice, 1601) [1601a] — 113
Works in 1585[5], 1592[1]

Numbers in the left-hand margin refer to Reese, 1954, pp.470ff; models are given in parentheses where known.

5   Ad coenam Agni (hymn), 5vv, 1554; H x, 105, C i, 125
29 Ad fugam, 4vv, 1567; H xi, 57, C iv, 74
72 Aeterna Christi munera (hymn), 4vv, 1590; H xiv, 1, C xv, 1 — 118
    Alma Redemptoris mater (ant), 6vv, 1600a; H xx, 106, C xxviii, 148 — 118
75 Ascendo ad Patrem (own motet, 1572), 5vv, 1601; H xxi, 38, C xxix, 54
10 Aspice Domine (Jacquet's motet, 1532), 5vv, 1567; H xi, 71, C iv, 91 — 115
82 Assumpta est Maria (own motet), 6vv; H xxiii, 97, C xxv, 209

44 Ave Maria (prayer), 4vv, 1594; H xvi, 1, C xxiii, 1 — 118
50 Ave Maria (c.f. unidentified), 6vv, 1596; H xv, 113, C xxi, 142 — 118
57 Ave regina coelorum (ant), 4vv, 1599a; H xviii, 1, C xxv, 1
85 Beatus Laurentius (ant), 5vv; H xxiii, 48, C xxiv, 194
91 Benedicta es (Josquin, 1520), 6vv; H xxiv, 72, C xxviii, 222 — 118
15 Brevis (free), 4vv, 1570; H xii, 50, C vi, 62 — 118
28 Confitebor tibi (own motet, 1572), 8vv, 1585[5]; H xxii, 110, C xxx, 163 — 111
98 De Beata Marie [Virginis] (i) [Mantuan], 5vv; C xviii, 83 — 118, 133
99 De Beata Marie [Virginis] (ii) [Mantuan], 5vv; C xviii, 126 — 118, 133
100 De Beata Marie [Virginis] (iii) [Mantuan], 5vv; C xviii, 162 — 118, 133
6   De beata virgine (Mass IX, Credo I, Mass XVII), 4vv, 1567; H xi, 1, C iv, 1 — 118
19 De beata virgine (Mass IX, Credo I, Mass XVII), 6vv, 1570; H xii, 135, C vi, 175 — 118
16 De feria (Mass XVIII), 4vv, 1570; H xii, 66, C vi, 84 — 118
68 Descendit angelus Domini (Penet, 1532), 4vv, 1600a; H xx, 1, C xxviii, 1
39 Dies sanctificatus (own motet, 1563), 4vv, 1593/4; H xv, 1, C xxi, 1 — *116, 117–18*
43 Dilexi quoniam (Maffoni), 5vv, 1593/4; H xv, 84, C xxi, 105 — 114
38 Dominicalis (Masses XI, XII, Credo) [Mantuan], 5vv, 1592[1]; H xxxiii, 1 (see H xxx, 28) — 118
55 Dum complerentur (own motet, 1569), 6vv, 1599; H xvii, 85, C xxiv, 117
52 Dum esset summus pontifex (ant), 4vv, 1599; H xvii, 23, C xxiv, 32
93 Ecce ego Joannes (unidentified), 6vv; H xxiv, 129, C xxix, 197
1   Ecce sacerdos magnus (ant), 4vv, 1554; H x, 3, C i, 1 — 97, 118
46 Emendemus in melius (unidentified), 4vv, 1594; H xvi, 44, C xxiii, 61
25 Eripe me de inimicis (Maillard, 1559), 5vv, 1582; H xiii, 59, C x, 79

90 Salve regina (ant), 5vv; H xxiv, 46, C xxviii, 185

11 Salvum me fac (Jacquet, 1538), 5vv, 1567; H xi, 97, C iv, 126 — 115

45 Sanctorum meritis (hymn), 4vv, 1594; H xvi, 22, C xxiii, 30

26 Secunda (anon. motet, Veni Sancte Spiritus, attrib. Palestrina in H xxxii, 137), 4vv, 1582; H xiii, 85, C x, 115 — 114

34 Sicut lilium inter spinas (own motet, 1569), 5vv, 1590; H xiv, 95, C xv, 130

8 Sine nomine, 4vv, 1567; H xi, 41, C iv, 53

95 Sine nomine [Mantuan], 4 'voci mutati' v; C xix, 168 — 118

60 Sine nomine, 5vv, 1599a; H xviii, 64, C xxv, 93

36 Sine nomine [Beata Dei genetrix in *D-As* 18] (anon. motet: Cantabo Domine in *I-Rsc* G 792–5), 6vv, 1591; H x, 153, C i, 182 — 114

13 Spem in alium (Jacquet, 1539), 4vv, 1570; H xii, 3, C vi, 1 — 115

62 Te Deum laudamus (hymn), 6vv, 1599a; H xviii, 119, C xxv, 172

48 Tu es pastor ovium (own motet), 5vv, 1594; H xvi, 85; C xxiii, 115

77 Tu es Petrus (ant), 6vv, 1601; H xxi, 86, C xxix, 123

92 Tu es Petrus (own motet, 1572), 6vv; H xxiv, 105, C xxviii, 268

20 Ut re mi fa sol la (hexachord), 6vv, 1570; H xii, 165, C vi, 216 — 113, 118

87 Veni creator Spiritus (hymn), 6vv; H xxiii, 122, C xxv, 246 — 118

58 Veni sponsa Christi (own motet, 1563), 4vv, 1599a; H xviii, 21, C xxv, 30

59 Vestiva i colli (own madrigal, 1566), 5vv, 1599a; H xviii, 38, C xxv, 54

78 Viri Galilaei (own motet, 1569), 6vv, 1601; H xxi, 111, C xxix, 159

3 Virtute magna (Lasson, 1532), 4vv, 1554; H x, 55, C i, 62 — 115

Et in terra, 12vv, and possibly Domine deus, 4vv (from Missa 'Cantantibus organis Caecilia'); C xxxi, 84

(*doubtful, considered authentic by Jeppesen, MGG, x, cols.673f*)

Escoutes, 8vv, *D-Mbs* 64
Octo vocum, 8vv, *Mbs* 64
Papae Marcelli, 4vv; H xxx, 15
Papae Marcelli, 12vv, *I-Rvat* C.S.469
Pilastrina, *MOd* VI
Sexti toni, 4vv, *E-P* 3
Sine nomine, 4vv, *MOe* D.303
Sine nomine, 16vv, *PS* B.21
Tu es Petrus, 18vv; C xxvi, 1

MOTETS, ETC — 119–126

Motecta festorum totius anni cum Communi Sanctorum . . . liber primus, 4vv (Rome, 1563); lost, see Baini, i, 210 [1563] — 100, 110, 112, 115, 119, 120

Liber primus motettorum, 5–7vv (Rome, 1569) [1569] — 100, 110, 112, 119

Motettorum liber secundus, 5, 6, 8vv (Venice, 1572) [1572] — 110, 112, 119

Motettorum liber tertius, 5, 6, 8vv (Venice, 1575) [1575] — 110, 112, 119

Motectorum liber secundus, 4vv (Venice, 1581); lost, 1581 according to Baini, ii, 128; 1584 according to Casimiri (1939), 253 [1581] — 110, 119

Motettorum liber quartus ex Canticis canticorum, 5vv (Rome, 1584); see Casimiri in C xi, p.xi (T, B dated 1583) [1583/4] — 102, 110, 111, 119, 127

Motectorum liber quintus, 5vv (Rome, 1584) [1584] — 110, 119, 124

Motettorum liber quintus, 5vv (Venice, 1595; as 1584 with 1 add. motet) [1595] — 111

Works in 1563[3]; 1586[2]; G. Guidetti, ed.: Cantus ecclesiasticus officii maioris hebdomadae (Rome, 1587); G. Bassano, ed.: Motetti, madrigali et canzoni francesi, a 4–6 (Venice, 1591); 1592[2]; G. B. Bovicelli, ed.: Regole, passaggi di musica, madrigali e motetti passeggiati (Venice, 1594); 1600[11]; 1607[6]; 1609[1]; 1616[7] — 111

Accepit Jesus, 6vv, 1575; H iii, 123, C viii, 160
Ad Dominum cum tribularer, 4vv, 1581; H v, 135, C xi, 26
Adjuro vos filiae, 5vv, 1583/4; H iv, 52, C xi, 157
Adoramus te Christe, 4vv, 1581; H v, 176, C xi, 78
Ad te levavi, 4vv, 1581; H v, 130, C xi, 20
Ad te levavi, 12vv; H xxvi, 139
Aegypti noli flere, 5vv, 1584; H iv, 121, C xii, 45
Alleluja. Tulerunt Dominum, 5vv, 1569; H i, 30, C v, 35
Alma Redemptoris mater, 4vv, 1581; H v, 156, C xi, 52
Alma Redemptoris mater, 4vv, *A-Wn* 16709
Alma Redemptoris mater, 8vv; H vi, 159
Alma Redemptoris mater, 8vv; H vii, 73
Angelus Domini, 5vv, 1575; H iii, 18, C viii, 23
Angelus Domini, 8vv, *I-Rvat* C.S.294
Apparuit caro, 5vv, 1584; H iv, 134, C xii, 64
Apparuit gratia, 8vv; H vii, 153
Ardens est, 5vv, 1584; H iv, 124, C xii, 49
Ascendens Christus, 4vv; H vii, 55
Ascendit Deus, 4vv, H xxxii, p.vi
Ascendo ad Patrem, 5vv, 1572; H ii, 33, C vii, 42
Asperges me, 4vv; H xxxii, 129
Asperges me, 4vv, *E-P* 3
Assumpta est Maria, 6vv; H vi, 28
Ave Maria, 4vv, 1563; H v, 20, H xxvi, 5, C iii, 23, C xx, 6

Dies sanctificatus, 8vv; H vii, 158
Dilectus meus descendit, 5vv, 1583/4; H iv, 58, C xi, 166
Dilectus meus mihi, 5vv, 1583/4; H iv, 47, C xi, 150
Disciplinam et sapientiam, 8vv; H vi, 129
Dixit Dominus, 4vv, Rvat 10776 (see Jeppesen, 1958)
Doctor bonus et amicus Dei, 4vv, 1563; H v, 80, C iii, 100
Domine Deus, qui conteris, 5vv, 1575; H iii, 85; C viii, 111
Domine in virtute, 8vv, 1572; H ii, 153, C vii, 205
Domine quando veneris, 4vv, 1581, H v, 117, C xi, 3
Domine quis habebit, 12vv; H xxvi, 166
Domine, secundum actum, 4vv; H vii, 57
Domine, secundum actum, 5vv, 1584; H iv, 106, C xiii, 23
Dominus Jesus in qua nocte, 5vv, 1572; H ii, 77, C vii, 102
Dum aurora finem daret, 4vv, 1563; H v, 77, C iii, 97
Dum complerentur, 4vv; H xxxi, 11
Dum complerentur, 6vv, 1569; H i, 111, C v, 149
Duo ubera tua, 5vv, 1583/4; H iv, 71, C xi, 185
Ecce merces sanctorum, 5vv, 1584; H iv, 137, C xii, 68
Ecce, nunc benedicite, 4vv, 1581; H v, 128, C xi, 17
Ecce, nunc benedicite, 4vv; H vii, 62
Ecce, nunc benedicite, 4, 5vv; H xxxi, 156
Ecce, nunc benedicite, 6vv, D-MÜs 1236
Ecce, nunc benedicite, 12vv; H vii, 35, C xxxii, 1
Ecce sacerdos, 6vv; H xxxi, 70
Ecce tu pulcher es, 5vv, 1583/4; H iv, 22, C xi, 116
Ego sum panis vivus … Patres vestri, 4vv, 1581; H v, 146, C xi, 39
Ego sum panis vivus qui, 5vv, 1569; H i, 43, C v, 54
Estote fortes, 6vv; H xxxi, 75
Et erexit, 4vv; H xxxii, 128
Exaudi Domine preces, 4vv; H v, 107, C iii, 135
Exaudi Domine preces, 4vv; H xxxi, p.iii (Haber doubts authenticity)
Exi cito in plateas, 5vv, 1572; H ii, 50, C vii, 65
Expurgate vetus fermentum, 8vv; H vi, 144
Exsultate Deo, 5vv, 1584; H iv, 151, C xii, 88
Fasciculus myrrhae, 5vv, 1583/4; H iv, 20, C xi, 113
Fili, non te frangant, 8vv; H vii, 80
Fratres ego enim accepi, 8vv; H vi, 6
Fuit homo missus a Deo, 5vv, 1575; H iii, 39, C viii, 49
Fuit homo missus a Deo, 4vv, 1563; H v, 38, C iii, 46

Fuit homo missus a Deo, arr. insts G. Bassano: Motetti (Venice, 1591); H xxxiii, 51 (see H v, 38)
Fundamenta ejus, 4vv, 1581; H v, 139, C xi, 30
Gaude, Barbara, 4vv; H vii, 70
Gaude, Barbara, 5vv, 1572; H ii, 59, C vii, 78
Gaude gloriosa, 5vv, 1584; H iv; 149, C xii, 84
Gaudent in coelis, 4vv, 1563; H v, 96, C iii, 121
Gloria Patri, 4vv; H xxxi, 15
Gloriosi príncipes, 4vv, 1581; H v, 180, C xi, 83
Guttur tuum, 5vv, 1583/4; H iv, 78, C xi, 193
Haec dies, 4vv, 1581; H v, 167, C xi, 66
Haec dies, 6vv, 1575; H iii, 114, C viii, 148
Haec dies, 8vv; H vii, 88
Haec est dies praeclara, 8vv; H vii, 163
Heu mihi Domine, 4vv, 1581; H v, 121, C xi, 8
Hic est beatissimus Evangelista, 6vv; H vi, 41
Hic est discipulus ille, 5vv, 1569; H i, 87, C v, 116
Hic est panis, 8vv; H vi, 14
Hic est vere martyr, 4vv, 1563; H v, 92, C iii, 116
Hodie beata virgo, 4vv, 1563; H v, 17, C iii, 19
Hodie beata virgo, arr. insts G Bassano: Motetti (Venice, 1591); H xxxii, 49 (see H v, 17)
Hodie Christus natus est, 4vv; H xxxi, 135
Hodie Christus natus est, 8vv, 1575; H iii, 155, C viii, 203
Hodie gloriosa, 8vv; H vi, 82
Hodie Maria virgo coelos, 4vv, 1616?
Hodie nata est, 5vv, 1569; H i, 64, C v, 83
Homo quidam fecit, 5vv, 1572; H ii, 39, C vii, 50
Illumina oculos (canon), 3vv, 1586[2]; H xxx, 3
Illumina oculos, 5vv, I-Rvat C.S.473
Inclytae sanctae virginis Catharinae, 5vv, 1575; H iii, 36, C viii, 45
In diebus illis mulier, 4vv, 1563; H v, 50, C iii, 61
In Domino laetabitur (canon), 4vv, 1586[2]; H xxx, 4
Ingrediente Domino, 4vv; H xxxi, 137
Ingrediente Domino, 5vv; H xxx, p.xi
In illo tempore egressus Jesus, 5vv, 1572; H ii, 18, C vii, 21
In manus tuas, 4vv; H xxxii, 49
Innocentes pro Christe, 4vv; H vii, 66

139

Si ignoras te, 5vv, 1583/4; H iv, 14, C xi, 105
Solve, jubente Deo, 6vv, 1569; H i, 123, C v, 165
Spiritus Sanctus replevit, 8vv; H vi, 76
Stabat mater, 4, 8vv; H vi, 96
Stabat mater, 8vv; H vi, 96
Stabat mater, 12vv; H vii, 130
Stella quam viderant Magi, 5vv, 1569; H i, 6, C v, 5
Sub tuum praesidium, 4vv, 1581; H v, 173, C xi, 75
Sub tuum praesidium, 8vv; H vi, 3
Super flumina Babylonis, 4vv, 1581; H v, 125, C xi, 14
Surgam et circuibo, 5vv, 1583/4; H iv, 50, C xi, 154
Surge, amica mea, 5vv, 1583/4; H iv, 44, C xi, 146
Surge illuminare Jerusalem, 8vv, 1575; H iii, 134, C viii, 174
Surge, Petre, 5vv, 1584; H iv, 130, C xii, 58
Surge, propera amica mea, et veni, 4vv, 1563; H iv, 47, C iii, 57
Surge, propera amica formosa mea, 5vv, 1583/4; H iv, 41, C xi, 142
Surge, sancte Dei, 5vv, 1584; H iv, 159, C xii, 100
Surrexit pastor bonus, 4vv, 1581; H v, 177, C xi, 79
Surrexit pastor bonus, 8vv; H vi, 57
Susanna ab improbis, 6vv, 1575; H iii, 100, C viii, 130
Suscipe verbum, virgo Maria, 5vv, 1569; H i, 22, C v, 25
Tempus est ut revertar, 5vv, 1584; H iv, 101, C xii, 16
Thomas unus, 4vv; H xxxii, 134
Tollite jugum meum, 4vv, 1563; H v, 87, C iii, 109
Tota pulchra es, 5vv, 1583/4; H iv, 25, C xi, 120
Tota pulchra es, arr. insts G. Bassano: Motetti (Venice, 1591;) H xxxiii, 52 (see H iv, 25)
Tradent enim vos, 5vv, 1575; H iii, 59; C viii, 75
Tradent enim vos, 6vv; H vi, 53
Trahe me post te, 5vv, 1583/4; H iv, 5, C xi, 93
Tria sunt numera, 8vv; H vii, 76
Tribulare si nescirem, 6vv, 1572; H ii, 81, C vii, 107
Tribulationes civitatum, 5vv, 1584; H iv, 154, C xii, 92
Tribus miraculis, 4vv, 1563; H v, 15, C iii, 15
Tu es pastor ovium, 4vv, 1563; H v, 41, C iii, 49
Tu es pastor ovium, 5vv; H vi, 21, H xxxi, 63
Tu es Petrus, 6vv, 1572; H ii, 121, C vii, 162
Tu es Petrus, 7vv, 1569; H i, 146, C v, 196
Unus ex duobus, 5vv, 1569; H i, 98, C v, 131

Valde honorandus est, 4vv, 1563; H v, 8, C iii, 8
Veni Domine, 6vv, 1572; H ii, 88, C vii, 117
Veni Sancte Spiritus, 4vv; H xxxii, 137
Veni Sancte Spiritus, 8vv; H vii, 117
Veni Sancte Spiritus, 8vv, 1575; H iii, 143, C viii, 186
Veni sponsa Christi, 4vv, 1563; H v, 105, C iii, 132
Venite exultemus, 5vv; H xxxii, 53
Venit Michael archangelus, 5vv, 1569; H i, 71, C v, 94
Veni, veni dilecti mi, 5vv, 1583/4; H iv, 81, C xi, 197
Veni, veni dilecti me, arr. insts G. Bassano: Motetti (Venice, 1591); H xxxiii, 58 (see H iv, 81)
Victimae paschali, 4, 8vv; H xxxii, 180
Victimae paschali, 8vv; H vii, 105
Victimae paschali, 8vv; H vii, 112
Victimae paschali, 8vv; H vii, 194
Videns secundus salvatorem, 5vv, 1584; H iv, 140, C xii, 72
Videntes stellam Magi, 8vv; H vii, 194
Vidi aquam, 4vv, E-P 3
Vidi turbam magnam, 6vv, 1569; H i, 129, C v, 174
Vineam meam, 5vv, 1583/4; H iv, 11, C xi, 101
Virgo prudentissima, 7vv, 1569; H i, 152, C v, 204
Viri Galilarei, 6vv, 1559; H i, 105, C v, 141
Vos amici mei, 8vv, 1592²; H xxxi, 42
Vox dilecti mei, 5vv, 1583/4; H iv, 39, C xi, 139
Vulnerasti cor meum, 5vv, 1583/4; H iv, 27, C xi, 124

HYMNS

Hymni totius anni secundum Sanctae Romanae Ecclesiae consuetudinem, necnon hymni religionum, 4vv (Rome, 1589) [1589]   111, 124, 305
Works in 1586²
Ad coenam Agni providi, 5vv, 1589; H viii, 42, C xiv, 54
Ad preces nostras, 5vv, 1589; H viii, 29, C xiv, 37
A solis ortus cardine, 5vv, 1589; H viii, 12, C xiv, 15
Audi benigne, 5vv; H xxxi, 119
Audi benigne, 4vv, A-Wn 16709
Audi benigne, 4vv, Wn 16199
Audi benigne, 5vv; H xxxii, 43
Aurea luce et decore, 5vv, 1589; H viii, 78, C xiv, 103
Ave maris stella, 5vv, 1589; H viii, 65, C xiv, 85

Christe, qui lux es, 5vv, 1589; H viii, 161, C xiv, 215
Christe redemptor . . . ex Patre, 6vv, 1589; H viii, 6, C xiv, 8
Christe redemptor . . . conserva, 5vv, 1589; H viii, 93, C xiv, 123
Christe redemptor omnium, 6vv, I-Rsg 59; see Casimiri (1919)
Coeli Deus, 4vv; H xxxi, 90
Conditor alme siderum, 6vv, 1589; H viii, 1, C xiv, 1
Conditor alme siderum, 4vv, Rsg 59; see Casimiri (1919)
Creator alme siderum, 4vv; H xxxi, 123
Decus morum, 5vv, 1589; H viii, 157, C xiv, 208
Deus tuorum militum, 5vv, 1589; H viii, 105, C xiv, 141
Deus tuorum militum (tempore Paschali), 4vv, 1589; H viii, 110, C xiv, 146
Deus tuorum militum, 5vv; H xxx, 129
Doctor egregie Paule, 4vv, 1589; H viii, 63, C xiv, 83
En gratulemur hodie, 5vv, 1589; H viii, 147, C xiv, 196
Exultet coelum laudibus, 5vv, 1589; H viii, 98, C xiv, 130
Exultet coelum laudibus, 5vv; H xxx, 133
Gloria laus, 4vv; H xxx, 138
Gloria laus, 4vv; H xxxi, 134
Hostis Herodes impie, 6vv, 1589; H viii, 19, C xiv, 23
Hostis Herodes impie, 4vv, Rsg 59; see Casimiri (1919)
Hujus obientu, 4vv, 1589; H viii, 131, C xiv, 175
Hymnis canoris, 4vv, 1589; H viii, 177, C xiv, 235
Immense coeli conditor, 4vv; H xxxi, 85
Iste confessor, 5vv, 1589; H viii, 119, C xiv, 158
Jesu, corona virginum, 5vv, 1589; H viii, 123, C xiv, 164
Jesu, corona virginum (tempore Paschali), 5vv, 1589; H viii, 127, C xiv, 169
Jesu, flos matris, 4vv, 1586²; H xxx, 5
Jesu, nostra redemptio, 6vv, 1589; H viii, 47, C xiv, 60
Jesu, rex admirabilis, 3vv, 1586²; H xxx, 2
Lauda, mater ecclesia, 4vv, 1589; H viii, 82, C xiv, 109
Lauda, mater ecclesia, 4vv; Bc Q31
Laudibus summis, 5vv, 1589; H viii, 142, C xiv, 190
Lucis Creator optime, 5vv, 1589; H viii, 23, C xiv, 28
Magnae Deus potentiae, 4vv; H xxxi, 93
Magne pater Augustine, 5vv, 1589; H viii, 138, C xiv, 184

Mensis Augusti, 4vv, 1589; H viii, 173, C xiv, 230
Monstra te esse, 3vv, 1605¹
Monstra te esse [Ave maris stella], 4vv; H xxx, 139
Nunc juvat celsi, 4vv, 1589; H viii, 169, C xiv, 228
O gloriosa domina, 4, 12vv; H xxx, 181
O lux beata Trinitas, 4vv, 1589; H viii, 27, C xiv, 33
Pange lingua gloriosi, 5vv, 1589; H viii, 57, C xiv, 74
Pange lingua, 4vv; H xxx, 142
Petrus beatus, 4vv; 1589; H viii, 85, C xiv, 112
Plasmator hominis, 4vv; H xxxi, 96
Prima lux surgens, 5vv, 1589; H viii, 165, C xiv, 220
Proles coelo prodiit, 5vv, 1589; H viii, 152, C xiv, 202
Quicumque Christum quaeritis, 4vv, 1589; H viii, 86, C xiv, 114
Quicumque Christum quaeritis, 4vv, Bc Q31
Quodcumque vinclis, 4vv, 1589; H viii, 62, C xiv, 80
Rex gloriose martyrum, 4vv, 1589; H viii, 117, C xiv, 155
Salvete flores martyrum, 4vv, 1589; H viii, 17, C xiv, 21
Salvete flores martyrum, 4vv, Bc Q31
Sanctorum meritis, 4vv, 1589; H viii, 113, C xiv, 150
Tantum ergo, 4vv, H xxx, 153
Tantum ergo, 4vv, D-MÜs 4283
Telluris ingens, 4vv; H xxxi, 87
Te lucis ante, 4vv; H xxxi, 47
Te lucis ante, 4vv, MÜs 1236
Tibi, Christe, splendor, 4vv, 1589; H viii, 90, C xiv, 119
Tibi, Christe, splendor, 4vv, I-Rsg 59; see Casimiri (1919)
Tristes erant apostoli, 5vv, 1589; H viii, 102, C xiv, 136
Tristes erant apostoli, 4vv; H xxx, 152
Tua Jesu dilectio, 3vv, 1586²; H xxx, 4
Urbs beata Jerusalem, 5vv, 1589; H viii, 132, C xiv, 177
Ut queant laxis, 5vv, 1589; H viii, 73, C xiv, 96
Veni Creator spiritus, 5vv, 1589; H viii, 51, C xiv, 67
Veni Creator spiritus, 4vv; H xxx, 155
Vexilla regis prodeunt, 5vv, 1589; H viii, 35, C xiv, 46
Vexilla regis prodeunt (tempore Paschali), 5vv, 1589; H viii, 70, C xiv, 91
Vexilla regis prodeunt, 4vv; H xxx, 160

LAMENTATIONS

Lamentationum Hieremiae prophetae liber primus (Rome, 1588) [1588]   111, 112, 122, 123, 124

Aleph. Ego vir, 4vv, 1588; H xxv, 20, C xiii, 22
Aleph. Ego vir, 4vv, I-SPd 9
Aleph. Ego vir, 5vv; H xxv, 65, C xiii, 74
Aleph. Ego vir, 6vv; H xxv, 124, C xiii, 142
Aleph. Ego vir, 6vv; H xxv, 187, C xiii, 213
Aleph. Quomodo obscuratum, 4vv, 1588; C xiii, 252
Aleph. Quomodo obscuratum, 4vv; H xxv, 28, C xiii, 31
Aleph. Quomodo obscuratum, 4vv, SPd 9
Aleph. Quomodo obscuratum, 5vv; H xxv, 74, C xiii, 86
Aleph. Quomodo obscuratum, 5vv; H xxv, 137, C xiii, 158
Aleph. Quomodo obscuratum, 5vv; H xxv, 200, C xiii, 231
Aleph. Quomodo sedet, 4vv, 1588; H xxv, 1, C xiii, 1
Aleph. Quomodo sedet, 4vv; H xxv, 39, C xiii, 42
Aleph. Quomodo sedet, 4vv, SPd 9
Aleph. Quomodo sedet, 5vv; H xxv, 91, C xiii, 103
Aleph. Quomodo sedet, 5vv; H xxv, 155, C xiii, 175
Aleph. Quomodo sedet, 8vv; H xxxii, 163
Heth. Cogitavit, 4vv, 1588; H xxv, 12, C xiii, 14
Heth. Cogitavit, 4vv; H xxv, 54, C xiii, 61
Heth. Cogitavit, 4vv; H xxxi, 4
Heth. Cogitavit, 4vv; H xxxi, 125, C xiii, 243
Heth. Cogitavit, 4vv, SPd 9
Heth. Cogitavit, 5vv; H xxv, 111, C xiii, 128
Heth. Cogitavit, 5vv; H xxv, 173, C xiii, 198
Heth. Misericordiae, 4vv, 1588; H xxv, 24, C xiii, 27
Heth. Misericordiae, 4vv; H xxv, 70, C xiii, 80
Heth. Misericordiae, 5vv; H xxv, 130, C xiii, 150
Heth. Misericordiae, 5vv; H xxv, 193, C xiii, 223
Heth. Peccatum peccavit, 4vv; H xxxi, 130, C xiii, 268
Jod. Manum suam, 4vv, 1588; H xxv, 8, C xiii, 9
Jod. Manum suam, 4vv, SPd 9
Jod. Manum suam, 5vv; H xxv, 49, C xiii, 54
Jod. Manum suam, 5vv; H xxv, 166, C xiii, 190
Jod. Manum suam, 6vv; H xxv, 104, C xiii, 120
Jod. Manum suam, 8vv; H xxxii, 172
Lamed. Matribus suis, 4vv, 1588; H xxv, 16, C xiii, 18

Lamed. Matribus suis, 4vv; H xxv, 60, C xiii, 68
Lamed. Matribus suis, 4vv; H xxxi, 16, C xiii, 249
Lamed. Matribus suis, 4vv, SPd 9
Lamed. Matribus suis, 5vv; H xxv, 116, C xiii, 134
Lamed. Matribus suis, 6vv; H xxv, 180, C xiii, 206
Pars mea, 4vv; H xxxi, 133
Recordare, 4vv, 1588; H xxv, 32, C xiii, 36
Recordare, 4vv, SPd 9
Recordare, 6vv; H xxv, 80, C xiii, 93
Recordare, 6vv; H xxv, 144, C xiii, 166
Recordare, 6vv; H xxv, 204, C xiii, 237
Recordare, 6vv; H xxxi, 161, C xiii, 258
Theth., 4vv; H xxxi, 132
Theth. Misericordiae, 4vv, SPd 9
Vau. Ei egressus, 4vv, 1588; H xxv, 4, C xiii, 5
Vau. Ei egressus, 4vv; H xxv, 43, C xiii, 47
Vau. Ei egressus, 4vv, SPd 9
Vau. Ei egressus, 5vv; H xxv, 97, C xiii, 110
Vau. Ei egressus, 5vv; H xxv, 160, C xiii, 181
Vau. Ei egressus, 8vv; H xxxii, 168

LITANIES

Litaniae deiparae virginis, quae in sacellis deiparae virginis ubique dictatis concinnuntur liber primus, 4vv (Rome, 1593); lost, see Baini, ii, 243 and ElmerQ [1593]
Litaniae liber secundus, 3, 4vv (?1593); lost, see Baini, ii, 243 [?1593]
Works in 1596?, 1620[1]

BVM, 3, 4vv, ?1593, 1596?; H xxvi, 33, C xx, 36
BVM, 4vv, 1593; H xxvi, 1, C xx, 1
BVM, 5vv; H xxvi, 67, C xx, 72
BVM, 6vv; H xxvi, 71, C xx, 77
BVM, 8vv; H xxvi, 78, C xx, 86
BVM, 8vv, 1620?; H xxvi, 95, C xx, 106
Domini, 8vv; H xxvi, 102, C xx, 116
Domini, 8vv; H xxvi, 113, C xx, 129
Domini, 8vv; H xxvi, 119, C xx, 136
Sacrae Eucharistiae, 8vv; H xxvi, 125, C xx, 144
Sacrae Eucharistiae, 8vv; H xxvi, 133, C xx, 154

MAGNIFICAT

Magnificat octo tonum liber primus (Rome, 1591) [1591]

(verses set given in parentheses)

Tone 1 (odd), 4vv; 1591; H xxvii, 1, C xvi, 1
Tone 1 (even), 4vv, 1591; H xxvii, 40, C xvi, 50
Tone 1 (even), 4vv; H xxvii, 79, C xvi, 98
Tone 1 (even), 5vv; H xxvii, 147, C xvi, 190
Tone 1 (both), 8vv; H xxvii, 235, C xvi, 323
Tone 2 (odd), 4vv, 1591; H xxvii, 6, C xvi, 7
Tone 2 (even), 4vv, 1591; H xxvii, 45, C xvi, 56
Tone 2 (even), 4vv; H xxvii, 88, C xvi, 111
Tone 2 (even), 5vv; H xxvii, 158, C xvi, 203
Tone 3 (odd), 4vv, 1591; H xxvii, 11, C xvi, 13
Tone 3 (even), 4vv, 1591; H xxvii, 49, C xvi, 62
Tone 3 (even), 4vv; H xxvii, 97, C xvi, 124
Tone 3 (even), 6vv; H xxvii, 168, C xvi, 215
Tone 4 (odd), 4vv, 1591; H xxvii, 15, C xvi, 19
Tone 4 (even), 4vv, 1591; H xxvii, 54, C xvi, 68
Tone 4 (even), 4vv; H xxvii, 105, C xvi, 136
Tone 4 (even), 6vv; H xxvii, 178, C xvi, 229
Tone 4 (even), 4 equal vv; H xxvii, 244, C xvi, 303
Tone 5 (odd), 4vv, 1591; H xxvii, 20, C xvi, 25
Tone 5 (even), 4vv, 1591; H xxvii, 58, C xvi, 74
Tone 5 (even), 4vv; H xxvii, 113, C xvi, 147
Tone 5 (even), 5vv; H xxvii, 191, C xvi, 246
Tone 6 (odd), 4vv, 1591; H xxvii, 26, C xvi, 32
Tone 6 (even), 4vv; 1591; H xxvii, 63, C xvi, 80
Tone 6 (even), 4vv; H xxvii, 121, C xvi, 157
Tone 6 (even), 6vv; H xxvii, 202, C xvi, 260
Tone 6 (even), 4vv; H xxvii, 251, C xvi, 312
Tone 7 (odd), 4vv, 1591; H xxvii, 30, C xvi, 38
Tone 7 (even), 4vv; 1591; H xxvii, 67, C xvi, 86
Tone 7 (even), 4vv; H xxvii, 128, C xvi, 168
Tone 7 (even), 5vv; H xxvii, 214, C xvi, 276
Tone 8 (odd), 4vv, 1591; H xxvii, 35, C xvi, 44
Tone 8 (even), 4vv, 1591; H xxvii, 72, C xvi, 93
Tone 8 (even), 4vv; H xxvii, 136, C xvi, 179
Tone 8 (even), 6vv; H xxvii, 225, C xvi, 290

OFFERTORIES

Offertoria totius anni secundum Sanctae Romanae Ecclesiae consuetudinem, 5vv (Rome, 1593) [1593]

(all for 5vv in 1593)

Ad te levavi; H ix, 3, C xvii, 1
Afferentur regi; H ix, 195, C xvii, 266
Angelus Domini; H ix, 75, C xvii, 103
Anima nostra; H ix, 24, C xvii, 30
Ascendit Deus, H ix, 87, C xvii, 120
Assumpta est; H ix, 173, C xvii, 233
Ave Maria; H ix, 13, C xvii, 14
Benedicam Dominum; H ix, 108, C xvii, 150
Benedicite gentes; H ix, 84, C xvii, 115
Benedictus es; H ix, 51, C xvii, 69
Benedictus sit Deus; H ix, 93, C xvii, 128
Benedixisti, Domine; H ix, 10, C xvii, 10
Bonum est confiteri; H ix, 46, C xvii, 61
Confessio et pulchritudo; H ix, 170, C xvii, 229
Confirma hoc, Deus; H ix, 90, C xvii, 123
Confitebor tibi; H ix, 66, C xvii, 90
Confitebuntur coeli; H ix, 182, C xvii, 246
Constitues eos; H ix, 179, C xvii, 241
De profundis; H ix, 161, C xvii, 217
Deus, Deus meus; H ix, 78, C xvii, 107
Deus enim firmavit; H ix, 29, C xvii, 38
Deus tu conversus; H ix, 6, C xvii, 5
Dextera Domini; H ix, 43, C xvii, 57
Diffusa est gratia; H ix, 200, C xvii, 272
Domine, convertere; H ix, 99, C xvii, 136
Domine Deus; H ix, 198, C xvii, 269
Domine, in auxilium; H ix, 140, C xvii, 187
Elegerunt Apostoli; H ix, 18, C xvii, 22
Exaltabo te; H ix, 125, C xvii, 167
Expectans exspectavi; H ix, 137, C xvii, 183
Illumina oculos meos; H ix, 105, C xvii, 145
Immittet angelus; H ix, 134, C xvii, 179
Improperium; H ix, 69, C xvii, 94
In omnem terram; H ix, 185, C xvii, 250

In te speravi; H ix, 131, C xvii, 175
Inveni David; H ix, 32, C xvii, 41
Jubilate Deo omnis terra; H ix, 37, C xvii, 49
Jubilate Deo universa terra; H ix, 40, C xvii, 53
Justitiae Domini rectae; H ix, 60, C xvii, 81
Justitiae Domini rectae; H ix, 117, C xvii, 162
Justorum animae; H ix, 187, C xvii, 254
Justus ut palma; H ix, 21, C xvii, 26
Justus ut palma; H ix, 164, C xvii, 221
Laetamini in Domino; H ix, 193, C xvii, 262
Lauda anima mea; H ix, 81, C xvii, 111
Laudate Dominum; H ix, 63, C xvii, 85
Meditabor; H ix, 57, C xvii, 77
Mihi autem; H ix, 167, C xvii, 225
Oravi ad Dominum; H ix, 143, C xvii, 191
Perfice gressus meos; H ix, 48, C xvii, 64
Populum humilem; H ix, 114, C xvii, 158
Posuisti Domine; H ix, 27, C xvii, 34
Precatus est Moyses; H ix, 128, C xvii, 175
Recordare mei; H ix, 158, C xvii, 213
Reges Tharsis; H ix, 35, C xvii, 45
Sacerdotes Domini; H ix, 96, C xvii, 132
Sanctificavit Moyses; H ix, 146, C xvii, 196
Scapulis suis; H ix, 54, C xvii, 73
Si ambulavero; H ix, 149, C xvii, 200
Sicut in holocaustis; H ix, 111, C xvii, 154
Sperent in te; H ix, 102, C xvii, 141
Stetit angelus; H ix, 176, C xvii, 237
Super flumina Babylonis; H ix, 152, C xvii, 205
Terra tremuit; H ix, 72, C xvii, 99
Tu es Petrus; H ix, 203, C xvii, 277
Tui sunt coeli; H ix, 16, C xvii, 18
Veritas mea; H ix, 190, C xvii, 258
Vir erat in terra; H ix, 155, C xvii, 209

MADRIGALS

Il primo libro di madrigali, 4vv (Rome, 1555) [formerly thought lost; inc. in US-R] [1555]   126-8

Il primo libro de madrigali, 5vv (Venice, 1581) [1581]   110, 126

145

Il secondo libro de madrigali, 4vv (Venice, 1586) [1586]
Delle madrigali spirituali libro secondo, 5vv (Rome, 1594) [1594]
Works in 1554[2b], 1557[2a], 1558[13], 1559[16], 1560[23], 1561[10], 1562[7]; 1562[22], 1563[3], 1566[17], 1568[16], 1570[16], 1574[4], 1576[5], 1577[1]; 1582[4], 1583[12], 1585[6], 1586[9], 1586[13], 1588[19], 1589[7], 1589[11]; 1591[16], 1591[12], 1592[11]; G. B. Bovicelli, ed.: Regole, passaggi di musica, madrigali, e motetti passeggiati (Venice, 1594); 1596[11]

(secular)

Ahi che quest'occhi, 3vv, 1589[11]; H xxviii, 135
Alla riva del Tebro, 4vv, 1586; H xxviii, 105, C xxxi, 47
Amor, ben puoi tu ormai, 4vv, 1586; H xxviii, 75, C xxxi, 7
Amor, che meco (Bembo), 4vv, 1555; H xxviii, 42, C ii, 40
Amor, fortuna (Petrarch), 4vv, 1555; H xxviii, 31, C ii, 30
Amor, quando fioriva (Petrarch), 4vv, 1586; H xxviii, 107, C xxxi, 50
Amor se pur sei Dio, 3vv, 1588[9]; H xxx, 47
Anima, dove sei, 5vv, 1577[7]; H xxx, 119
Ardo lungi ed dapresso, 4vv, 1586; H xxviii, 129, C xxxi, 77
Beltà se com'in ment'io, 4vv, 1586; H xxviii, 110, C xxxi, 54
Che debbo far (Petrarch), 4vv, 1555; H xxviii, 34, C ii, 33
Che non fia che giammai, 4vv, 1555; H xxviii, 7, C ii, 7
Chiare, fresche, e dolci acque (Petrarch), 4vv, 1558[13]; H xxx, 48, C ii, 107
Chiaro, sì chiaro, 4vv, 1555; H xxviii, 19, C ii, 18
Chi dunque fia, 4vv, 1586; H xxviii, 92, C xxxi, 31
Chi estinguerà il mio foco, 4vv, 1555; H xxviii, 21, C ii, 20
Com'in più negre tenebre, 5vv, 1561[10]; H xxviii, 143
Con dolce, altiero ed amoroso cenno, 4vv, 1554[2b], H xxx, 93, C ii, 64
Così la fama scriva, 4vv, 1586; H xxviii, 71, C xxxi, 1
Da così dotta man, 3vv, 1589[11]; H xxviii, 136
Da fuoco così bel, 4vv, 1557[2a], H xxx, 61, C ii, 67
Da poi ch'io vidi, 4vv, 1562[7]; H xxviii, 76
Deh, fuss'or qui madonna, 4vv, 1586; H xxviii, 119, C xxxi, 65
Deh, or foss'io (Petrarch), 4vv, 1555; H xxviii, 1, C ii, 1
Dido chi giace, 5vv, 1586[9]; H xxviii, 146
Dolor non fu, 5vv, 1561[10]; H xxviii, 149, C ii, 148
Donna bell'e gentil, 5vv, 1560[2a] H xxviii, 153, C ii, 144
Donna gentil, 4vv, 1586; H xxviii, 85, C xxxi, 20
Donna presso al cui il viso, 5vv, 1596[11]; H xxx, 107, H xxxiii, 67

E con i raggi tuoi, 1594; H xxix, 179, C xxii, 82
E dal letto, 1594; H xxix, 163, C xxix, 66
Ed arda ogn'hor, 1594; H xxix, 166, C xxii, 70
Eletta Mirra, che soave odore, 1594; H xxix, 119, C xxii, 22
E quella certa speme, 1594; H xxix, 172, C xxii, 76
E questo spirto, 1594; H xxix, 160, C xxii, 63
E, se fur già, 1594; H xxix, 110, C xxii, 13
E, se 'l pensier, 1594; H xxix, 116, C xxii, 19
E, se mai voci, 1594; H xxix, 100, C xxii, 4
E, se nel foco, 1594; H xxix, 134, C xxii, 37
E tua mercé, 1594; H xxix, 169, C xxii, 73
E tu, anima mia, 1581; H xxix, 87, C ix, 111
E tu Signor, 1594; H xxix, 190, C xxii, 94
Fa, che con l'acque tue, 1594; H xxix, 126, C xxii, 28
Figlio immortal, 1594; H xxix, 97, C xxii, 1
Giammai non resti, 1581; H xxix, 74, C ix, 97
Ma so ben, Signor mio, 1581; H xxix, 84, C ix, 108
Non basta ch'una volta, 1581; H xxix, 79, C ix, 102
Novella Aurora, 1594; H xxix, 157, C xxii, 60
O cibo di dolcezza, 1581; H xxix, 49, C ix, 67
O Jesu dolce, 1581; H xxix, 70, C ix, 93
O manna saporito, 1581; H xxix, 65, C ix, 86
O refrigerio acceso, 1581; H xxix, 52, C ix, 70

Orto che sei si chiuso, 1594; H xxix, 132, C xxii, 34
Or tu, sol, che, 1594; H xxix, 103, C xxii, 7
O sol'incoronato, 1581; H xxix, 45, C ix, 63
Paraclito amoroso, 1581; H xxix, 58, C ix, 78
Per questo, Signor mio, 1581; H xxix, 90, C ix, 114
Quanto più T'offend'io, 1581; H xxix, 76, C ix, 99
Regina della vergini, 1594; H xxix, 182, C xxii, 86
Santo altare, 1594; H xxix, 144, C xxii, 46
S'amarissimo fele, 1594; H xxix, 129, C xxii, 31
Signor, dammi scienza, 1581; H xxix, 67, C ix, 39
S'io non Ti conoscessi, 1581; H xxix, 82, C ix, 106
Specchio che fosti, 1594; H xxix, 151, C xxii, 54
Spirito santo, amore, 1581; H xxix, 42, C ix, 58
Tu di fortezza torre, 1594; H xxix, 147, C xxii, 50
Tu sei soave fiume, 1581; H xxix, 55, C ix, 70
Vello di Gedeon, 1594; H xxix, 154, C xxii, 57
Vergine bella (Petrarch), 1581; H xxix, 1, C ix, 1
Vincitrice de l'empia idra, 1594; H xxix, 137, C xxii, 40

OTHER WORKS
(*doubtful*)

Esercizi XI sopra la scala, a 4; H xxxi, 99
Ricercari VIII sopra li toni, a 4; H xxxii, 80

BIBLIOGRAPHY

GENERAL STUDIES OF LIFE AND WORKS

G. Baini: *Memorie storico-critiche della vita e delle opere di Giovanni Pierluigi da Palestrina* (Rome, 1828/*R*1966)

C. von Winterfeld: *J. Pierluigi von Palestrina* (Breslau, 1832)

F. S. Kandler: *Über das Leben und die Werke des G. Pierluigi da Palestrina . . . nach den Memorie storico-critiche des Abbate G. Baini verfasst* (Leipzig, 1834)

G. Cascioli: *La vita e le opere di G. P. da Palestrina* (Rome, 1894)

Z. K. Pyne: *Palestrina: his Life and Times* (London, 1922)

A. Cametti: *Palestrina* (Milan, 1925/*R*)

K. G. Fellerer: *Palestrina* (Regensburg, 1930, 2/1960)

H. Coates: *Palestrina* (London, 1938/*R*1949)

K. Jeppesen: 'Palestrina, Giovanni Pierluigi da', *MGG*

BIOGRAPHY, BACKGROUND, HISTORICAL POSITION

A. Adami da Bolsena: *Osservazioni per ben regolare il coro dei cantori della Cappella pontificia* (Rome, 1711)

G. Pitoni: *Notitia de contrapuntisti e de compositori di musica* (MS, *I-Rvat*: C.G., I/1–2, *c*1725)

M. Fornari: *Narrazione istorica dell'origine, progressi, e privilegi della Pontificia cappella* (MS, *I-Rvat*: C.S., 606, dated 1749)

G. Campori: *Delle relazioni di Orlando di Lasso e G. P. da Palestrina coi principi estensi* (Rome, 1870)

P. Canal: *Della musica in Mantova* (Venice, 1881), 655–774

F. X. Haberl: 'Das Archiv der Gonzaga in Mantua', *KJb*, i (1886), 31

——: *Die römische 'Schola cantorum' und die päpstlichen Kapellsänger bis zur Mitte des XVI. Jahrhunderts* (Leipzig, 1888)

A. Bertolotti: *Musici alla corte dei Gonzaga in Mantova dal secolo XV al XVIII* (Milan, 1890/*R*1969)

A. Cametti: *Cenni biografici di Giovanni Pierluigi da Palestrina* (Milan, 1894)

——: 'Un nuovo documento sulle origini di G. P. da Palestrina', *RMI*, x (1903), 517

K. Weinmann: *Palestrinas Geburtsjahr* (Regensburg, 1915)

R. Casimiri: *G. P. da Palestrina: nuovi documenti biografici* (Rome, 1918–22)

A. Cametti: 'Le case di G. P. da Palestrina in Roma', *RMI*, xxviii (1921), 419

——: 'Rubino Mallapert', *RMI*, xxix (1921), 335

——: 'Giovanni Luigi da Palestrina e il suo commercio di pelliccere', *Archivio della R. Società romana di storia patria*, xliv (1921), 207

Bibliography

G. Cascioli: 'Nuove ricerche sul Palestrina', *Psalterium*, vi (1923)

———: 'Un ritratto di Palestrina', *NA*, i (1924), 113

R. Casimiri: 'Memorie musicali prenestine del secolo XVI', *NA*, i (1924), 7–56

A. Mercati: 'Melchior Major, l'autore del vibrante necrologio di Giovanni Pierluigi da Palestrina', *NA*, i (1924), 57

R. Casimiri: 'Diarii Sistini', *NA*, i–xvii (1924–40)

O. Ursprung: 'Palestrina und Palestrina-Renaissance', *ZMw*, vii (1924–5), 530

———: 'Palestrina und Deutschland', *Festschrift Peter Wagner* (Leipzig, 1926/*R*1969), 190–221

R. Casimiri: ' "Disciplina musicae" e "mastri di capella" dopo il Concilio di Trento nei maggiori istituti ecclesiastici di Roma: Seminario romano – Collegio germanico – Collegio inglese (secoli XVI–XVII)', *NA*, xii–xx (1935–43)

———: 'Il Palestrina e il Marenzio in un privilegio di stampa del 1584', *NA*, xvi (1939), 253

P. H. Lang: 'Palestrina across the Centuries', *Festschrift Karl Gustav Fellerer* (Regensburg, 1962), 294

H. Hucke: 'Palestrina als Autorität und Vorbild im 17. Jahrhundert', *Congresso internazionale sul tema Claudio Monteverdi e il suo tempo: Venezia, Mantova e Cremona 1968*, 253

T. C. Day: *Palestrina in History* (diss., Columbia U., 1970)

WORKS AND STYLE

BurneyH; HawkinsH

J. J. Fux: *Gradus ad Parnassum* (Vienna, 1725, 2/1742; partial Eng. trans., 1943 as *Steps to Parnassus: the Study of Counterpoint*, rev. 2/1965 as *The Study of Counterpoint*)

H. Bellermann: *Der Kontrapunkt* (Berlin, 1862)

A. W. Ambros: *Geschichte der Musik*, iv (Leipzig, 1881, rev. 3/1909 by H. Leichtentritt)

F. X. Haberl: 'Die Cardinalskommission von 1564 und Palestrinas *Missa Papae Marcelli*', *KJb*, vii (1892), 82

P. Wagner: 'Das Madrigal und Palestrina', *VMw*, viii (1892), 423–98

C. Respighi: *G. P. da Palestrina e l'emendazione del Graduale romano* (Rome, 1900)

R. Molitor: *Die nach-tridentinische Choral-Reform zu Rom* (Leipzig, 1901–2)

R. Schwartz: 'Zu den Texten der weltlichen Madrigale Palestrinas', *JbMP 1905*, 95

P. Wagner: *Geschichte der Messe* (Leipzig, 1913)

K. Weinmann: 'Zur Geschichte der Palestrinas Missa Papae Marcelli', *JbMP 1916*, 23

R. Casimiri: *Il Codice 59 dell'Archivio musicale lateranense, autografo di G. P. da Palestrina* (Rome, 1919)

K. Weinmann: *Das Konzil von Trient und die Kirchenmusik* (Leipzig, 1919)

K. Jeppesen: *Palestrinastil med saerligt henblik paa dissonansbehandlingen* (Copenhagen, 1923; Ger. trans., 1925; Eng. trans., 1927, 2/1946, as *The Style of Palestrina and the Dissonance*)

——: 'Das "Sprunggesetz" des Palestrinastils bei betonten Viertelnoten (halben Taktzeiten)', *Kongressbericht: Basel 1924*, 221

A. Einstein: 'Ein unbekanntes Madrigal Palestrinas', *ZMw*, vii (1924–5), 530

R. Casimiri: 'I "XXVII Responsoria" di M. A. Ingegneri, attribuiti a G. P. da Palestrina', *NA*, iii (1926), 17

K. Jeppesen: 'Das isometrische Moment in der Vokalpolyphonie', *Festschrift Peter Wagner* (Leipzig, 1926/*R*1969), 87

——: 'Über ein Brief Palestrinas', *Festschrift Peter Wagner* (Leipzig, 1926/*R*1969), 100

K. G. Fellerer: *Der Palestrinastil und seine Bedeutung in der vokalen Kirchenmusik des 18. Jahrhunderts* (Augsburg, 1929/*R*1972)

K. Jeppesen: *Kontrapunkt (vokalpolyfoni)* (Copenhagen, 1930, 3/1962; Ger. trans., 1935, 5/1970; Eng. trans., 1939)

——: 'Wann entstand die Marcellus-Messe?', *Studien zur Musikgeschichte: Festschrift für Guido Adler* (Vienna, 1930/*R*1971), 126

W. Widmann: 'Die sechsstimmige Messen Palestrinas', *KJb*, xxvi (1930), 94

R. Casimiri: 'La "Missa Cantantibus organis Caecilia" a 12 voci di Giovanni Pierluigi da Palestrina', *NA*, viii (1931), 233

O. Ursprung: *Die katholische Kirchenmusik* (Potsdam, 1931)

W. Kurthen: 'Ein Zitat in einer Motette Palestrinas', *KJb*, xxix (1934), 50

H. J. Moser: ' "Vestiva i colli" ', *AMf*, iv (1939), 129

O. Strunk: 'Some Motet-types of the Sixteenth Century', *PAMS 1939*, 155; repr. in O. Strunk: *Essays on Music in the Western World* (New York, 1974)

J. Samson: *Palestrina, ou La poésie de l'exactitude* (Geneva, 1940)

A. Auda: 'La mesure dans la messe "L'homme armé" de Palestrina', *AcM*, xiii (1941), 39

——: 'Le "tactus" dans la messe "L'homme armé" de Palestrina', *AcM*, xiv (1942), 27–73

R. Casimiri: *La polifonia vocale* (Rome, 1942)

K. Jeppesen: 'Marcellus-Probleme', *AcM*, xvi–xvii (1944–5), 11; Eng. trans. in *Giovanni Pierluigi da Palestrina: Pope Marcellus Mass*, Norton Critical Score (New York, 1975)

O. Strunk: 'Guglielmo Gonzaga and Palestrina's *Missa Dominicalis*',

Bibliography

MQ, xxxiii (1947), 228; repr. in O. Strunk: *Essays on Music in the Western World* (New York, 1974)

A. Einstein: *The Italian Madrigal* (Princeton, 1949/*R*1971)

P. Hamburger: 'The Ornamentations in the Works of Palestrina', *AcM*, xxii (1950), 128

K. Jeppesen: 'The Recently Discovered Mantova Masses of Palestrina', *AcM*, xxii (1950), 36

H. Rahe: 'Thema und Melodiebildung der Motetten Palestrinas', *KJb*, xxxiv (1950), 62

W. Lipphardt: *Die Geschichte des mehrstimmigen Proprium Missae* (Heidelberg, 1950)

M. Antonowytsch: *Die Motette Benedicta es von Josquin des Prez und die Messen super Benedicta von Willaert, Palestrina, de la Hêle und de Monte* (Utrecht, 1951)

H. Anglès: 'Palestrina y los "Magnificat" de Morales', *AnM*, viii (1953), 153

K. Jeppesen: 'Pierluigi da Palestrina, der Herzog Guglielmo Gonzaga und die neugefundenen Mantovaner-Messen Palestrinas: ein ergänzender Bericht', *AcM*, xxv (1953), 132–79

J. Klassen: 'Untersuchungen zur Parodiemesse Palestrinas', *KJb*, xxxvii (1953), 53

——: 'Das Parodieverfahren in der Messe Palestrinas', *KJb*, xxxviii (1954), 24–54

G. Reese: *Music in the Renaissance* (New York, 1954, rev. 2/1959)

R. Bobbitt: 'Harmonic Tendencies in the *Missa Papae Marcelli*', *MR*, xvi (1955), 273

P. Hamburger: *Subdominante und Wechseldominante* (Wiesbaden, 1955)

J. Klassen: 'Zur Modellbehandlung in Palestrinas Parodiemessen', *KJb*, xxxix (1955), 41

H. C. Wolff: 'Die Variationstechnik in den frühen Messen Palestrinas', *AcM*, xxvii (1955), 59

P. Hamburger: *Studien zur Vokalpolyphonie* (Wiesbaden, 1956)

K. Schnürl: 'Die Variations-Technik in den Choral-Cantus firmus Werken Palestrinas', *SMw*, xi (1956), 11–66

E. Apfel: 'Zur Entstehungsgeschichte des Palestrinasatzes', *AMw*, xiv (1957), 30

A. C. Haigh: 'Modal Harmony in the Music of Palestrina', *Essays on Music in Honor of Archibald Thompson Davison* (Cambridge, Mass., 1957), 111

E. Paccagnella: *Palestrina: il linguaggio melodico e armonico* (Florence, 1957)

H. K. Andrews: *An Introduction to the Technique of Palestrina* (London, 1958)

K. Jeppesen: 'Palestriniana: ein unbekanntes Autogramm und einige unveröffentlichte Falsibordoni des Giovanni Pierluigi da Palestrina', *Miscelánea en homenaje a Monseñor Higinio Anglés*, i (Barcelona, 1958), 417

E. Ferraci: *Il Palestrina* (Rome, 1960)

S. Hermelink: *Dispositiones modorum* (Tutzing, 1960)

R. Schlötterer: 'Struktur und Kompositions-Verfahren in der Musik Palestrinas', *AMw*, xvii (1960), 40

R. L. Marshall: 'The Paraphrase Technique of Palestrina in his Masses based on Hymns', *JAMS*, xvi (1963), 347

J. Haar: '*Pace non trovo*: a Study in Literary and Musical Parody', *MD*, xx (1966), 95–149

S. W. Klyce: *Palestrina and his 'Missa Papae Marcelli': an Analysis for Performance* (diss., Indiana U., 1969)

L. Lockwood: *The Counter-Reformation and the Masses of Vincenzo Ruffo* (Venice, 1970)

H. Federhofer: 'Ist Palestrina ein Manierist?', *Convivium musicorum: Festschrift Wolfgang Boetticher* (Berlin, 1974), 44

H. S. Powers: 'The Modality of "Vestiva i colli" ', *Studies in Renaissance and Baroque Music in Honor of Arthur Mendel* (Kassel and Hackensack, 1974), 31

L. Comes: *La melodia palestriniana e il canto gregoriano* (Venice, 1975)

L. Lockwood: Introduction to *Giovanni Pierluigi da Palestrina: Pope Marcellus Mass*, Norton Critical Score (New York, 1975)

F. Luisi, ed.: *Atti del convegno di studi palestriniani: Palestrina 1975*

O. Mischiati: ' "Ut verba intelligerentur": circostanze e connessioni a proposito della "Missa Papae Marcelli" ', *Atti del convegno di studi palestriniani: Palestrina 1975*, 415

G. Rostirolla: 'La Cappella Giulia in San Pietro negli anni del magistero di G. P. da Palestrina', *Atti del convegno di studi palestriniani: Palestrina 1975*, 99–284

G. Reese: 'The Opening Chant for a Palestrina Magnificat', *A Musical Offering: Essays in Honor of Martin Bernstein* (New York, 1977), 239

Q. W. Quereau: 'Sixteenth-century Parody: an Approach to Analysis', *JAMS*, xxxi (1978), 404–41

A. M. Monterosso Vacchelli: *La messa l'homme armé di Palestrina: studio paleografico ed edizione critica*, IMa, vii (1979) [incl. facs. and transcr.]

H. S. Powers: 'Tonal Types and Modal Categories in Renaissance Polyphony', *JAMS*, xxxiv (1981), 428–70

K. G. Fellerer: *Palestrina-Studien* (Baden-Baden, 1982) [collection of previously pubd essays]

Bibliography

H. S. Powers: 'Modal Representation in Polyphonic Offertories', *Early Music History*, ii (1982), 43–86

Q. W. Quereau: 'Aspects of Palestrina's Parody Procedures', *Journal of Musicology*, i/2 (1982), 198

I. Godt: 'A New Look at Palestrina's *Missa Papae Marcelli*', *College Music Symposium*, xxiii (1983), 22

D. Lewin: 'An Interesting Global Rule for Species Counterpoint', *In Theory Only*, vi/8 (1983), 19

T. Ford: *Dubious Masses by Palestrina: a Study in Authenticity* (in preparation)

ORLANDE DE LASSUS

James Haar

Life

I Early years

Orlande de Lassus was born in 1530 or, more probably, 1532 at Mons in Hainaut, a Franco-Flemish province notable for the number of distinguished musicians born and trained there during the Renaissance. Also known as Roland de Lassus and, in Italy in particular, as Orlando di Lasso, he was one of the most prolific and versatile of 16th-century composers, and in his time the best-known and most widely admired musician in Europe.

Nothing definite is known about Lassus's parents, nor is there any solid proof that he was a choirboy at the church of St Nicholas – much less for the legend that he was three times abducted because of the beauty of his voice. The first known fact about him, attested to by his contemporary and earliest biographer, Samuel Quickelberg, is that at about the age of 12 he entered the service of Ferrante Gonzaga, a cadet of the Mantuan ducal house and a general in the service of Charles V. Gonzaga was in the Low Countries in summer 1544; when he headed south the boy Lassus presumably accompanied him. After a stop near Paris Gonzaga returned to Italy, where he visited Mantua before proceeding to Sicily late in 1545. Thus Lassus's first Italian experience was at the Mantuan court. From Palermo, Gonzaga went to Milan, where Lassus apparently spent the years 1546–9. It is likely that at this time he met other musicians in the service of the Gonzaga, particularly Hoste da Reggio, a madrigalist who headed whatever musical establishment Ferrante Gonzaga maintained.

According to Quickelberg, Lassus next went to Naples, where he entered the service of Constantino Castrioto and lived in the household of G. B. d'Azzia della Terza, a man of letters who introduced him into the Accademia de' Sereni. It is thought that Lassus began to compose while in Naples, and that the villanellas printed in Antwerp in 1555 may have been written at this time. From Naples he went to Rome; after a period in the household of Antonio Altoviti, Archbishop of Florence but then resident in Rome, he became *maestro di cappella* at St John Lateran in spring 1553 (succeeding Paolo Animuccia and preceding, by two years, Palestrina). Though young and as yet not well known as a composer – at least in print – Lassus must by this time have acquired a certain reputation as a musician in order to get a post such as this.

A little over a year later Lassus left Rome, for a visit to his parents who were ill, but he found them dead on his arrival. His whereabouts for a short period after this are unknown, and it has been claimed, though not proved (he himself never spoke of it), that he visited France and England in the company of the singer–diplomat–adventurer G. C. Brancaccio. Early in 1555 Lassus was in Antwerp. Although he is not known to have held any official post, he seems to have made friends quickly here, and with helpful people such as the printers Tylman Susato and Jean de Laet. In that year Susato printed what has been called Lassus's 'op.1', a collection of 'madrigali, vilanesche, canzoni francesi e motetti' for four voices; meanwhile Antonio Gardane in Venice had issued Lassus's first book of five-part madrigals. In 1556 the first book of five- and six-part motets appeared in Antwerp; it seems that Lassus had waited to publish his music until he had accumulated a substantial number of pieces. How much other music he had written up to this time we do not know; but it is probable that some of the madrigals appearing in Antonio Barré's Roman anthologies of the late 1550s date from Lassus's stay in Rome, that at least one mass, *'Domine secundum actum meum'*, may have been written before 1556, and that the *Sacrae lectiones novem ex propheta Iob*, though not printed until 1565, belong to this period. The *Prophetiae Sibyllarum*, a collection of highly chromatic settings of humanistic Latin texts that was not published until after Lassus's death although it had periods of notoriety during his lifetime – including the amazed response of Charles IX of France in 1571 – may also belong to Lassus's Italian years (it survives in a manuscript containing a portrait of the composer at the age of 28).

II Munich

In 1556 Orlande de Lassus received and accepted an invitation to join the court of Duke Albrecht V of Bavaria in Munich. The circumstances of this appointment are not clear, but it is evident that Dr Seld, the imperial vice-chancellor at Brussels, played a part in the negotiations (having first recommended Philippe de Monte for the post). Lassus was engaged as a tenor in a chapel headed by Ludwig Daser; a half-dozen other newly engaged Flemish singers also arrived in Munich in 1556–7, the result of a deliberate plan to 'netherlandize' a chapel which had perhaps come to seem too provincially German in character (Albrecht V's ambitions to revitalize his chapel may have been spurred by news of the dissolution of Charles V's chapel in 1555).

During the next few years Lassus's salary began to rise, but as late as 1568 he was still referred to in the chapel records as 'cantor' and 'tenor 2us'. On the other hand the title-pages of prints such as the *Libro quarto de madrigali* for five voices of 1567 referred to him as *maestro di cappella* of the Bavarian court. Whether for musical reasons or political and religious ones (Daser was a Protestant and Albrecht V, who had for some time tolerated and even encouraged reformers in Bavaria, had turned back to Catholicism, sending a representative to the Council of Trent in 1563), Lassus, who appears to have remained Catholic though he was no Counter-Reformation zealot, took over the leadership of the chapel when Daser was pensioned in 1563, a position he was to hold for 30 years. During this period the make-up of the chapel changed as more and more Italians were recruited. There was much fluctuation in numbers of singers and instrumentalists, the highpoint being reached in 1568 at the time of the young Duke Wilhelm's marriage, the low occurring after the latter's accession to the throne in 1579. But Lassus's position ended only with his death, and so firm was his hold on it that it could be inherited by his two sons in turn – Ferdinand (*c*1560–1609) and Rudolph (*c*1563–1625), both composers. In 1629 Ferdinand's son, also called Ferdinand (1592–1630), still represented the family in the chapel.

Lassus's duties included a morning service, for which

polyphonic masses, elaborate or simple as the occasion required, were prepared. Judging from his enormous output of *Magnificat* settings, Vespers must have been celebrated solemnly a good deal of the time. It is less clear for what services much of the repertory of motets was created, though many could have fitted into celebrations of the Mass and Offices. Music for special occasions was provided by the ducal chapel; this included state visits, banquets for which 'Tafelmusik' was customary and hunting parties. Indeed Albrecht's love of musical display and his munificence towards musicians was much criticized in some court quarters. In addition Lassus supervised the musical education of the choirboys; he saw to copying of manuscripts and perhaps to the collection of printed music for the ducal library; and he became a friend and companion to the duke and especially to his heir, the future Wilhelm V.

In 1558 Lassus married Regina Wäckinger, the daughter of a Bavarian court official. He settled into what seems to have been a stable and comfortable existence, apparently one that he never seriously considered changing. This was varied by journeys undertaken at ducal behest. Thus in 1560 he went to Flanders to recruit singers; in 1562 he was in Frankfurt for the coronation of the Emperor Maximilian II; Andrea Gabrieli joined Lassus's chapel for this visit, and may have remained in Munich for a year or two thereafter. In 1567 Lassus was in northern Italy, visiting Ferrara and Venice – and reminding Italians that, as he said in the dedication to his fourth book of five-part madrigals, good Italian music could be written even in far-off 'Germania'.

Lassus's fame was steadily growing, at home and

*5. Orlande de Lassus: woodcut from his 'Livre de chansons nouvelles'
(1571)*

abroad. He began, perhaps at the duke's request, to
collect and put in order his own compositions, particularly the motets. The Venetian and Flemish printers
who published his first works continued to issue
madrigals, chansons and sacred music; in the 1560s
Berg in Munich, Montanus and Neuber in Frankfurt,
and Le Roy & Ballard in Paris began to print individual

works, then series of volumes devoted to the music of the man becoming known as 'princeps musicorum' and the 'divin Orlande'.

In 1568 Lassus played an important part in the festivities for the wedding of Wilhelm V with Renée of Lorraine; in addition to composing music and supervising performances he is said to have performed the role of a 'magnifico' in Italian comedies. He was becoming something of a genuine 'magnifico': in 1570 Maximilian II conferred upon him a patent of nobility; in 1571 and again in 1573 he paid a visit to the French court at the invitation of Charles IX; in 1574 he was made a Knight of the Golden Spur by Pope Gregory XIII. Such honours were rarely bestowed on musicians. Still, Lassus was content to remain in Munich; there seems to be no proof that in 1574 he seriously thought of moving to France, and turned back only on hearing of the death of Charles IX.

In 1574–9 Lassus made a number of journeys, visiting Venice, Trent, Ferrara, Mantua, Bologna and Rome. His motet *Domine Jesu Christe* was awarded a prize at Evreux in 1575, and he was awarded the 'silver organ' again in 1583 for his Cecilian motet *Cantantibus organis*. He may have had as a pupil Giovanni Gabrieli, who was in Munich during the 1570s. From these years a charming correspondence between the composer and Duke Wilhelm, Albrecht's son and heir, survives; these letters, and some correspondence between Wilhelm and his father, are proof of the high regard felt by both men for Lassus. Before his death, Albrecht V provided that the composer was to receive his salary for the rest of his life. The five magisterial volumes of sacred works called *Patrocinium musices* (see fig.6, p.165) appeared during these years and numerous reprints of his earlier music testify to Lassus's continuing popularity all over Europe.

On the accession of Wilhelm V in 1579 the ducal chapel was much reduced in size. Whatever Lassus may have felt about this, he did not consider leaving. Refusing an invitation (1580) to succeed Antonio Scandello in Dresden, he told the Duke of Saxony that he did not want to leave his house, garden and other good things in Munich, and that he was now beginning to feel old. His activity as a composer did not diminish, however; the years 1581–5 are marked by a number of new publications, of masses, *Magnificat* settings, motets, psalms and German lieder. In 1584 Ferdinand Lassus took over some of his father's duties, and the next year Lassus made a pilgrimage to Loreto. On this journey he visited Verona and Ferrara, where he heard new Italian music of an advanced style. The conservatism of his own later music was the result of deliberate choice, viewed by the composer himself with some wryness, and not because of ignorance of what was happening in Italy.

Although Lassus's final years were marked by some poor health and by a 'melancholia hypocondriaca' for which he sought the help of a physician, Thomas Mermann, he was occasionally active, accompanying Wilhelm V to Regensburg in 1593; and he continued to write music, if only intermittently. Shortly before his death in Munich on 14 June 1594, he dedicated to Pope Clement VIII his last cycle of compositions, the *Lagrime di S Pietro*, adding to it a seven-voice motet, *Vide homo quae pro te patior*.

III Letters
A series of letters that were written by Lassus to Duke

6. Title-page of Lassus's 'Patrocinium musices: missae aliquot'
(Munich: Adam Berg, 1589)

Wilhelm, son and heir of Albrecht V, survives. The letters, dated between 1572 and 1579 and for the most part written from Munich to the duke's establishment at Landshut, are celebrated for their mixture of languages, passing back and forth from a playful, half-macaronic Latin to Italian, French and German. A few are partly in doggerel verse, strengthening the supposition that Lassus wrote some of his own texts for occasional and humorous pieces. The tone of these letters and their amusing signatures ('Orlando Lasso col cor non basso'; 'Orlandissimo lassissimo, amorevolissimo'; 'secretaire publique, Orlando magnifique') show Lassus to have been on terms of easy familiarity with Wilhelm. Occasionally there is a reference to music, as in a letter of 22 March 1576, when he wrote: 'I send a copy of *Io son ferito*; if it seems good to you, I will hope to hear my work at Landshut or elsewhere' (this must refer to Lassus's mass written on Palestrina's well-known madrigal and published in 1589). Wilhelm apparently knew a good deal about music and liked to talk about it; thus Lassus could send him a letter (11 March 1578; see fig.7) entirely made up of musical puns and jokes, mentioning other composers such as Rore, Clemens and Arcadelt, and referring jokingly to musical terms, as in the description of 'una baligia senza pause, coperta di passagi di molte cadenze fatte in falso bordone a misura di macaroni' ('a valise without rests, covered with passage-work of many cadences made from *falsibordoni* the size of macaroni'). These letters suggest that Lassus had read Italian epistolary writers such as Pietro Aretino and Antonfrancesco Doni; and they confirm his reputation as – when the occasion required and perhaps when the mood was on him – an amusing friend and boon companion.

verdelott cosa che portarebbe damno a le longhe senza coda pur si
spera chel dissimulare di cipriano Amolliva il core ale seste
maggiore per essere un poco dure di cervuello, Il s.r contrapunto
moderno a fatto ligare molte quarte per terza persona pur le
potra lasciare sciolte con l'occasione di qualche bona parola
che le sia data ben e vero che a cacciato de la sua corte quelli
che dauano recapito a le consonante perfette vestite dun medesimo
panno perche tali gente fanno bonissimi effetti praticandosi di
raro, perche il conuersar insieme nihil valet quando poi si
passeggia per terza compagnia sta bene esser serrati insieme
& accordarsi dolcemente ligando lun'a laltro con amoreuole
et usata concordia ma tornando a quando io penso al
martire dauchadelt s'intende che se neandato per dispeyato
a farsi frate e questa noua ha portato un benedicamus dno
coperto dormesino, quale ha trouato per strada un agnus
dei de isaac qual da quatro todeschi e stato mangiato
a voce parj se dice di piu che certe crome fastidiose
se ne vanno a la volta di fiandra in compagnia de molti
melli sospirj : la capis : il resto che seguira presto si sapera:
per adesso io humilissimamente baso le many di vra Ex.tia
supplicandola a pigliar i miei capricci in bona parte e tenermi
sempre nella sua bona gratia nro s.re la conserui insieme
con la s.ra principessa renea in sanita et allegrezza quanto
dchilera Di monaco adi 11 di marzo 1578:

Di vra Ex.tia
humiliss.o seruitor:
orlando de lassus

7. *Part of an autograph letter (11 March 1578) from Lassus to Duke Wilhelm*

CHAPTER TWO

Sacred Latin works

I Masses

The earliest surviving printed volume of masses by Lassus was issued by Claudio Merulo in Venice in 1570 and is a 'volume two'; an earlier first volume must have existed. Some of Lassus's masses belong to the first years of his residence in Munich in the late 1550s; the latest, a five-voice mass based on Gombert's *Triste depart*, was written as a kind of valedictory gesture near the end of his life. The 60 or so masses known to be authentic (there are a number of doubtful works in this genre) make up a not inconsiderable part of his oeuvre. Since their publication in the new Lassus edition, the traditional view that Lassus's masses are of peripheral importance in his work, and indeed of largely perfunctory character, has been modified. Certainly they were not considered of negligible value during the late 16th and early 17th centuries. Although no single mass attained the popularity of some of the more celebrated motets, many were reprinted during and after his lifetime; several groups were included in the *Patrocinium musices*; and Le Roy & Ballard's resplendent *Missae variis concentibus ornatae ab Orlando de Lassus* of 1577–8 suggests that the Parisian publishers planned (although they did not carry out) a complete edition of his masses.

Most of Lassus's settings are parody masses, based

on motets (chiefly his own), French chansons (by Nicolas Gombert, Adrian Willaert, Monte and members of the Parisian school), or Italian madrigals (by Sebastiano Festa, Jacques Arcadelt, Cipriano de Rore and Palestrina). They provide an instructive anthology of parody techniques. His rearrangement and recomposition of his own music, as in the *Missa 'Locutus sum'*, show Lassus's technical prowess; his striking transformation of a rather simple model, such as Daser's motet for the *Missa 'Ecce nunc benedicite'*, illustrates his ability to raise the level of music of his lesser contemporaries. More remarkable still is the sensitivity he displayed in adapting secular models as diverse as Arcadelt's *Quand'io pens'al martire*, the densely polyphonic texture of Gombert's chansons, and the supple and subtle flow of Rore's madrigals. The masses based on these pieces are reminiscent of their models in style yet show no musical incongruity or technical strain. A work like the *Missa 'Qual donna attende'*, based on Rore's distinguished madrigal, must have provided a rich treat for connoisseurs of this genre.

At the other extreme in Lassus's masses are the short, syllabic *missae breves*. Some of these are parodies of works, like Claudin de Sermisy's *La la Maistre Pierre*, themselves in concise syllabic style. The shortest of all is the 'Jäger' Mass or *Missa venatorum*, a work designed for a brief service on days the court spent hunting. Some of the masses based on plainchant are of this succinct type; an exception is the impressive five-voice *Missa pro defunctis* with its curious bass intonations. Whether or not because they fit post-Tridentine ideas about music for the Mass (Lassus is known to have been stubborn about changing things at Munich to conform with new ideas coming from Rome), some of the shortest and simplest of Lassus's masses were among his most popular works in the genre. It should be stressed, however, that these works do not represent him fully or entirely characteristically as a composer of masses.

II Passions

Lassus's four settings of the Passions are responsorial and of the kind cultivated by north Italian composers throughout most of the 16th century. In two of them (the *St Matthew* and *St John*) the words of the turbae and of the various individuals are set polyphonically, the first group for five-part chorus and the second for solo duos and trios; the words of Christ and the evangelists' narrative are to be chanted. The Passions according to St Mark and St Luke are shorter works in which chordal polyphony is provided only for the turbae. In the *St Matthew Passion*, first published in 1575, a clear stylistic distinction is made between the music of the turbae – chordal successions with ponderously decorated cadences – and the supple imitative style of the duos and trios used for the words of Peter, Judas and other characters. This work enjoyed great and lasting popularity. Various later Passions borrowed from it, and a manuscript dated 1743, complete with added thoroughbass part, shows that it was still performed 150 years after its composition. The other three Passions survive only in manuscript, with convincing though not absolutely definitive attribution to Lassus.

III Magnificat settings

Lassus's 101 settings of the *Magnificat*, collected in a posthumously published edition (1619) by his son

Rudolph, far outnumber those of any other 16th-century composer (Palestrina, for example, wrote 35). Their wide circulation in print and manuscript is testimony to their lasting popularity; only those of Morales had anything like this success. All but a few are *alternatim* settings of the even verses, leaving the odd verses to be chanted, as was customary, or perhaps played on the organ.

In 1567 Lassus published three cycles each containing a six-verse setting for all eight tones. He went on to write two more such cycles; all are based on the appropriate chant tones of the *Magnificat*, with widely varied use of cantus firmus technique. Some 60 settings use the psalmodic tones; a number of others have monophonic tunes used as cantus firmi. He respected the *Magnificat* tones in his choice of mode, and tended not to embellish the cantus firmus when using it intact; but no brief description could do justice to the flexible virtuosity with which the time-honoured device of the cantus firmus is used in these works. There is of course much integration of cantus firmus with other voices through melodic paraphrase and contrapuntal imitation.

A *Magnificat* parodying Rore's celebrated madrigal *Ancor che col partire* was published in the collection of 1576. Some 25 of the *Magnificat* settings appearing in subsequent years are parody works; Lassus was the first to make consistent use of parody technique in this genre, and he seems to have liked using the procedure almost as much as he did in the masses. His own motets (and an occasional chanson) were favoured sources, but he ranged widely through 16th-century literature, from Josquin (whose *Praeter rerum seriem* served as model for a magnificently elaborate six-voice work) to Alessandro Striggio and Orazio Vecchi, from motets to madrigals. As in the masses, parody technique is used here in almost bewilderingly varied fashion, and with a sure instinct for blending the style of the model with that of the 'copy'.

Lassus's settings of the *Magnificat* vary greatly in length and complexity, from concise settings resembling *falsibordoni* to resplendently contrapuntal works over 200 bars long. His tendency generally to write more compact, harmonically conceived works in his later years may be seen in these pieces, but not in any easily predictable way. The opening and closing verses are generally closer to their melodic or contrapuntal models, the middle verses correspondingly freer. All voices respect to some degree the bipartite structure of the psalm verses.

IV Other liturgical works
There are a large number of liturgical and quasi-liturgical works in other genres. Some were printed in the composer's lifetime: the Offices for Christmas, Easter and Pentecost in the third volume of the *Patrocinium musices* (1574); the Christmas Lessons of volume iv (1575) in that series; the Lamentations of Jeremiah, some of which were printed in 1585; the Lessons from Job (two sets, printed in 1565 and 1582); and the seven *Psalmi Davidis poenitentiales* (printed in 1584 but composed much earlier). Posthumously published works include 12 litanies (1596; two others survive in manuscript copies). None of these works was included in the *Magnum opus musicum* and none therefore appears in Haberl's edition. Only the penitential psalms have been much studied.

An important category of Office polyphony in Lassus's works is the *Nunc dimittis*. 12 settings survive, none of them ever printed: four, based on chant, date from about 1570, and eight (not all confirmed as genuine), of which five are known to be parody works based on motets and madrigals, from the last period of his life. Still other groups of liturgical pieces survive only in manuscript and were apparently never printed (they were perhaps considered in a way the private property of the Bavarian court chapel): these include a group of *falsibordoni*, an important hymn cycle (*c*1580) and a group of responsories (1580s). These have been described briefly (by Boetticher), but await publication and thorough investigation.

V Motets

Specially difficult to assess simply by reason of their enormous number, the motets of Lassus as they appear in Haberl's edition pose an additional problem: they are printed in the order assigned to them by Rudolph and Ferdinand Lassus in the *Magnum opus musicum* of 1604, and thus arranged by number of voices rather than in chronological order of publication (the new Lassus edition is fortunately proceeding on quite different principles). Studies of Lassus's music based on chronology have been made (Boetticher), but much remains to be done. It is not easy to be sure about relative composition dates for much of this music; the publication date is of course not an infallible guide, sometimes not even a useful one. Details of stylistic growth and change can probably be seen and analysed, but the criteria for such a study have yet to be fully developed.

In motet composition, as in the writing of madrigals, Lassus began by assimilating the styles fashionable in Italy in his youth. Cipriano de Rore and the Roman school around Barré seem the two most important of these influences, as seen in the carefully conceived declamatory rhythms in all voice parts. The bold yet tonally controlled chromaticism of motets such as *Alma nemes*, and the use of distinctive, finely chiselled thematic material in *Audi dulcis amica mea* (both printed in 1555), certainly show that Lassus knew Rore's work. The motets of the Roman and Antwerp years, and also those of the first decade in Munich, are dazzlingly virtuoso in invention and the handling of vocal textures. *Videntes stellam*, a two-section motet for five voices printed in 1562, is a good example of Lassus's brilliant early style. The melodic material, distantly derived from a *Magnificat* antiphon for Epiphany week, transforms gentle hints in the chant into dramatically descriptive motifs that rocket through the texture, a texture that is constantly varied but always clear, and always well grounded harmonically. It is no wonder that the composer of pieces such as this rapidly won for himself first place at the Bavarian court and an international reputation soon to surpass that of all his contemporaries.

Imitation plays a large role in the contrapuntal technique of Lassus's early work, as does voice pairing; he did not of course observe these techniques as strictly as did Josquin's generation, but neither did he favour the thick texture and close-set imitation cultivated by Gombert. Everywhere there is harmonic clarity and solidity, equally apparent in pieces such as the *Prophetiae Sibyllarum*, which use the chromatic vocabulary fashionable in the 1550s, as in completely diatonic works.

It has been said that Lassus made little use of canon or other constructivist elements. This is true in a statistical sense, but when he chose he could show off Netherlands skills; for example, the seven-part *In omnibus requiem quaesivi* (published 1565) has a three-part canon, with one of the voices in contrary motion. Cantus firmus writing is rarer in Lassus than in Palestrina, but on occasion Lassus could revert to the kind of cantus firmus procedure used by Josquin and Obrecht; *Homo cum in honore esset* (six voices; published 1566) has a *soggetto cavato* as cantus firmus on the text 'Nosce te ipsum', heard successively in breves, semibreves and minims. In this eclectic revival of earlier techniques, and in many individual passages where archaisms like fauxbourdon or use of outmoded long notes are seen, Lassus may have been using elements of an older Netherlands style for expressive reasons, making a musical allusion to support the meaning of a phrase of text.

Like all Lassus's music, the motets are immensely varied in musical invention and expressive detail. Nonetheless a recognizable stylistic 'set' may be observed in all the motets of the period *c*1555–70: thematic originality is blended with a contrapuntal fluidity that in less distinguished pieces approaches formula; there is plenty of chordal declamation, always marked by strength and clarity of harmony; expressive word-painting abounds but does not dominate or upset the equilibrium of a piece; and a certain succinctness – the economy of utterance that was to become increasingly evident in Lassus's later works – is noticeable (the famous six-part

Timor et tremor, published 1564, is as surprising for brevity as it is celebrated for expressive power). Lassus's capacity for obtaining iridescent changes of colour in the plainest of diatonic palettes through skilful vocal scoring, a trait very marked in his later works, is present in his early motets; it is indeed one of the most characteristic of his stylistic traits (see ex.1, the opening of *O Domine salvum me fac*, published 1562).

In his motets of the 1570s and 1580s, as in other works of this period, Lassus made much use of chordal declamation on short note values, varied by quickly alternating points of imitation of rather neutral melodic character. This 'villanella' style (see Boetticher) may indicate a desire for a more up-to-date vocabulary on Lassus's part. If so, that is about as far as he went; the works of the last decade are less markedly declamatory, more complex in texture and marked by a certain denseness and concentration of style that is not so much progressive as it is highly individual, a final style seen to good advantage in the six-part *Musica Dei . donum optimi* (published 1594), a moving tribute to the composer's art (this text was also set by other 16th-century composers).

Although they cannot be categorized in any very neat way, Lassus's motets can be divided roughly under a few general headings.

(*i*) *Didactic works.* The 24 duos of 1577 and many of the pieces for three voices must have been intended for students. In this the duos are particularly interesting. Compared with other famous 16th-century collections of duos such as those of Jhan Gero or of Bernardino Lupacchino – both sets reprinted so often as to leave

Ex.1 *O Domine salvum me fac*

no doubt about their pedagogical usefulness – Lassus's psalm settings and textless bicinia are surprising in their individuality of style: they are not generic counterpoint but rather illustrations of his own contrapuntal practice. They were popular enough to be reprinted and even to be 'modernized' (in a Parisian reprint of 1601 with an

177

added third voice), but they did not rival Gero's in longevity of use; they have about them too much of the finished and idiosyncratic composition, too little of the contrapuntal exercise. For Lassus's own pupils they must have been of great value since the writing of duos was probably the most important part of a 16th-century composer's training. It may be noted that the two-part pieces illustrate the D, E, F and G modes but not those on A and C; this supports the remark of Leonhard Lechner, Lassus's pupil, that his teacher used only the traditional eight modes.

(*ii*) *Ceremonial motets*. There are a surprising number of pieces written for special occasions or to honour rulers and dignitaries; these are mostly grouped together in the *Magnum opus musicum*, near the beginning or end of the divisions by number of voices. Some of them provide clues to the composer's life; thus the five-part *Te spectant Reginalde Poli* (published 1556) may indicate that Lassus knew the English Cardinal Pole in Rome in the 1550s. Many occasional pieces honouring the Habsburgs and various secular and religious potentates throughout Germany were doubtless commissioned by the Bavarian court. By far the largest number of these are addressed to Albrecht V, to his eldest son (the future Wilhelm V) and to other members of the ducal family (one of these, *Unde revertimini*, started its existence under a slightly different name as a work in praise of Henri d'Anjou, the future Henri III of France). They vary in length and scoring (from three to ten voices) but as a matter of course are uniformly bright and festive in nature. Some, like the nine-section *Princeps Marte potens, Guilelmus*, are little more than a series of acclamations (in this instance addressed to Wilhelm V, his bride, and members of the imperial and ducal families); others are in full polyphonic style. A distinguishing feature of Lassus's ceremonial pieces honouring the Wittelsbachs is their personal tone, evident proof of the composer's close relationship with his employers. This is seen in *Multarum hic resonat*, addressed to Wilhelm on his name day in 1571, and in *Haec quae ter triplici*, the dedicatory piece of a collection of motets for three voices (1577) honouring Albrecht's three sons, on a text ending 'Lassus mente animoque dicat' ('Lassus' set to the composer's musical signature of *la–sol*). Most appealingly personal of all is *Sponsa quid agis*, for five voices, thought to have been composed for Lassus's marriage in 1558; here the colouristic harmony on the words 'Non me lasciviae veneris', in an otherwise diatonic framework, is a charming bit of musical allusion.

(*iii*) *Humorous motets.* Pieces with texts ranging from playfulness to burlesque are to be found among the works with Latin texts. Their music is appropriate and often witty in itself, but almost never broadly farcical; Lassus, rather like Mozart, tended to clothe his verbal jokes in exquisite musical dress. One exception is the travesty of 'super flumina Babylonis', beginning 'SU-su-PER-per' and proceeding haltingly and confusedly through both text and music, perhaps mocking the efforts of inexpert singers. Of a similar nature is *Ut queant laxis*, for five voices, in which the tenor sings the isolated notes of the hexachord between snatches of four-voice polyphony. In many apparently serious motets the tone-painting of individual words is so literal

179

that one suspects a half-humorous intent, and occasionally one is sure of it: the concertato performance of motets is parodied in *Laudent Deum cythara*, in which five instrumental families are named, to music characteristic for each, in the space of a dozen bars (the total length of the piece).

There are drinking-songs in Latin in his output, as there are in German and French. These may be elaborate, as in the eight-part double chorus *Vinum bonum*. Perhaps the most amusing is the macaronic *Lucescit jam o socii*, whose independently rhymed series of alternating Latin and French lines sounds so much like some of the composer's letters to Duke Wilhelm that Lassus must surely be author of both text and music.

(*iv*) *Classical and classicistic texts.* The ceremonial motets are full of classical phrases. Other pieces setting either classical texts (Virgil, Horace) or humanistic 16th-century verse are to be found; there is a whole group of these near the end of the five-part section of the *Magnum opus musicum*. Lassus made his contribution to the list of Renaissance composers who set Dido's lament *Dulces exuviae*; his version is in correctly quantitative declamatory chords with little ornament, a style not far from that used for classical choruses (as in Andrea Gabrieli's music for *Edippo tiranno*). Most of these pieces are less academic in character, closer to the composer's normal motet style. There are, however, examples of almost completely literal quantitative settings; the five-voice setting of *Tragico tecti syrmate coelites* looks very much like the settings of Horatian odes used in German schools, a genre with which Lassus was evidently familiar. Related to this genre are the *Prophetiae Sibyllarum*, famous for their chordal chromaticism but also showing careful declamatory exactness in setting the curious half-Christian, half-pagan humanistic verse.

(*v*) *Religious works*. There are hints of ordering within the liturgical calendar in sections of the *Magnum opus musicum* (examples are the four-part offertories, roughly nos.124–68 in Haberl's edition, and the section in the five-part motets beginning with the Christmas antiphon *Angelus ad pastores*, no.192; the six-part motets also show traces of liturgical sequence). The collection also has groupings by category such as hymns, Marian antiphons, Gospel or Epistle motets etc, which are convenient for study but of little help in determining liturgical usage. As Lassus's sons included in their huge anthology a good many pieces which are motets only by virtue of being contrafacta of secular works, their methods of assemblage and editing appear too arbitrary to serve as the basis for study of the religious function of their father's motets.

A large proportion of the motets must of course have been used in performance of the Mass and Offices in the court chapel. The number of settings of Marian antiphons, some of which are very elaborate, suggest that portions of the Office were sung with great solemnity. This is also true of settings of the *Pater noster*, the *Ave Maria*, and hymns included in the *Magnum opus musicum*; the six-part settings of *Veni Creator Spiritus* and *Veni Sancte Spiritus* are particularly resplendent. When one recalls that many of Lassus's motet prints carried the rubric 'apt for voices and instruments' it is easy to imagine concerted performances of motets using some of the forces depicted in Hans Mielich's miniature, which shows the court chapel as assembled for chamber performance (see fig. 8). Among the motets appearing in tablatures, chiefly of German origin, are a group in Johannes Rühling's keyboard book (1583) which are arranged in liturgical order for Sundays and great feast days throughout the year, and thus are clearly intended for use in the liturgy.

Whether motets on religious texts were used as liturgical works, for private devotional purposes or in concert is hard to determine. Marian antiphons, for example, could certainly have been used as devotional pieces. Style may offer some clue; the Gospel motets (six voices, nos.549–58) are severely conservative and thus 'sound' liturgical whereas the Epistle motets adjacent to them are highly expressive (*Cum essem parvulus*, nos.570–71, with its touching delineation of the cardinal virtues and especially of charity, is one of the composer's most moving works in any genre) and thus appear devotional in character. The many psalm settings, some of them free compilations from various psalms (the celebrated *Timor et tremor* is among them), are difficult to judge in this regard. A thorough study of the liturgical practices at Munich might help to place many works whose function is now not clear.

The motets of Lassus were admired in their own day not only for their beauty and technical perfection but also for their rhetorical power – their ability to move the affections through the use of rhetorical devices transferred into musical idioms. Joachim Burmeister's celebrated rhetorical analysis of *In me transierunt* (published 1562) in his *Musica poetica* (1606; an expanded version of the *Musica autoschediastikou*, 1601) com-

8. *The Bavarian court chapel assembled for chamber music: miniature by Hans Mielich from the Mielich Codex, 16th century; Lassus is at the keyboard, surrounded by musicians playing viola da gamba, viole da braccia, bass recorder, flute, trombone, cornetts, racket and lute*

pares the motet to a classically ordered speech. 40 years earlier Quickelberg had praised Lassus's ability to 'describe an object almost as if it were before one's eyes'. One has only to think of the many striking, sharply individualized openings of motets – the *exordia* of classical rhetoric – in Lassus's work to see that both expressiveness and the rhetorician's trick of catching attention can hardly be missed in this music. Whether the composer proceeded as deliberately, even pedantically, as Burmeister would have it may be doubted. But if one recalls Lassus's carefully precise declamation of classical texts it becomes clear that he knew something of the German didactic tradition linking music with the study of classical metres; it is not a large step from this to assume that he also knew how classical rhetoric was studied in the schools. The 'speaking' quality of much of this music cannot be a fortuitous property; it is not only expressive in a general sense but affective in a precise way, clearly perceptible to the composer's contemporaries.

CHAPTER THREE

Other works

I Madrigals

Included in the mixed print issued in Antwerp by Tylman Susato in 1555 and often referred to as Lassus's 'op.1', there are seven madrigals for four voices showing the composer's grasp of the genre as a result of his Italian, particularly his Roman, years. His poetic tastes – a quatrain and a canzone stanza of Petrarch, an ottava by Ariosto, a Sannazaro poem and a pastoral in sestina (a form he particularly liked) – are typical of the period. *Del freddo Rheno*, a complete sestina rather in the style of the cyclic madrigals of Arcadelt and Berchem, opens the group on a note of simple tunefulness (this piece was popular with intabulators); in other madrigals the style varies from Willaert-like seriousness (*Occhi piangete*), through supple contrapuntal writing resembling Rore (*Per pianto la mia carne*), to the chordal declamation typical of the Roman *madrigale arioso* (*Queste non son più lagrime*). A certain clarity and succinctness of utterance are Lassus's personal stamp; in other respects this collection is highly eclectic. These madrigals, together with a few others including the chanson-like *Appariran per me le stell'*, reappeared in Lassus's first book of four-part madrigals, published by Dorico in Rome and then by Gardane in Venice, both in 1560. The strong resemblance of Lassus's early madrigals to those of his contemporaries may be illustrated by the fact that one piece in this volume, *Non vi vieto*, credited to Lassus and included in Sandberger's edition, is actually the work of Hoste da Reggio, part of a cycle in the latter's second book for four voices (1554). Lassus's volume was a popular one, reprinted a dozen times over the next 30 years and supplying favourite materials for lutenists' intabulations. Other early four-part madrigals appeared in Barré's Roman anthologies of *madrigali ariosi*.

Also highly successful, to judge by the frequency with which they were reprinted, were the first book for five voices, first issued by Gardane in Venice in 1555, and the second, printed by Barré in Rome in 1557 after having long been held in private hands (so says the dedicatory letter of G. B. Bruno, who is known to have been in Rome in 1554). These madrigals and, in all probability, most of those in the third book for five voices (brought out by Barrè in Rome in 1563 after, says the publisher, a diligent search for works by Orlande) must have been written before Lassus's departure from Rome in 1554. Petrarch dominates the first volume and is well represented in the others, with a six-section canzone cycle (*Standomi un giorno*) in a 'narrative', vibrantly declamatory style opening the second book.

The Petrarchan sonnets receive on the whole the most serious treatment, with sharply expressive thematic material in the tradition of Rore (see ex.2, the opening of *Sol'e pensoso*). Other forms such as the sestina, cyclic or in individual stanzas, are given lighter polyphonic dress; and the chordal declamation of the arioso madrigal may be seen (Bernardo Tasso's *Vostro fui vostro son*). Some works, particularly a group near the end of the second book, are clearly in an easy, 'popular'

Madrigals

Ex.2 *Sol'e pensoso*

style. Even the most ambitious Petrarchan settings, however, are marked by Lassus's ever-present clarity of tonal palette and attractiveness of melody. These madrigals are distinguished by free use of material (there is little exact imitative writing) and by much variety of speed and character in declamation, despite the fact that the *misura cromatica* (C) is used in only a few pieces. They do not perhaps equal the work of Rore in intensity but they do rival the older master in variety of mood and seamless technical perfection – no mean achievement for a man in his twenties. The frequent choice of texts in which the word 'lasso' appears (in six pieces scattered through the three volumes), and the invariable *la–sol* setting it receives, suggest a youthful desire to 'sign' his works; Lassus as a young Roman clearly wanted the world to know who he was.

From the first decade in Munich come the contents of the fourth book for five voices, written to show, in the composer's words, that the Muses were cherished and could flourish in 'Germania' as well as in Italy. Lassus visited Venice in May 1567; while there (when he was described in a letter as 'lively and a good companion') he saw to the printing of this fourth book, which he dedicated to Duke Alfonso II d'Este and then took to Ferrara to present to him. Lassus's inclination towards the cyclic madrigal is again seen here; there is a complete sestina by Petrarch at the beginning, sonnets in two parts, and another sestina (*Qual nemica fortuna oltra quest'Alpe*) that seems to combine local Ferrarese reference (the Po river) with a laboured geography-of-love image.

Lassus's madrigal output slowed down after this. He contributed to the anthologies of Bavarian court madrigals assembled by Massimo Troiano (1569) and Cosimo Bottegari (1575); the discovery in Dublin of the missing tenor partbook of the 1569 volume (*RISM* 1569[19]) will allow publication and study of these works. Whether a true 'middle period' in stylistic terms can be seen in these and other individual pieces appearing in various anthologies of the 1570s remains to be demonstrated.

In 1585 Lassus was again in Italy; the dedication of his volume of five-part madrigals printed in Nuremberg in that year (reissued in Venice in 1587 as the *Libro quinto*) is to the great Veronese patron Mario Bevilacqua, whose *ridotto* the composer may have visited at this time. Here serious Petrarchan texts alternate with religious sonnets by Gabriel Fiamma. In style these madrigals, separated from the fourth book by nearly 20 years, show definite awareness of the newer Italian madrigal: not that of the chromaticists but rather that of Marenzio, with brief contrast motifs, declamation on short note values and counterpoint that is chiefly figured chordal progressions (*Io che l'età più verde* is an example). Lassus's older style is not completely absorbed by these novelties, and in a few pieces his earlier madrigals are recalled (the sestina *Quando il giorno*). How well he could write in a newer style is demonstrated by the amusing *La non vol esser più mia* (published 1584), a work in fully-fledged canzonetta idiom.

The madrigals for four, five and six voices dedicated to Lassus's friend the physician Thomas Mermann (Nuremberg, 1587) show some of the traits seen in the volume of 1585 but are more varied in style (at least one, *Pensier dicea*, is an older work), often suggesting the compression and individuality of his late motet style. In this volume a five-section religious cycle to text by Beccuti ('il Copetta'), *Signor le colpe mie*, has been shown (see Boetticher) to be missing its first stanza, *Di terrena armonia*, a piece for some reason printed separately in *Continuation du mellange* issued by Le Roy & Ballard in 1584.

At the very end of his life Lassus set the 21 ottava stanzas of Tansillo's *Lagrime di S Pietro*. This cycle of seven-voice spiritual madrigals is one of the most remarkable artistic testaments in the history of music. Deliberately restrained in mood and character, planned as a magnificent tonal arch covering the whole range of 16th-century sound, the work is at once musically unified and expressively varied. Lassus's lifelong habits of concision and balance, subordinating vivid declamation and rhetorical power to inexorable musical clarity, are here given their definitive statement. The transcendentally synthetic quality of this music, blending styles as diverse as the *Prophetiae Sibyllarum* and the late madrigals, stands in the sharpest possible contrast to what was in other hands already becoming the drily academic *stile antico*.

Among Lassus's most popular Italian-texted works are the six four-voice villanellas in the 'op.1' of 1555 (these pieces are often found in anthologies of lute intabulations) and the contents of the *Libro de villanelle, moresche, et altre canzoni* for four, five, six and eight voices (Paris, 1581), a volume said by the composer to have been written in his old age when he should have known better. The famous *Matona mia cara* may serve as an example of pieces to be found in this volume, although some of the other pieces are equally amusing. All are reworkings of older material, following the time-honoured principle of using pre-existing melodies in this genre; the most outrageous texts receive elegant if simple musical setting, in its own way a final statement about this sub-species of the madrigal.

II Chansons

Although they are fewer in number than his madrigals, Lassus's chansons, about 150 in all, are nonetheless

considerable in bulk and, more important, highly characteristic of the composer, who never entirely left off
being a Frenchman. He wrote a number of chansons in
his youth and did not by any means stop when he moved
to Munich; French was in common use at the court, and
chansons of various types were evidently in demand
from his patrons as well as from his publishers.

To judge by their dates of publication, Lassus wrote
chansons from the 1550s into the 1580s; a greater
proportion than of most other categories are early
works. Just as the madrigals were brought out for the
most part by Roman and Venetian printers, so the chansons were published chiefly in the Netherlands (Phalèse,
Susato, Laet) and in Paris (Le Roy & Ballard, Du
Chemin). Their wide popularity can be seen from the
frequent reprints and from their appearance in print
in Lyons, La Rochelle, Strasbourg and London
(Vautrollier, 1570). Some of the later reprints bear
the proud description of the composer as 'Prince des
musiciens de nostre temps'. The chansons were much in
favour with keyboard, cittern and especially lute intabulators; the *Theatrum musicum* of Phalèse and Bellère
(*RISM* 1568[23], 1571[16]) is particularly rich in Lassus's
works. The English translation of Le Roy's lute tutor
(London, 1574) contains 11 chansons by Lassus. A
very large number of chansons, including some of the
bawdiest, were 'spiritualized' in French and German
religious collections (Pasquier, 1576; Berg, 1582). The
bulk of Lassus's chanson output was collected in two
volumes of 'meslanges' issued by Le Roy & Ballard
(1576, 1584). Of the chansons not included in these
volumes or in the important *Livre de chansons nouvelles*
issued by Phalèse in 1571, some have not survived

191

complete; among these are a set of religious chansons on texts by Guy du Faur de Pibrac, published in 1581. Fortunately two of these pieces, illustrating the sobriety of Lassus's late chanson style, have been reassembled through the discovery (by Bernstein) of a set of manuscript parts in Edward Paston's library (in the Fitzwilliam Museum, Cambridge).

Lassus turned to some of the most famous of 16th-century French poets for texts: Marot, Ronsard, Du Bellay and Baïf. The fact that he often set texts already known in musical settings is reflected in his occasional choice of Mellin de Saint-Gelais, a favourite poet among composers of the preceding generation, and also in his fondness for light verse from popular anthologies such as *La fleur de poesie francoyse* (1542). Occasional choice of much earlier poetry (Chartier, Villon) can also be seen. The subject matter ranges from dignified nature-poetry (Du Bellay) and Petrarchesque lyrics (Ronsard), through sententious and moralizing texts, to the familiar drinking-songs, some macaronic texts, and Rabelaisian amorous and bawdy narratives; no one wrote more amusing chansons of this last type (*En un chasteau* and *Il esteoit une religieuse* are excellent examples). There are also biblical and religious texts (the famous *Susanne un jour*, for example) – these apart from the contrafacta imposed by other hands on nearly all the secular chansons. There are a few real love-lyrics, some occasional pieces, and isolated soundings of familiar chanson-like themes such as 'faulte d'argent' (in *Je suis quasi prest d'enrager*).

In musical style the chansons are more varied than the usual blanket description given them – as either 'Parisian' patter chansons or motet-like serious pieces –

would suggest. Lassus could and often did write chansons, usually light narratives or dialogues, in the classically clear and succinct style made popular in Attaingnant's anthologies. How directly and economically he went about this can be seen in a work such as *Un advocat dit à sa femme* (ex.3). These pieces are usually for four voices, but Lassus, who in all genres preferred five-part texture, could manage 'Parisian' style just as easily in five voices (*La terre les eaux*, for example). He could even write a piece that resembles, paradoxically, an instrumental *canzona alla francese*

Ex.3 *Un advocat dit à sa femme*

193

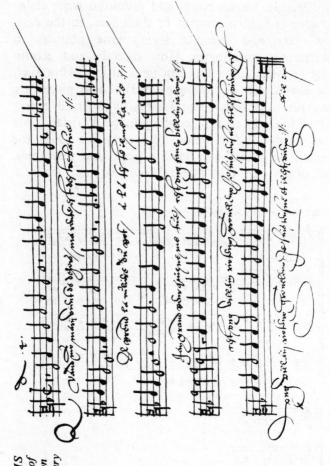

9. Autograph MS
of the alto part of
Lassus's chanson
'Quand mon mary', 1564

194

transcribed for voices (*Si pour moy avez du souci*). The light chansons are not always written in 'Parisian' fashion; the Italian patter style infecting so much of Lassus's work in his middle years may also be seen here (there is one outright 'villanelle', to Baïf's *Une puce j'ay dedans l'oreill'*).

Many chansons begin, as do so many of the lieder, with a contrapuntal *exordium*, sharply delineating the character of the piece through distinctive melodic shapes; then follow patter chords or lightweight texture in which short motifs are constantly thrown back and forth among the voices. Sometimes the music changes character with every flicker of meaning in the text, as in the setting of Marot's *Qui dort icy*. The declamation in all the lively chansons is good; in some it is extraordinarily vivid – Marot's *Bon jour et puis quelles nouvelles* is given a setting of such conversational immediacy that on hearing it all barriers separating us from the 16th century seem to drop away.

The more serious chansons resemble the reflective, affective madrigals of Rore and his successors more than they do motets. Chansons such as *Le temps passé* (with its 'soupir' figures), *Mon coeur ravi d'amour* and *Comme la tourterelle* (with its madrigalian chromaticism) are madrigals in all but their very Gallic declamatory diction. Use of madrigalian style is sometimes but not always influenced by the text; thus Ronsard's *J'espère et crains*, with its laboured Petrarchan oxymora, is given a quite restrained setting, while *Vray dieu disoit une fillette*, a very French text, is given such Italian touches as a long final pedal point. In a category by themselves are pieces such as *La nuict froide et sombre* (Du Bellay), set as an expansive, colouristic tone poem in style even though characteristically brief in actual duration.

German schoolmasters would not have picked chansons by Lassus as examples of rhetorical organization and affective power; the genre was not sufficiently grand. Many of the chansons would nevertheless make good examples of the musician as rhetorician; Marot's *Fleur de quinze ans*, for instance, is in Lassus's hands a seduction speech of extraordinarily tight organization and persuasive musical diction.

III German lieder

For a composer like Lassus who was French by birth and Italian by musical training, composition in a German vein must have posed problems. He published no lieder until 1567; by that time he was surely fluent in setting German texts, enough for him to have written for private use, at the court, pieces Duke Albrecht liked too well to allow to circulate in print (preface to the 1567 collection). But the native tradition was very strong in Munich, where Ludwig Senfl had worked until his death (1542–3); the song collections of Hans Ott, Georg Forster and others remained popular, and the need for new works was correspondingly less great during Lassus's early years at the Bavarian court.

The lieder are few in number only by the standards of Lassus's prolific output in other genres; if one counts the German psalms for three voices (1588) there are over 90 compositions, including several multipartite six-part sacred compositions larger in scale than most of the motets. Many of the secular pieces were famous in the composer's time and are among his best-known works today (*Audite nova*, for example). The proportion of sacred pieces among the lieder is high, even without counting the volume of psalms; this suggests that the German collections were intended for a somewhat different audience from that for the madrigals and the chansons.

In the preface to the third book of five-part lieder (1576), Lassus contrasted the Italian and German styles, emphasizing (and defending) the roughness of the latter. He evidently tried to cultivate a specifically German style. The results were good, certainly; but his position in the history of the lied has been described (by Osthoff) as that of an innovator who discarded German tradition, that of the Tenorlied, in favour of a style mixing elements of the madrigal, the villanella and the chanson. This is true primarily of the secular lieder; the sacred works use traditional melodies in, on the whole, as strict an adherence to cantus firmus writing as Lassus showed in any genre.

In some respects Lassus was conservative as a composer of lieder. He chose texts for the most part already known in sacred and secular songbooks (one exception is the setting of Hans Sachs's *Ein Körbelmacher in eim Dorff*), and inclined towards folklike ones. His German settings are rhythmically lively and correct in declamation, but not exaggeratedly so; nor are there experiments in chromaticism in the lieder. His preference for five-part texture (which he felt he had to justify as a novelty in the preface to the 1567 collection) was merely carrying over into the lieder a general preference typical of his generation.

The sacred lieder use texts and melodies common to Lutheran and Catholic songbooks (the Ulenberg psalm translations are, however, Catholic and even anti-

Protestant in intent), with Luther's *Vater unser im Himmelreich* opening the first collection. The psalm settings range from the rather simple tricinia of the 1588 collection (where they alternate with similar settings by his son Rudolph) to the great six-part psalm-motets such as *Ich ruff zu dir*, using paraphrased and cantus firmus versions of the borrowed melodies, in the French–German volume of 1590.

Among the secular texts chosen by Lassus are drinking-songs and lieder in which the bad effects of liquor are lamented (*Mein Fraw hilgert*); possibly the constantly expressed preference for wine over beer was a personal one. Comic rustic narrative encounters (*Baur, was tregst im Sacke?*) are among the most famous of the lieder. There are also melancholy and satirical pieces (*Die Zeit, so jetzt vorhanden ist*), some love-songs of narrative character, and a few songs of nature-love. The traditional vein of elegiac introspection seen in the lied from Paul Hofhaimer to Senfl was on the whole avoided by Lassus.

Many lieder begin with an imitative *exordium* followed by lively patter. Relationships to the villanella and lighter madrigal may of course be seen (Lassus knew the celebrated German villanella collections of Jacob Regnart), and chanson-like rhythms occur with frequency. The combination is a natural and convincing one; Lassus did not so much break with German tradition as simply set texts in his own style, a somewhat eclectic one in every genre. In any event the triumphantly German character of the best lieder is proof enough that he mastered the lied in his own way.

IV Lassus and Palestrina

In a comparison of Lassus and Palestrina, certain similarities could be cited: each had a flawless technique and each revelled in its use; both were conservative musicians, perhaps by temperament but certainly in accord with the demands of the positions they held. Many stylistic details, such as frequent use of imitative melismas based on cambiata figures, are common to both men's work. What sets them apart are Lassus's greater variety of style and genre, his greater economy of utterance (occasionally verging on the perfunctory, but nearly always effective aesthetically by its very brevity), his liking for highly individual opening subjects and his preference for clearcut and strongly directed chordal harmony.

WORKS

Editions: *O. de Lassus: Sämtliche Werke*, ed. F. X. Haberl and A. Sandberger (Leipzig, 1894–1926) [S]
O. de Lassus: Sämtliche Werke: neue Reihe, ed. S. Hermelink and others (Kassel, 1956–) [H]

Numbers in right-hand margins denote references in the text.

Il primo libro di madrigali, 5vv (Venice, 1555) [1555a]	159, 186
Il primo libro dove si contengono madrigali, vilanesche, canzoni francesi, e motetti, 4vv (Antwerp, 1555⁹)[1555b]	158–9, 175, 190
Il primo libro de mottetti, 5, 6vv (Antwerp, 1556) [1556]	159, 175
Secondo libro delle muse, madrigali...con una canzone del Petrarca, 5vv (Rome, 1557²²) [1557]	
Il primo libro di madrigali, 5vv (Venice, 1560) [enlarged edn. of 1555a] [1560a]	
Liber decimus quintus ecclesiasticarum cantionum ... ex omnibus tonis, 5, 6vv (Antwerp, 1560) [enlarged edn. of 1556] [1560b]	
Tiers livre des chansons, 4–6vv (Louvain, 1560) [1560c]	
[25] Sacrae cantiones, 5vv (Nuremberg, 1562) [1562]	
Il terzo libro delli madrigali, 5vv (Rome, 1563¹³) [1563]	
Le premier livre de chansons, auquel sont ving et sept chansons nouvelles, 4vv (Antwerp, 1564) [1564a]	
Primus liber concentuum sacrorum, 5, 6vv (Paris, 1564) [1564b]	
Quatriesme livre des chansons, 4, 5vv (Louvain, 1564) [1564c]	
Dixhuitcieme livre des chansons, 4, 5vv (Paris, 1565) [1565a]	
Modulorum ... modulatorum secundum volumen, 4–8, 10vv (Paris, 1565) [1565b]	
Quinque et sex vocibus perornatae sacrae cantiones ... liber secundus, 5, 6vv (Venice, 1565) [1565c]	159, 172
Sacrae lectiones novem ex propheta Iob, in officiis defunctorum cantari solitae, 4vv (Venice, 1565) [1565d]	
Liber missarum ... liber primus, 4–6vv (Venice, 1566?), lost [1566a]	
Sacrae cantiones ... liber secundus 5, 6vv (Venice, 1566) [1566b]	
Sacrae cantiones ... liber tertius 5, 6vv (Venice, 1566) [1566c]	
Sacrae cantiones ... liber quartus 6, 8vv (Venice, 1566) [1566d]	160, 161, 188, 189
Libro quarto de madrigali, 5vv (Venice, 1567) [1567a]	
Magnificat octo tonorum, 4–6vv (Nuremberg, 1567) [1567b]	171
Neue teütsche Liedlein, 5vv (Munich, 1567) [1567c]	196, 197
Selectissimae cantiones, 6 and more vv (Nuremberg, 1568) [1568a]	
Selectissimae cantiones, 4, 5vv (Nuremberg, 1568) [1568b]	
Cantiones aliquot, 5vv (Munich, 1569) [1569a]	
Liber secundus sacrarum cantionum, 4vv (Louvain, 1569) [1569b]	
Disieme livre de chansons, 4vv (Paris, 1570⁹) [1570a]	
Mellange d'Orlande de Lassus, contenant plusieurs chansons, tant en vers latins qu'en ryme francoyse, 4, 5vv (Paris, 1570) [1570b]	
Praestantissimorum divinae musices auctorum missae decem, 4–6vv (Louvain, 1570?) [1570c]	
Premier livre des chansons, 4, 5vv (Louvain, 1570⁹) [1570d]	
Quinque missae suavissimis modulationibus refertae...liber secundus, 4, 5vv (Venice, 1570) [1570e]	168
Second livre des chansons, 4, 5vv (Louvain, 1570⁹) [1570f]	
Selectiorum aliquot cantionum sacrarum, 6vv, fasciculus adiunctis in fine tribus dialogis, 8vv (Munich, 1570) [1570g]	
Viginti quinque sacrae cantiones, 5vv (Nuremberg, 1570)[enlarged edn. of 1562] [1570h]	
Livre de chansons nouvelles, 5vv, avec 2 dialogues, 8vv (Paris, 1571) [1571a]	162, 191–2
Moduli nunquam hactenus editi, 5vv (Paris, 1571) [1571b]	
Der ander Theil teutscher Lieder, 5vv (Munich, 1572) [1572a]	
Moduli, 4, 8vv (Paris, 1572) [1572b]	
Moduli, 6, 7, 12vv (Paris, 1573) [1573a]	
Patrocinium musices ... cantionum ... prima pars, 4–6vv (Munich, 1573) [1573b]	
6 cantiones latinae, 4vv, adiuncto dialogo, 8vv: 6 teutsche Lieder, 4vv, sampt einem Dialogo, 8vv: 6 chansons françoises nouvelles, 4vv, avecq un dialogue, 4vv, con un dialogo, 8vv (Munich, 1573) [1573c]	163, *165*, 168
Patrocinium musices ... missae aliquot, secunda pars, 5vv (Munich, 1574) [1574a]	
Patrocinium musices ... officia aliquot, de praecipuis festis anni ... tertia pars, 5vv (Munich, 1574) [1574b]	172
Patrocinium musices ... passio, 5vv, idem lectiones Iob, et lectiones matutinae de nativitate Christi, 4vv, quarta pars (Munich, 1575) [1575]	172
Der dritte Theil schöner, neuer, teutscher Lieder, sampt einem zu End gesetzten frantzösischen frölichen Liedlein, 5vv (Munich, 1576) [1576a]	197

Les meslanges ... contenantz plusieurs chansons, tant en vers latins qu'en ryme francoyse, 4–6, 8, 10vv (Paris, 1576, earlier edn. 1570, lost, repr. with sacred contrafacta, London, 1570) [1576b] — 191, 238

Patrocinium musices ... Magnificat aliquot, quinta pars, 4–6, 8vv (Munich, 1576) [1576c] — 171

Thresor de musique ... contenant ... chansons, 4–6vv (Geneva, 1576) [1576d]

Liber mottetarum, 3vv (Munich, 1577) [1577a] — 176

Missae variis concentibus ornatae ... cum cantico beatae Mariae octo modis variato, 4–6, 8vv (Paris, 1577–8) [1577b] — 168

Moduli, 4–9vv (Paris, 1577) [1577d]

Novae aliquot et ante hac non ita usitatae cantiones suavissimae, 2vv (Munich, 1577) [also incl. 12 textless bicinia] [1577d] — 176

Altera pars selectissimarum cantionum, 4, 5vv (Nuremberg, 1579) [1579]

Liber missarum, 4, 5vv (Nuremberg, 1581) [1581a]

Libro de villanelle, moresche, et altre canzoni, 4–6, 8vv (Paris, 1581) [1581b] — 190

Fasciculi aliquot sacrarum cantionum, 4–6, 8vv (Nuremberg, 1582) [1582a]

Lectiones sacrae novem, ex libris Hiob excerptae, 4vv (Munich, 1582) [1582b] — 172

Missa ad imitationem moduli (Quand'io penso al martire), 4vv (Paris, 1582) [1582c]

Mottetta typis nondum uspiam excusa, 6vv (Munich, 1582) [1582d]

Sacrae cantiones, 5vv (Munich, 1582) [1582e]

Neue teutsche Lieder, geistlich und weltlich, 4vv (Munich, 1583) [1583a]

Teutsche Lieder, zuvor unterschiedlich, jetzund aber ... inn ein Opus zusammen getruckt, 5vv (Nuremberg, 1583) [1583b] — 189, 191

Continuation du mellange, 3–6, 10vv (Paris, 1584) [1584a] — 172

Psalmi Davidis poenitentiales, modis musicis redditi ... his accessit psalmus Laudate Dominum de coelis, 5vv (Munich, 1584/R1970) [1584b]

Cantica sacra, recens numeris et modulis musicis ornata, 6, 8vv (Munich, 1585) [1585a] — 172

Hieremiae prophetae lamentationes, et aliae piae cantiones, 5vv (Munich, 1585) [1585b]

Madrigali novamente composti, 5vv (Nuremberg, 1585) [1585c] — 189

Sacrae cantiones ... recens singulari industria compositae, 4vv (Munich, 1585) [1585d]

Madrigali novamente composti, 4–6vv (Nuremberg, 1587) [1587a] — 189

Missa ad imitationem moduli Beatus qui intelligit, 6vv (Paris, 1587) [1587b]

Patrocinium musices: Beatissimae deiparaeque Virginis Mariae canticum Magnificat, ad imitationem cantilenarum quarundam, 4–6vv (Munich, 1587) [1587d] — 171

Missae ... liber primus, 4, 5vv (Milan, 1588?) [1588a]

Tertium opus musicum, continens lectiones Hiob et motectas seu cantiones sacras, 4–6vv (Nuremberg, 1588?) [1588b]

Teutsche Psalmen: geistliche Psalmen, 3vv (Munich, 1588?) [1588c] — 196, 198

Patrocinium musices: missae aliquot, 5vv (Munich, 1589) [1589]

Neue teutsche, und etliche frantzösische Gesäng, 6vv (Munich, 1590) [1590]

Cantiones sacrae, 6vv (Graz, 1594) [1594]

Lagrime di S Pietro ... con un mottetto nel fine, 7vv (Munich, 1595) [1595] — 164, 189–90

Musica nuova dove si contengono madrigali, sonnetti, stanze, canzoni, villanelle et altri compositioni, 3vv (Munich, 1595), lost

Cantiones ab Orlando di Lasso et huius filio Ferdinando di Lasso compositae, 5vv (Munich, 1597?) [1597] — 159

Prophetiae Sibyllarum ... chromatico more singulari confectae, 4vv (Munich, 1600) [1600]

Liber primus cantiones sacrae Magnificat vocant, 5, 6vv (Paris, 1602?) [1602]

Magnum opus musicum ... complectens omnes cantiones, 2–10, 12vv (Munich, 1604) [1604] — 172, 173, 178, 180, 181

Missa ad imitationem moduli Dixit Joseph, 6vv (Paris, 1607) [1607a]

Missa ad imitationem moduli Or sus à coup, 4vv (Antwerp, 1607) [1607b]

Missae posthumae, 6, 8vv (Munich, 1610) [1610] — 170–71

Iubilus beatae virginis, hoc est centum Magnificat, 4–8, 10vv (Munich, 1619) [1619]

Further printed works, 1555[30] 1557[20] 1558[13] 1559[12] 1559[13] 1560[14] 1561[5] 1561[10] 1562[7] 1563[3] 1564[1] 1564[2] 1564[3] 1564[4] 1564[5] 1566[2] 1566[17] 1567[1] 1567[11] 1567[13] 1567[16] 1568[2] 1568[4]

Scarco di doglia, 5vv, 1574a (on Rore's madrigal); H iii, 175
Se salamandre, 4vv, MS c1570 (doubtful, possibly by Lockenburg) (on Crecquillon's chanson); H xi, 113
Sesquialtera, 4vv, MS 1579; H x, 69
Sidus ex claro, 5vv, 1574a (on own motet); H iii, 217
Si me tenez, 6vv, MS c1560 (doubtful, possibly by J. Vaet) (on Crecquillon's chanson); H xi, 179
Si rore aenio, 5vv, MS 1572; H ix, 101
Surge propera, 6vv, 1577b (on own motet); H iv, 157
Surrexit Pastor bonus (i), 5vv, MS c1576 (doubtful, possibly by Ivo de Vento) (on Lassus's motet); H xi, 135
Surrexit Pastor bonus (ii), 5vv (inc.) (on own motet); H xii, 15
Susanne un jour, 5vv, 1577b (on own chanson); H iv, 121
Tempus est ut revertar, 6vv, frag. (B only of Kyrie and Gloria) (on own motet); H xii, 159
Tous les regretz, 6vv, 1577b (on Gombert's chanson); H v, 3
Triste depart, 6vv, MS 1592 (on Gombert's chanson); H x, 115
Veni in hortum meum, 5vv, 1581a (on own motet); H v, 185
Vinum [Verbum] bonum, 8vv, 1577b (on own motet); H v, 105

PASSIONS

Passio Domini nostri Jesu Christi secundum Mattheum, 5vv, 1575; H ii, 3 — 170
Passio Domini nostri Jesu Christi secundum Marcum, 4vv, MS 1582; H ii, 27 — 170
Passio Domini nostri Jesu Christi secundum Lucam, 4vv, MS 1582; H ii, 37 — 170
Passio Domini nostri Jesu Christi secundum Johannem, 5vv, MS 1580; H ii, 47 — 170

MAGNIFICAT SETTINGS — 170-72

Alma real se come fide stella (octavi toni), 5vv, 1619 (on Rore's madrigal)
Amor ecco colei (septimi toni), 6vv, 1587d
Ancor che col partire (quarti toni), 5vv, 1576c (on Rore's madrigal)
Aria di un sonetto (octavi toni), 5vv, 1587d (on D. Ortiz's Aria di Ruggiero)
Aurora lucis rutilat (octavi toni), 10vv, 1619 (on own motet)
Beau le cristal (sexti toni), 4vv, 1619 (on own chanson)

Benedicta es caelorum regina (octavi toni), 6vv, 1602 (on Josquin's motet)
Dalle belle contrade (sexti toni), 5vv, 1619 (on Rore's madrigal)
Dessus le marché d'Arras (primi toni), 6vv, 1587d (on own chanson)
Deus in adjutorium (septimi toni), 6vv, 1587d (on own motet)
Dies est laetitia (sexti toni), 6vv, 1602
D'ogni gratia e d'amor (septimi toni), 6vv, 1619 (on Striggio's madrigal)
Ecco ch'io lasso il core (secundi toni), 6vv, 1587d (? on Striggio's madrigal)
Erano capei d'oro (septimi toni), 5vv, 1619 (on G. M. Nanino's madrigal)
Hélas j'ai sans merci (septimi toni), 5vv, 1619 (on own chanson)
Il est jour (secundi toni), 4vv, 1587d (on Sermisy's chanson)
Las je n'iray plus (secundi toni), 5vv, 1619 (on own chanson)
Mais qui pourroit (secundi toni), 6vv, 1587d (on own chanson)
Margot labourez les vignes (septimi toni), 4vv, 1619 (on own chanson)
Memor esto (secundi toni), 6vv, 1619 (on own motet)
Mort et fortune (tertii toni), 5vv, 1587d (on Gombert's chanson)
O che vezzosa aurora (secundi toni), 6vv, 1619 (on Vecchi's madrigal)
Omnis enim homo (primi toni), 6vv, 1587d (on own motet)
Omnis homo primum bonum vinum ponit (sexti toni), 6vv, 1602 (on Wert's motet)
O s'io potessi (secundi toni), 4vv, 1619 (on Berchem's madrigal)
Pange lingua gloriosa (septimi toni), 4vv, 1619
Praeter rerum seriem (secundi toni), 6vv, 1602 (on Josquin's motet)
Quando lieta sperai (quarti toni), 6vv, 1587d (on a madrigal attrib. Rore)
Quanti in mille anni il ciel (secundi toni), 6vv, 1587d (on Nollet's madrigal)
Recordare Jesu pie (septimi toni), 6vv, 1619 (on own motet)
S'io credessi per morte (tertii toni), 4vv, 1619 (on A. de Reulx's madrigal)
S'io esca vivo (septimi toni), 6vv, 1619 (on own madrigal)
Si par souhait (primi toni), 4vv, 1587d (on own chanson)
Si vous estes m'amie (sexti toni), 6vv, 1619 (on own chanson)
Susanne un jour (primi toni), 6vv, 1587d (on Lupi's chanson)
Tant vous allez doux (sexti toni), 6vv, 1619 (on Ebran's chanson)
Ultimi miei sospiri (secundi toni), 6vv, 1619 (on Verdelot's madrigal)
Vergine bella (primi toni), 5vv, 1619 (on Rore's madrigal)
Vola vola pensier [Aeria a la italiana] (octavi toni), 5vv, 1602
Vous perdez temps (septimi toni), 5vv, 1619 (on Sermisy's chanson)

Primi toni, 4vv, 1576c; Primi toni (i), 5vv, 1619; Primi toni (ii), 5vv, 1619; Primi toni (iii), 5vv, 1619
Secundi toni (i), 5vv, 1619; Secundi toni (ii), 5vv, 1619; Secundi toni, 6vv, 1619
Tertii toni, 5vv, 1619
Quarti toni (i), 5vv, 1619; Quarti toni (ii), 5vv, 1619; Quarti toni (iii), 5vv, 1619; Quarti toni, 8vv, 1619
Quinti toni, 5vv, 1619; Quinti toni, 6vv, 1619
Sexti toni (i), 5vv, 1619; Sexti toni (ii), 5vv, 1619; Sexti toni (iii), 5vv, 1619; [Sexti toni], 5vv, MS c1582, D-Mbs; Sexti toni, 8vv, 1576c
Septimi toni (i), 5vv, 1619; Septimi toni (ii), 5vv, 1619; Septimi toni, 7vv, 1619; Septimi toni, 8vv, 1576c; Septimi toni, 8vv, 1619
Octavi toni (i), 5vv, 1619; Octavi toni (ii), 5vv, 1619; Octavi toni, 6vv, 1619; Octavi toni (i), 8vv, 1619; Octavi toni (ii), 8vv, 1619
8 settings, octo tonorum, 6vv, 1567b; 8 settings, octo tonorum, 5vv, 1567b; 8 settings (i), octo tonorum, 4vv, 1567b; 8 settings (ii), octo tonorum, 4vv, 1576b

OFFICES
(all printed works in 1574b)

Asperges me (i), 5vv
Asperges me (ii), 5vv
Cibavit eos (Officium corporis Christi), 5vv
Puer natus est (Officium natalis Christi), 5vv
Resurrexit (Officium paschale), 5vv
Spiritus Domini (Officium pentecostes), 5vv
Vidi aquam, 5vv
Officium in purificatione Beatae Mariae Virginis, 4vv, c1583–5, Mbs

LESSONS
Sacrae lectiones ex propheta Iob, 4vv, 1565d; ed. H.J.Therstappen, Die Klagen des Hiob (Berlin, 1948)
Lectiones matutinae de nativitate Christi, 4vv, 1575
Lectiones sacrae novem ex libris Hiob, 4vv, 1582b

LAMENTATIONS
9 Lamentationes Hieremiae, 4vv, c1588, Mbs
9 Lamentationes Hieremiae, 5vv, 1585b; ed. in Musica sacra, xii (Berlin, 1867)

LITANIES
(all printed works in 1596²; for some edns. see Boetticher)

De gloriosissima Dei genitrice (i), 4vv
De gloriosissima Dei genitrice (i), 5vv
De gloriosissima Dei genitrice (ii), 5vv
De gloriosissima Dei genitrice (iii), 5vv
De gloriosissima Dei genitrice (iv), 5vv
De gloriosissima Dei genitrice, 6vv
De gloriosissima Dei genitrice, 8vv
De gloriosissima Dei genitrice, 9vv
De gloriosissima Dei genitrice, 9vv, c1590, D-Mbs
De gloriosissima Dei genitrice, 10vv, c1580, Mbs
De nomine Jesu, 5vv
De omnibus sanctis, 4vv
De omnibus sanctis, 5vv
De omnibus sanctis, 7vv

NUNC DIMITTIS
(all MSS in D-Mbs)

Come havran fin, 4vv, c1592
Heu mihi Domine, 5vv, c1592
Io son si stanco, 5vv, c1592
Oculi mei semper ad Dominum, 6vv, c1592
S'el mio sempre per voi, 4vv, c1592
Secundi toni, 4vv, c1570
Quarti toni, 4vv, c1570
Quarti toni, 5vv, c1592
Septimi toni, 4vv, c1570
Octavi toni, 4vv, c1570
[without title], 5vv, c1592
[without title], 7vv

FALSIBORDONI
(all in D-Mbs, c1578)

Advena (primi toni), 5vv
Donec ponam (primi toni stravaganti), 5vv
Donec ponam (sexti toni), 5vv
Nisi Dominus (quinti toni), 5vv
Quoniam confortavit (septimi toni), 5vv

Sit nomen Domini (secundi toni), 5vv
Stantes erant pedes nostri (tertii toni), 5vv
[textless] (quarti toni), 4vv
[textless] (sexti toni), 5vv
[textless] (octavi toni), 5vv

173

HYMNS

(all in D-Mbs, c1580)

Aurem benignam protinus, 4vv; Beata quoque agmina, 4vv; Colludamus venerantes, 4vv; Cuius corpus sanctissimum, 4vv; Gloria Deo per immensa, 4vv; Hic nempe mundi, 4vv; Hi sunt quos retinens, 4vv; Ibant magi quam, 5vv; Illustre quiddam cernimus, 4vv; Janitor coeli doctor, 4vv; Maria soror Lazari, 4vv; Nova veniens ex coelo, 4vv; Nuntius celso veniens, 4vv; Pange lingua gloriosi, 5vv; Procul recedant somnia, 4vv; Quae te vicit clementia, 4vv; Qui condolens interitu, 5vv; Qui mane junctum, 4vv; Qui paracletus diceris, 5vv; Qui pascis inter lilia, 4vv; Qui pius prudens, 4vv; Quo volneratus insuper, 4vv; Respice clemens solio, 4vv; Scrutator alme cordium, 4vv; Sermone blando angelus, 4vv; Sit trinitatis sempiterna, 4vv; Sumen illud ave, 4vv; Te mane laudum, 4vv; Tu lumen tu splendor, 5vv; Vos prima Christi victima, 4vv; Vos secli justi, 4vv

173

RESPONSORIES
In nativitate Domini, 5vv, ?1580–85, *Mbs*
Pro Triduo sacro in nocturno II et III, 4vv, ?1580–85. *Mbs*

173–84

MOTETS
Accipe daque (2p. of Anna mihi dilecta veni)
Accipe qua recrees (2p. Quo fers), 6vv, 1604; S xi, 101
Accipite Spiritum (2p. of Jam non dicam vos)
Ad Dominum cum tribularer (2p. Heu mihi), 6vv, 1594; S xvii, 49
Adoramus te Christe (i), 3vv, 1604; S i, 57
Adoramus te Christe (ii), 3vv, 1604; S i, 57
Adoramus te Christe, 4vv, 1604; S i, 112
Adoramus te Christe, 5vv, 1604; S v, 63
Adorna thalamum, 4vv, 1585d; S i, 91
Ad primum morsum, 6vv, 1594; 5vv, 1556; S ix, 150
Ad te Domine levavi (2p. Vias tuas), 5vv, 1556; S ix, 150

Ad te igitur (3p. of Infelix ego)
Ad te levavi animam meam, 6vv, 1582d; S xvii, 121
Ad te levavi oculos meos (2p. Miserere nostri), 6vv, 1570g; S xvii, 125
Ad te perenne gaudium, 3vv, 1604; S i, 60
Adversum me loquebantur, 5vv, 1562; S ix, 40
Aegra currit (2p. of Lauda mater ecclesia)
Agimus tibi gratias, 3vv, 1604; S i, 59
Agimus tibi gratias, 4vv, 1604; S i, 131
Agimus tibi gratias, 5vv, 1576d; S v, 98
Agimus tibi gratias, 5vv, 1579; S v, 100
Agimus tibi gratias, 6vv, 1573b; S xiii, 103
Alia est enim (2p. of Quicumque vult salvus esse)
Alleluja (2p. of Surrexit Dominus)
Alleluja laus et gloria, 4vv, 1604; S i, 68
Alma nemes quae sola [Alme Deus qui cuncta tenes], 4vv, 1555b; S iii, 93

174

Alma parens dilecta Deo (2p. Qua sina coelestis; 3p. Nos pia turba; 4p. Tu modo diva; 5p. Aspicent invictos), 5vv, 1604; S v, 128
Alma Redemptoris mater, 5vv, 1597; S v, 102
Alma Redemptoris mater, 6vv, 1582d; S xiii, 105
Alma Redemptoris mater, 6vv, 1604; S xiii, 108
Alma Redemptoris mater, 8vv, 1604; S xxi, 14
Alma Venus [Christe Patris verbum] (2p. Nunc elegos divae [Tu poteris]), 5vv, 1560b; S v, 37
Amen dico vobis, 4vv, 1564³; S i, 119
Andreas Christi famulus, 6vv, 1585a; S xv, 1
Angelus ad pastores iat, 5vv, 1562; S iii, 139
Angelus Domini descendit (2p. Nolite timere), 6vv, 1585a; S xiii, 1
Angelus Domini locutus est, 5vv, 1571b; S v, 51
Anima mea liquefacta, 5vv, 1582e; S ix, 42
Animam meam dilectam (2p. Congregamini), 5vv, 1565b; S v, 29
Anna mihi dilecta veni [Christe Dei soboles] (2p. Accipe daque), 4vv, 1579; S iii, 95
Anni nostri sicut, 6vv, 1566d; S xv, 53
Ante me non est formatus, 6vv, 1573b; S xi, 131
Aspicent invictos (5p. of Alma parens dilecta Deo)
At illi (2p. of Cum natus esset)
Audi benigne conditor (2p. Multum quidem), 5vv, 1568²; S vii, 86
Audi dulcis [filia] amica mea, 4vv, 1555b; S i, 99

181

174

175

182

175

Lauda Jerusalem Dominum (2p. Qui emitit; 3p. Emittit verbum; 4p. Non fecit taliter), 6vv, 1565c; S xvii, 70
Lauda mater ecclesia, 5vv, 1597; S v, 171
Lauda mater ecclesia (2p. Aegra currit; 3p. Surgentem cum victoria), 6vv, 1582d; S xv, 3
Lauda Sion salvatorum (2p. Dies enim; 3p. Quod non capis; 4p. Ecce panis), 6vv, 1577c; H i, 75
Laudate Dominum de coelis (2p. Laudate Dominum de terra; 3p. Juvenes et virgines; 4p. Laudate eum), 5vv, 1565b; S ix, 161
Laudate Dominum de terra (2p. of Laudate Dominum de coelis)
Laudate Dominum omnes gentes, 6vv, 1604; S xv, 156
Laudate Dominum omnes gentes, 12vv, 1573a; S xxi, 152
Laudate Dominum quoniam bonus est (2p. Magnus Dominus; 3p. Praecinite; 4p. Non in fortitudine), 7vv, 1568a; S xix, 106
Laudate eum (4p. of Laudate Dominum de coelis)
Laudate pueri Dominum, 7vv, 1568a; S xix, 94
Laudavi igitur, 6vv, 1604; S xv, 154
Laudent Deum cythara, 4vv, 1604; S iii, 58
Laus honor (4p. of Jesu corona virginum)
Legem pone mihi (2p. Da mihi intellectum), 5vv, 1562; S ix, 73
Legitimo ergo (2p. of Gratia soli Dei pie)
Levabo oculos meos, 4vv, 1582c; S iii, 29
Levavo oculos meos, 8vv, 1566d; S xxi, 71
Libera me Domine, 6vv, 1568a; S xv, 109
Libet jacere (3p. of Beatus ille qui procul)
Locutus sum in lingua mea (2p. Fac mecum signum), 6vv, 1568a; S xvii, 62
Lucescit jam o socii (see 'Chansons')
Lucescit jam pariter, 4vv, 1584a (doubtful)
Luna velut (6p. of Princeps Marte potens)
Luxuriosa res vinum, 6vv, 1594; S xv, 85
Magnanimus princeps (3p. of Princeps Marte potens)
Magnus Dominus (2p. of Laudate Dominum quoniam bonum est)
Manum nomen Domini (3p. of Resonet in laudibus)
Maria Magdalena (4p. of Surrexit Dominus)
Martini festum celebremus (2p. Plebs igitur), 5vv, 1573b; S v, 153
Matronarum decus (4p. of Princeps Marte potens)

Media vita in morte sumus (2p. Sancte Deus), 6vv, 1573b; S xiii, 90
Meditabor in mandatis, 4vv, 1582b; S iii, 83
Memento peccati tui, 5vv, 1597; S vii, 58
Me miserum (2p. of Quis mihi quia te rapuit)
Memor esto, 6vv, 1585a; S xvii, 32
Mens male (2p. of Heu quos dabimus miseranda)
Mirabile mysterium, 5vv, 1556; S v, 18
Mira loquor, 10vv, 1604; S xxi, 126
Miserere mei Deus, 9vv, MS 1580s, Mbs
Miserere mei Deus (4p. of Psalmi Davidis poenitentiales)
Miserere mei Domine, 4vv, 1585d; S iii, 31
Miserere nostri (2p. of Ad te levavi oculos)
Misericordias Domini, 5vv, 1573b; S ix, 9
Misit eos (2p. of Hodie completi sunt)
Missus est angelus (2p. Ne timeas Maria; 3p. Dixit autem; 4p. Dixit autem), 5, 6vv, 1565c; S vii, 16
Momenta quaevis temporis, 6vv, 1604; S xix, 58
Mors tua mors Christi (2p. Quisquid eril), 5vv, 1585b; S vii, 43
Mortalium jucunditas, 5vv, 1597; S xi, 20
Mox importuno (2p. of Hispanum ad coenam)
Multarum hic resonat, 5vv, 1571b; S iii, 112
Multe tribulationes, 6vv, 1604; S xv, 65
Multifariam multisque modis, 6vv, 1594; S xi, 161
Multum quidem (2p. of Audi benigne conditor)
Musica Dei donum optimi, 6vv, 1594; S xix, 63
Narrate omnia (2p. of Confitemini Domino)
Ne avertas (2p. of Exaudi Dominum vocem meam)
Nec minus effulget Salome (7p. of Princeps Marte potens)
Nectar et ambrosiam, 6vv, 1594; S xi, 109
Ne derelinquas amicus, 6vv, 1604; S xv, 134
Ne reminiscaris, 4vv, 1577c; S i, 109
Ne reminiscaris, 7vv, 1577c; S xix, 78
Ne timeas Maria (2p. of Missus est angelus)
Nisi Dominus (2p. Cum dederit), 5vv, 1562; S ix, 66
Nisi ego abiero (2p. of Tempus est ut revertar)
Noli regibus o Lamuel (2p. Date siceram), 5vv, 1571b; S vii, 47
Nolite timere (2p. of Angelus Domini descendit)

180

180

Princeps Marte potens, Guilelmus (2p. Gloria pontificum Ernestus; 3p. Magnanimus princeps; 4p. Matronarum decus; 5p. Virginitatis honos; 6p. Luna velut; 7p. Nec minus effulget Salome; 8p. Princeps egregius; 9p. Vive Pater patriae], 4, 8vv, 1604; S i, 61

Proba me Deus, 4vv, 1579; S iii, 35

Prolongati sunt dies mei (2p. Inveterata sunt; 3p. Si ergo fas), 6vv, 1594; S xvii, 1   178

Pronuba Juno tibi [Gratia summi; Qui regit astra], 4vv, 1570a; H i, 3

Prophetiae Sibyllarum (1p. Virgine matre; 2p. Ecce dies venient; 3p. Non tarde; 4p. In teneris; 5p. Ecce dies nigras; 6p. Jam mea; 7p. Dum meditor; 8p. Ipsa Deum; 9p. Virginis aeternum; 10p. Verax ipse; 11p. Cerno Dei; 12p. Summus erit], 4vv, 1600; ed. in Cw, xlviii (1937/R)   174–5, 181, 190

Propterea Deus (2p. of Quid gloriaris)

Propter fratres (4p. of Laetatus sum)

Providebam Dominum, 7vv, 1604; S xix, 98

Psalmi Davidis poenitentiales (1p. Domine ne in furore tuo . . . miserere; 2p. Beati quorum remissae sunt; 3p. Domine ne in furore tuo . . . quoniam; 4p. Miserere mei Deus; 5p. Domine exaudi . . . non avertas; 6p. De profundis; 7p. Domine exaudi . . . auribus percipe), 5vv, 1584b/R1970; ed. W. Bäuerle (Leipzig, 1905)

Pulvis et umbra sumus, 4vv, 1573b; S i, 127

Quam benignus es (2p. O beatum hominem), 4vv, 1562; S ix, 30

Quam bonus Israel Deus (2p. Quia non est respectus), 6vv, 1594; S xix, 1

Quam magnificata sunt (2p. Beatus homo), 6vv, 1564³; S xvii, 7

Quam multa multitudo (2p. of Illustra faciem)

Quam pulchra es (2p. Guttur tuam), 6vv, 1585a; S xiii, 149

Quanti mercenarii (2p. of Pater peccavi)

Quare tristis es anima mea, 4vv, 1573c; S i, 154

Quare tristis es anima mea, 6vv, 1564b; S xvii, 12

Quasi cedrus, 4vv, 1564⁵; S i, 93

Qua sina coelestis (2p. of Alma parens)

Quemadmodum desiderat cervus, 6vv, 1569a; S xix, 18

Quem dicunt homines (2p. Tu es Christus), 5vv, 1567³; S vii, 6

Quem vidistis pastores, 5vv, 1569a; S v, 1

Quia delectasti (3p. of Deus canticum novum)

Quia illic (3p. of Laetatus sum)

Quia non est respectus (2p. of Quam bonus Israel Deus)

Quia vidisti me, 4vv, 1563³; S i, 137

Quicumque vult salvus esse (2p. Alia est enim; 3p. Et tamen; 4p. Haec est fides), 5vv, 1577c; H i, 32

Qui cupit, 4vv, 1564⁵; S i, 125

Quid estis pusillanimes, 4vv, 1573c; S i, 121

Quid facies, 4vv, 1582b; S iii, 100

Quid gloriaris (2p. Propterea Deus), 5vv, 1566c; S ix, 81

Quid prodest homini (2p. Futurum est), 5vv, 1571b; S vii, 70

Quid prodest stulto, 5vv, 1564b; S vii, 41

Quid tamen [Sponsa quid agis] (2p. Non me lasciviae), 5vv, 1571b; S xi, 64   179

Quid trepidas (2p. Gaudeat exultetque), 6vv, 1570g; S xi, 111

Quid vulgo memorant, 8vv, 1604; S xix, 122

Qui emitit (2p. of Lauda Jerusalem Dominum)

Qui maris terrae (2p. of Sidus ex claro veniet)

Qui moderatur sermones suos, 6vv, 1604; S xv, 142

Qui novus aethereo, 5vv, 1569a; S v, 80

Qui patiens est, 6vv, 1604; S xv, 137

Qui ponit aquam (2p. of Jam lucis orto)

Qui replet (2p. of Benedic anima mea Domino)

Quis enim cognovit (2p. of O altitudo divitiarum)

Qui sequitur me, 2vv, 1577d; S i, 3

Quis est homo, 5vv, 1567³; S ix, 53

Quis mihi det lacrimis, 5vv, 1573b; S v, 44

Quis mihi quis te rapuit [Quid tibi quidnam] (2p. Me miserum; 3p. Nunc juvat immensi), 5vv, 1565b; S xi, 30

Quis non timet (2p. of Cantabant canticum Moysi)

Quisquid erit (2p. of Mors tua mors Christi)

Qui sunt hi sermones (2p. Tu solus peregrinus), 5vv, 1582e; S vii, 9

Qui valet eloquio, 5vv, 1565b; S xi, 78

Qui timet Deum, 6vv, 1594; S xv, 56

Qui tribulant me (2p. Unam petii), 4vv, 1582b; S i, 145

Qui viderit (2p. of Vincenti dabo edere)

Qui vult venire, 2vv, 1577d; S i, 5

Quocumque loco fuero (2p. Jam quod quae sivi), 5vv, 1585b; S v, 65

Quocumque pergis (2p. of Jesu corona virginum)

Quod licet id libeat, 5vv, 1604; S xi, 16

Quod non capis (3p. of Lauda Sion salvatorem)

Quo fers (2p. of Accipe qua recres)

179

179

214

185

Come sei stat' o ciel (2p. of Ove sei vita mia)
Come va 'l mondo (Petrarch) (2p. Ma 'l cieco amor), 5vv, 1567a; S iv, 101

Con lei fuss'io (Petrarch), 5vv, 1555a; S ii, 63
Con le stell' (2p. of Del auro crin de la Tassinia bella)
Così aspettando (2p. of Mentre fioriv'amor)
Così cor mio vogliate (Ariosto), 4vv, 1587a; S vi, 80
Così quel che m'avanza (5p. of Per aspro mar di notte)
Crudel acerba inesorabil morte (Petrarch), 5vv, 1555a; S ii, 44
Dappoi che sott'il ciel (Petrarch), 5vv, 1584a; H i, 172
Deh che fuss'io (5p. of Non ha tante)
Deh hor foss'io co'l vago (Petrarch), 4vv, 1558¹³, S viii, 26
Deh lascia anima homai (Fiamma), 4vv, 1587a; S vi, 85
Deh non rinovellar (2p. of Che fai che pensi)
Deh perche voglio anco (Ariosto) (2p. Dunque fia ver), 5vv, 1584a; H i, 183

Deh sol che sei si chiaro, 4vv, 1570f; S viii, 61
Del auro crin de la Tassinia bella (2p. Con le stell'), 5vv, 1570f; S viii, 112
De l'eterne tue sante (Fiamma) (2p. Per questa), 5vv, 1585c; S vi, 1   185
Del freddo Rheno (2p. Ch'il credera; 3p. Rotava ed è pur ver; 4p. Si fe cristallo; 5p. Et io qual; 6p. Hor su la nuda terra), 4vv, 1555b; S viii, 3

Dicesi che la morte (A. Marsi), 5vv, 1563; S iv, 22
Di pensier in pensier (Petrarch), 6vv, 1579²; S x, 3
Di persona era tanto ben formata (Ariosto), 4vv, 1573c; S viii, 72
Di qua di là (Ariosto), 5vv, 1584a; H i, 176
Ditemi vita mia, 7vv, 1584⁴ S x, 5
Di terrena armonia (Beccuti) (2p. Signor le colpe mia; 3p. Padre rivolgi; 4p. Stanco di lagrimar; 5p. Voi che di prave; 6p. Fugga), 5vv, 1584a   189
[repr. without 1st stanza as Signor le colpe mie, 1587a]; H i, 179
Diviso m'ha (2p. of Poi che 'l'iniquo e fero mio destino)
Dunque fia ver (2p. of Deh perche voglio anco)
Ecco che pur vi lasso, 5vv, 1587a; S vi, 92
Ed a noi restare (2p. of Volgi cor mio la tua speranza)
E puro bene (2p. of Tanto e quel ben eterno amor)
Errai scorrendo (3p. of Per aspro mar di notte)

E sarebbe hora (2p. of O tempo o cielo)
Et in sembiante (2p. of Evro gentil)
Et io qual (5p. of Del freddo Rheno)
Et mentre (2p. of Quant'invidia vi port'aure)
Evro gentil se d'amoroso ardore (G. B. d'Azzia) (2p. Et in sembiante), 5vv, 1557; S ii, 121
Fiera stella s'el ciel ha forza (Petrarch) (2p. Ma tu prendi), 5vv, 1555a; S ii, 50
Fugga (6p. of Di terrena armonia)
Già mi fiu co'l desir (Petrarch), 5vv, 1555a; S ii, 14
Già senz'affan' (5p. of Si come al chiaro giorno)
Guarda 'l mio stat'a le vaghezze (Petrarch), 5vv, 1555a; S ii, 6
Hai Lucia buona cosa, 4vv, 1581b; S x, 86
Hor a cantar (2p. of Più volte un bel desio)
Hora per far (2p. of Io son si stanco sotto il grave peso)
Hor ch'a l'albergo de monton (Fiamma), 6vv, 1587a; S vi, 105
Hor che la nuova e vaga primavera, 10vv, 1575¹¹, S x, 43
Hor come i rai (3p. of Quando il giorno da l'onde)
Hor qui son lasso e voglio esser (Petrarch), 5vv, 1555a; S ii, 22
Hor su la nuda terra (6p. of Del freddo Rheno)
Hor vi riconfortate (Petrarch), 5vv, 1585c; S vi, 26
Hor vi riconfortate (Petrarch), 6vv, 1584a; S x, 14
Huomini e Dei (4p. of La ver' l'aurora)
Il grave de l'età (Fiamma) (2p. Alma tu che 'l furor), 6vv, 1587a; S vi, 126

Il mondo muta (5p. of Quando il giorno da l'onde)
Il tempo passa e l'hore (Petrarch), 5vv, 1567a; S iv, 92
Indi gl'acuti strali (2p. of Viene dolc'hymeneo)
Indi per altro (2p. of In qual parte del ciel)
In divina bellezza (2p. of In qual parte del ciel)
In dubbio di mio stato (Petrarch), 4vv, 1560c; S viii, 35
In dubbio di mio stato (Petrarch), 4vv, 1562?; S viii, 42
In qual parte del ciel (Petrarch) (2p. In divina bellezza), 5vv, 1557; S ii, 134

In sonno eterno (2p. of Non ha tante)
In un boschetto (3p. of Standomi un giorno)
Io che l'età più verde (Fiamma) (2p. Ma conven), 5vv, 1585c; S vi, 6
Io ho più tempo (2p. Almen nel suo fuggir), 5vv, 1575¹¹; S viii, 117

Io non sapea di tal vista (Petrarch), 5vv, 1585c; S vi, 33
Io son si stanco sotto il fascio antico (Petrarch), 5vv, 1585c; S vi, 45
Io son si stanco sotto il grave peso (Guidiccioni) (2p. Hora per far), 5vv, 1557; S ii, 139
Io ti vorria contar, 4vv, 1581b; S x, 85
Io vo fuggendo (4p. of Non ha tante)
I'vo piangendo i miei passati tempi (Petrarch) (2p. Si che s'io vissi), 5vv, 1567a; S iv, 116
La cortesia voi donne predicate, 4vv, 1555b; S x, 66
Lagrime di S Pietro (Tansillo), 7vv, 1595; ed. in Cw, xxxiv, xxxvii, xli (1935-6/R)
L'alto signor, dinanzi a cui (Petrarch), 5vv, 1563; S iv, 3
L'altr'hier sul mezzo giorno, 5vv, 1555a; S ii, 79
La non vol esser più mia, 5vv, 1584a; H i, 152
La notte che segui l'horribil (Petrarch) (2p. Riconosci; 3p. Come non conosch'io), 5vv, 1561[10]; S viii, 88
Lasso che (2p. of Qual nemica fortuna)
Lasso che par (2p. of Tutto 'l di piango)
La ver l'aurora (Petrarch) (2p. Temprar potess'io; 3p. Quante lagrime; 4p. Huomini e Dei; 5p. All'ultimo bisogno; 6p. Ridon hor), 5vv, 1567a; S vi, 65
La vita fugge (Petrarch), 5vv, 1563; S iv, 44
Le voglie e l'opre mie (Fiamma), 5vv, 1585c; S vi, 17
Lucia celu hai biscamia, 4vv, 1581b; S x, 97
Ma ben veggi'hor (2p. of Voi ch'ascoltate in rime)
Ma che morta (2p. of Spent'è d'amor)
Ma conven (2p. of Io che l'età più verde)
Madonna mia pietà, 4vv, 1555b; S x, 61
Madonna sa l'amor, 5vv, 1576b; H i, 156
Ma 'l cieco amor (2p. of Come va 'l mondo)
Malvaggio horrido gelo, 4vv, 1570f; S viii, 63
Ma quel ch'una (2p. of Chi non sa come spira)
Ma quel gran re (4p. of Per aspro mar di notte)
Ma sarò spento (6p. of Non ha tante)
Ma se con l'opr' (2p. of Bella guerriera mia)
Matona mia cara, 4vv, 1581b; S x, 93
Ma tu prendi (2p. of Fiera stella s'el ciel ha forza)
Mentre che 'l cor da gl'amorosi vermi (Petrarch) (2p. Quel fuoco), 5vv, 1555a; S ii, 27

Mentre fioriv'amor (2p. Cosi aspettando), 5vv, 1557; S ii, 111
Mia benigna fortun'e 'l viver lieto (Petrarch), 5vv, 1555a; S ii, 37
Mi me chiamere, 5vv, 1581b; S x, 108
Miser qui speme in cose mortal pone (Petrarch), 5vv, 1567a; S iv, 90
Misera che farò, 5vv, 1576[5]; S viii, 129
Mostran le braccia sue (Ariosto), 4vv, 1573c; S viii, 81
Ne però (2p. of O invidia nemica di virtute)
Nessun visse giamai (Petrarch), 5vv, 1584a; S viii, 137
No giorno t'haggio havere, 4vv, 1555b; S x, 65
Non hanno tante (2p. of Per aspro mar di notte)
Non ha tante (2p. In sonno eterno; 3p. Secchi vedransi; 4p. Io vo fuggendo; 5p. Deh che fuss'io; 6p. Ma sarò spento), 3, 5, 6vv, 1563; S iv, 6
Non hebbe (2p. of Quando il giorno da l'onde)
Non s'incolpi 'l desire, 5vv, 1563; S iv, 53
Non vi vieto per questo (Ariosto), 4vv, 1560a (by Hoste da Reggio); S viii, 29   185-6
O bella fusa, 4vv, 1581b; S x, 89
O beltà rara, 5vv, 1567a; S iv, 82
Occhi piangete accompagnate il core (Petrarch), 4vv, 1555b; S viii, 19   185
O che lieve è (2p. of Quel rossignuol che si soave piagne)
O d'amarissime onde, 5vv, 1561[10]; S viii, 97
O dolci parolette (Cassola), 5vv, 1564c; S viii, 107
O fugace dolcezza (Petrarch), 5vv, 1584a; S vi, 127
Ogni giorno m'han ditt', 4vv, 1581b; S x, 91
O invidia nemica di virtute (Petrarch) (2p. Ne però), 5vv, 1555a; S ii, 39
O là o che bon eccho, 8vv, 1581b; S x, 140
O Lucia miau, 3vv, 1560[14]; S x, 70
O occhi manza mia, 4vv, 1581b; S x, 103 [previously pubd 1557[20], 3vv (inc.)]
Onde come colui (2p. of Quando 'l voler)
O noiosa mia vita (2p. of Ov'è condott'il mio amoroso stile)
Ornando come suole, 6vv, 1587a; S vi, 154
O sempre vagh' (2p. of Si come al chiaro giorno)
O tempo o cielo (Petrarch) (2p. E sarebbe hora), 5vv, 1585c; S vi, 11
Ov'è condott'il mio amoroso stile (2p. O noiosa mia vita), 4vv, 1562[7]; S viii, 38
Ove d'altra montagn' ombra tocchi, 4vv, 1567[16]

Ove le luci giro, 5vv, 1576b; H i, 163
Ove sei vita mia (2p. Come sei stat' o ciel), 5vv, 1561[10], S viii, 102
O voi già stanchi (6p. of Per aspro mar di notte)
Padre rivolgi (3p. of Di terrena armonia)
Parch'hai lasciato, 4vv, 1581b; S x, 82
Parmi che sempre sian' (4p. of Quando il giorno da l'onde)
Passan vostri trionfi (Petrarch), 10vv, 1584a; S x, 53
Pensier dica che 'l cor (Ariosto), 5vv, 1569[10], S vi, 123
Per aspro mar di notte (Fiamma) (2p. Non hanno tante; 3p. Errai scorrendo; 4p. Ma quel gran re; 5p. Così quel che m'avanza; 6p. O voi già stanchi), 4vv, 1587a; S vi, 70
Perché qual peregrin (2p. of Come pianta)
Perché sempre nimica mia, 5vv, 1555a; S ii, 83
Perch'io veggio (Petrarch), 4vv, 1555b; S viii, 23
Per pianto la mia carne (Sannazaro), 4vv, 1555b; S viii, 13
Per questa (2p. of De l'eterne tue sante)
Pien d'un vago pensier (Petrarch), 5vv, 1555a; S ii, 75
Più volte un bel desio (Fiamma) (2p. Hor a cantar), 6vv, 1587a; S vi, 132
Poggi, valli (6p. of Quando il giorno da l'onde)
Poi che 'l camin m'è chiuso (Petrarch), 5vv, 1555a; S ii, 25
Poi che l'iniquo e fero mio destino (2p. Diviso m'ha), 5vv, 1555a; S ii, 32
Poi che 'l mio largo pianto (Petrarch), 4vv, 1583[15]; S viii, 84
Poi che si grand' (2p. of Ben sono i premi tuoi)
Pon fren' al gran dolor (Petrarch), 5vv, 1555a; S ii, 46
Prendi l'aurata lira (Fiamma), 6vv, 1587a; S vi, 158
Qual nemica fortuna (2p. Lasso che; 3p. Sol'io quanto; 4p. Talhor dico; 5p. Talhora parmi la luce; 6p. Re de gli altri), 5, 6vv, 1567a; S iv, 128
Quando fia mai quel giorno, 4vv, 1570f; S viii, 65
Quando il giorno da l'onde (Fiamma) (2p. Non hebbe; 3p. Hor come i rai; 4p. Parmi che sempre sian'; 5p. Il mondo muta; 6p. Poggi, valli), 5vv, 1585c; S vi, 50
Quando la sera scaccia (Petrarch), 5vv, 1555a; S ii, 35
Quando 'l voler (Petrarch) (2p. Onde come colui), 5vv, 1555a; S ii, 17
Quante lagrime (3p. of La ver' i'aurora)
Quant'invidia (2p. of Quant'invidia ti porto avara terra)

Quanto il mio duol, 4vv, 1560a; S viii, 31
Quant'invidia ti porto avara terra (Petrarch) (2p. Quant'invidia), 5vv, 1563; S iv, 18
Quant'invidia vi port'aure (C. Besalio) (2p. Et mentre), 5vv, 1563; S iv, 32
Quel chiaro sol (2p. Che se la ver'), 5vv, 1557; S ii, 116
Quel fuoco (2p. of Mentre che 'l cor da gl'amorosi vermi)
Quel rossignuol che si soave piagne (Petrarch) (2p. O che lieve è), 5vv, 1567a; S iv, 85
Que piangon (2p. of Soleasi nel mio cor)
Queste contrarie tempre (2p. of Signor se la tua grazia è fuoco)
Queste non son più lagrime (Ariosto), 4vv, 1555b; S viii, 15
Questi ch'inditio fan (Ariosto), 5vv, 1557; S ii, 132
Questo son lasso de la mia spem', 5vv, 1563; S iv, 28
Questo e disceso (2p. of Tra verdi rami)
Re de gli altri (6p. of Qual nemica fortuna)
Riconosci (2p. of La notte che segui l'horribil)
Ridon hor (6p. of La ver' i'aurora)
Rotava ed è pur ver (3p. of Del freddo Rheno)
Saccio 'na cosa, 4vv, 1581b; S x, 8
Scorgo tant'altro il lume (Tansillo), 5vv, 1563; S iv, 57
Se ben l'empia mia sorte, 4vv, 1555b; S viii, 17
Se ben non veggion gl'occhi, 4vv, 1570f; S viii, 67
Secchi vedransi (3p. of Non ha tante)
Segui già le speranze (Petrarch), 5vv, 1584a; S viii, 141
Se si alto por gir mie stanche rime (Petrarch), 5vv, 1563; S iv, 59
Si che s'io vissi (2p. of I vo piangendo)
Si ch'io mi credo (2p. of Sol'e pensoso i più deserti campi)
Si come'al chiaro giorno (2p. O sempre vagh'; 3p. Tal ch'io possa; 4p. Al'hor nel; 5p. Già senz'affan'; 6p. Altri non vedra), 4vv, 1566[2]; S viii, 46
Si com'i fiori da l'ardente sole, 5vv, 1570[15]; H i, 168
Si fe cristallo (4p. of Del freddo Rheno)
Signor da l'alto trono, 5vv, 1584a; H i, 150
Signor le colpe mie (2p. of Di terrena armonia)
Signor se la tua grazia è fuoco (Tansillo) (2p. Queste contrarie tempre), 5vv, 1567a; S iv, 106
Silen di rose ha 'l volto (C. Camilli), 6vv, 1594[4]; S x, 18
S'io esca vivo (Petrarch), 6vv, 1579[2]; S x, 9
S'io fusse ciaul', 4vv, 1581b; S x, 92

Un jour vis un foulon [On ne peut le fol amour], 4vv, 1570b; S xii, 39
Un mesnagier, 5vv, 1570b; S xiv, 54
Un [Mon] triste coeur rempli, 5vv, 1560c; S xiv, 80
Veux-tu ton mal [Puis qu'en mon mal], 5vv, 1559¹²; SS xiv, 71
Vignon vignon vignette, 6vv, 1584a; S xvi, 144
Vive sera et toujours perdurable, 5vv, 1570f; S xiv, 11
Voir est beaucoup, 4vv, 1559¹³; H i, 126
Vous qui aymez les dames, 5vv, 1560c; S xiv, 45
Vray dieu disoit une fillette [une ame sainte], 4vv, 1555b; S xii, 72

(German contrafacta)   195

Al mein Anfang (= Le temps peut bien); Auss tiefer Not (= Si le long temps); Bewar mich Herr (= Ton feu s'esteint); Das sawer Tranck (= La mort est jeu pire); Frölich und frey (= Quand mon mary vient); Gott ist mein Schütz (= A ce matin); Gross Angst und Not (= Trop endurer); Gunst geht für gspunst (= Soyonsjoyeux); Herr Jesu Christ (= Le vray amy); Hilff uns, o Herr (= Si froid et chault); Ich rieff zu dir Herr Jesu Christ (= Au feu verez-moy); Ich ruff zu dir, hilff mir (= Monsieur l'abbé); Id quid? fit, sit, Wie kann ich dirs abschlagen (= Je ne veux rien); Kein Lieb noch treu ist (= En un lieu)
Laetamini in Domino und singt in dulci jubilo (= Je l'ayme bien); Mein aininger Trost (= Petite folle); Mein Hoffnung (= Fleur de quinze ans); Merck schönes (= Hélas quel jour); O Herre Gott mein Not (= Bon mon coeur); O trewer Gott (= Ung doulx nenny); Seit frisch (= Margot labourez); Thue dich, o Herr (= Du corps absent); Vor Zeiten was ich lieb gehalten (= Hátez-vous); Wenn wir recht thun betrachten (= Du fond de ma pensée); Wer singen wil (= En m'ovant chanter); Wer sucht der findt (= Qui dort icy); Wolauff gut Gsellen (= Un jeune moine); Zu aller Stund (= Ardant amour souvent)

LIEDER

Allein Gott (3p. of Auss meiner sünden Tieffe)
Als Holophernes (6p. of Die Gnad kombt oben her)
Am Abent spat, beim khiellen Wein, 5vv, 1567c; S xviii, 33
Annelein, du singst fein, 4vv, 1573c; S xx, 46
Audite nova Der Bawr von Eselskirchen, 4vv, 1573c; S xx, 51
Auff dich, mein heber Herr und Gott (Ulenberg), 3vv, 1588c; S xx, 63
Auff ihen wil ich vertrawen (3p. of Von Gott wil ich nit lassen)
Auss gutem Grundt, 4vv, 1573c; S xx, 47
Auss härtem Weh, 6vv, 1590; S xx, 99

   196–8   196

Auss meiner sünden Tieffe (2p. Wann sich ein grimmer zoren; 3p. Allein Gott; 4p. Von Gott kein Mensch), 4vv, 1583a; S xx, 17
Bald ich von Gelt (6p. of Ich hab ein Mann)
Baur, was tregst im Sacke?, 4vv, 1583a; S xx, 29
Christ ist erstanden, 4vv, 1583a; S xx, 3
Da das der Herr (2p. of Im Lant zu Wirtenberg)
Da lagens (3p. of Mit Lust thet ich aussreitten)
Daniel geworfen war (9p. of Die Gnad kombt oben her)
Daniels Knaben drey (8p. of Die Gnad kombt oben her)
Dann bey dem Herren (5p. of Ich ruff zu dir mein Herr und Gott)
Dann eh er's hat begert (3p. of Der König wirdt seyn Wolgemut)
Darauff hat Gott gesandt (7p. of Die Gnad kombt oben her)
Darumb, o frommer Gott (10p. of Die Gnad kombt oben her)
Das ein das Annelein (2p. of Mit Lust thet ich aussreitten)
Das Meidlein (2p. of Einmal ging ich spatzieren)
Das Volck von Israel (4p. of Die Gnad kombt oben her)
Der g'winnen will (3p. of Hort zu eins news Gedicht)
Derhalben dann nichts (2p. of In viel Trübsal)
Der Herr, dir ist mit dir (2p. of Maria voll Genad)
Der Herr erhöre deine Klag (Ulenberg), 3vv, 1588c; S xx, 68
Der König wirdt seyn Wolgemut (Ulenberg) (2p. Du hast ihm geben; 3p. Dann eh er's hat begert), 6vv, 1590; S xx, 128
Der Meye bringt uns der Blümlein vil (J. Klieber), 5vv, 1572a; S xviii, 75
Der richter lacht (3p. of Im Lant zu Wirtenberg)
Der starcke Gott im Himmelreich (Ulenberg), 3vv, 1588c; S xx, 80
Der Tag der ist so frewdenreich, 5vv, 1572a; S xviii, 71
Der Wein, der schmeckt mir also, 5vv, 1567c; S xviii, 11
Der Welte Pracht ist hoch geacht, 5vv, 1576a; S xviii, 147
Die Fassnacht ist ein schöne Zeit, 5vv, 1567c; S xviii, 6
Die Gnad kombt oben her (2p. Wer Gott vertrauen thut; 3p. Wir armes Volck; 4p. Das Volck von Israel; 5p. Joseph verkauffet; 6p. Als Holophernes; 7p. Darauff hat Gott gesandt; 8p. Daniels Knaben drey; 9p. Daniel geworfen war; 10p. Darumb, o frommer Gott; 11p. Wer diss Lied hat gemacht; 12p. Hierauf sey nun gepreiset), 4vv, 1583a; S xx, 4
Die Thoren sprechen wohl (Ulenberg), 3vv, 1588c; S xx, 66
Die Welt und all ir Reichethumb (Ulenberg), 3vv, 1588c; S xx, 70
Die Zeit, so jetzt vorhanden ist, 5vv, 1567c; S xviii, 14

Do ich lang stilt (4p. of Mein Fraw hilgert)
Dort aber wirdt (2p. of O Mensch gedenck)
Du best gebenedeyd (3p. of Maria voll Genad)
Du hast ihm geben (2p. of Der König wirdt seyn Wolgemut)
Ein Esel und das Nüssbawmholtz, 4vv, 1573c; S xx, 45
Ein guten Raht wil geben ich (2p. In Glück und Frewd), 6vv, 1590; S xx, 83

Ein guter Wein ist Lobens werd, 5vv, 1567c; S xviii, 44
Ein Körbelmacher in eim Dorff (H. Sachs), 6vv, 1590; S xx, 124
Einmal ging ich spazieren (2p. Das Meidlein), 5vv, 1572a; S xviii, 98
Ein Meidlein zu dem Brunnen gieng (2p. Ich sprach o Fraw; 3p. Die Fraw gantz höflich; 4p. So danck ich Gott), 5vv, 1572a; S xviii, 82
Erzürn dich nicht o frommer Christ (L. Hätzer), 5vv, 1572a; S xviii, 65
Es jagt ein Jeger vor dem Holtz, 5vv, 1572a; S xviii, 88
Es sind doch selig alle die (M. Greiter), 5vv, 1572a; S xviii, 77
Es thut sich als verkeren, 4vv, 1573c; S xx, 49
Es zeugen des gottlosen Wercke (Ulenberg), 3vv, 1588c; S xx, 75
Fraw ich bin euch von hertzen Hold, 5vv, 1567c; S xviii, 31
Frölich und frey on alle Rey, 5vv, 1576a; S xviii, 149
Frölich zu sein ist mein Manier, 5vv, 1567c; S xviii, 38
Gebenedeyt auch (4p. of Maria voll Genad)
Gelt, Welt, dir wird (2p. of Welt, Gelt, dir wird einmal)
Gott ist auf den wir immer hoffen (Ulenberg), 3vv, 1588c; S xx, 79
Gott nimbt und geit zu jeder Zeit, 5vv, 1576a; S xviii, 130
Gross ist der Herr im heiligen Thron (Ulenberg), 3vv, 1588c; S xx, 79
Halt mich o Herr in deiner Hut (Ulenberg), 3vv, 1588c; S xx, 66
Herr der du meine Stercke bist (Ulenberg), 3vv, 1588c; S xx, 67
Herr Gott mein Hort (Ulenberg), 3vv, 1588c; S xx, 72
Hierauf sey nun gepreiset (12p. of Die Gnad kombt oben her)
Hilff lieber Herr die heilig Frommen (Ulenberg), 3vv, 1588c; S xx, 65
Hort zu ein news Gedicht (2p. So fundt man; 3p. Der g'winnen will), 5vv, 1576a; S xviii, 151
Ich armer Mann was hab ich than, 5vv, 1576a; S xviii, 113
Ich armes Weib (5p. of Ich hab ein Mann)
Ich hab dich lieb das weist du wol (2p. Und wann du freundlich bist), 5vv, 1572a; S xviii, 93
Ich hab ein Mann (2p. Wann er auffsteht; 3p. Nach dem Frühmal; 4p. Umb fünffte hin; 5p. Ich armes Weib; 6p. Bald ich von Gelt; 7p. Wann ich dann sag; 8p. Nun wars umb mich), 4vv, 1583a; S xx, 31

Ich harr auf Gott (3p. of Ich ruff zu dir mein Herr und Gott)
Ich harre auff Gott (Ulenberg), 3vv, 1588c; S xx, 76
Ich ruff zu dir mein Herr und Gott (Ulenberg) (2p. Wann du Herr wolltest; 3p. Ich harr auf Gott; 4p. Mein Hoffnung steht; 5p. Dann bey dem Herren), 6vv, 1590; S xx, 88
Ich sprach o Fraw (2p. of Ein Meidlein zu dem Brunnen gieng)
Ich sprich wan ich nit leuge, 5vv, 1576a; S xviii, 159
Ich weiss ein hübsches Frawelein, 5vv, 1572a; S xviii, 91
Ich weiss nur ein Meidlein, 4vv, 1583a; S xx, 28
Ich will auss gantzem Hertzen mein (Ulenberg), 3vv, 1588c; S xx, 64
Ich will dich Herr gebürlich loben (Ulenberg), 3vv, 1588c; S xx, 73
Ich will Gott unaußhörlich preisen (Ulenberg), 3vv, 1588c; S xx, 74
Im Lant zu Wirtenberg (2p. Da das der Herr; 3p. Der richter lacht), 5vv, 1567c; S xviii, 19
Im Mayen hört man die Hanen krayen, 5vv, 1567c; S xviii, 24
In Glück und Frewd (2p. of Ein guten Raht wil geben ich)
In viel Trübsal (2p. Derhalben dann nichts), 6vv, 1590; S xx, 116
In wölches Hauss (3p. of Mein Mann, der ist in Krieg)
Ist doch Gott gar (2p. of Wach auff o Menschenkind)
Ist keiner hie, der sprich zu mir, 5vv, 1567c; S xviii, 2
Joseph verkauffet (5p. of Die Gnad kombt oben her)
Kombt her zu mir spricht Gottes Son (G. Grünwald), 5vv, 1572a; S xviii, 73
Man sieht nun wol wie stet du bist, 5vv, 1572a; S xviii, 81
Maria voll Genad (2p. Der Herr, der ist mit dir; 3p. Du best gebenedeyd; 4p. Gebenedeyt auch), 6vv, 1590; S xx, 108
Mein Fraw hilgert (2p. Mein Fraw unmilt; 3p. Mein Fraw unrein; 4p. Do ich lang stilt; 5p. Sie raufft jr gnug), 5vv, 1576a; S xviii, 132
Mein Fraw unmilt (2p. of Mein Fraw hilgert)
Mein Fraw unrein (3p. of Mein Fraw hilgert)
Mein Gott, mein heber trewer Gott (Ulenberg), 3vv, 1588c; S xx, 69
Mein Hoffnung steht (4p. of Ich ruff zu dir mein Herr und Gott)
Mein Mann, der ist in Krieg (2p. Was soll ich euch; 3p. In wölches Hauss; 4p. Wolstu mich), 5vv, 1572a; S xviii, 51
Mit Lust thet ich aussreitten (2p. Das ein das Annelein; 3p. Da lagens), 5vv, 1576a; S xviii, 124
Nach dem Frühmal (3p. of Ich hab ein Mann)
Nun grüss dich Gott, 8vv, 1573c; S xx, 54
Nun wars umb mich (8p. of Ich hab ein Mann)

BIBLIOGRAPHY

FasquelleE

R. Eitner: 'Chronologisches Verzeichniss der gedruckten Werke von H. L. Hassler und Orlandus de Lassus', *MMg*, v, vi (1874), suppls.

C. van den Borren: *Orlande de Lassus* (Paris, 1920/R1975)

A. Sandberger: *Ausgewählte Aufsätze zur Musikgeschichte* (Munich, 1921), 1–168

E. Lowinsky: *Das Antwerpener Motettenbuch O. di Lasso's und seine Beziehungen zum Motettenschaffen der niederländischen Zeitgenossen* (The Hague, 1937)

H. Osthoff: *Die Niederländer und das deutsche Lied* (Berlin, 1938/R1967), 139ff

A. Einstein: *The Italian Madrigal* (Princeton, 1949/R1971), 477ff

K. Levy: ' "Susanne un jour": the History of a 16th Century Chanson', *AnnM*, i (1953), 375–408

B. Meier: 'Alter und neuer Stil in lateinisch textierten Werken von Orlando di Lasso', *AMw*, xv (1958), 51

W. Boetticher: *Orlando di Lasso und seine Zeit, 1532–1594* (Kassel, 1958)

H. Leuchtmann: *Die musikalische Wortausdeutungen in den Motetten des Magnum opus musicum von Orlando di Lasso* (Strasbourg, 1959)

W. Boetticher: 'Lasso, Orlando di', *MGG* [incl. detailed bibliography to c1958]

W. Frei: 'Die bayerische Hofkapelle unter Orlando di Lasso: Ergänzungen und Berichtigungen zur Deutung von Mielichs Bild', *Mf*, xv (1962), 359

W. Boetticher: *Aus Orlando di Lassos Wirkungskreis* (Kassel, 1963)

——: 'Wortausdeutung und Tonalität bei Orlando di Lasso', *KJb*, xlvii (1963), 75

R. Ears: 'Zur Deutung von Mielichs Bild der bayerischen Hofkapelle', *Mf*, xvi (1963), 364

S. Hermelink: 'Jägermesse: Beitrag zu einer Begriffsbestimmung', *Mf*, xvii (1965), 29

W. Boetticher: 'Über einige neue Werke aus Orlando di Lassos mittlerer Madrigal- und Motettenkomposition (1567–1569)', *AMw*, xxix (1965), 12

——: 'New Lasso Studies', *Aspects of Medieval and Renaissance Music: a Birthday Offering to Gustave Reese* (New York, 1966), 17

K. Morawska: 'Kompozycje Orlanda di Lasso w repertuarze instrumentalnym', *Muzyka*, xiii/3 (1968), 3

W. Boetticher: 'Weitere Beiträge zur Lasso-Forschung', *Renaissancemuziek 1400–1600: donum natalicium René Bernard Lenaerts* (Louvain, 1969), 61

S. Hermelink: 'Die Gegenquintsprungkadenz, ein Ausdrucksmittel der Satzkunst Lassos', *GfMKB, Bonn 1970*, 435

Bibliography

D. Kämper: *Studien zur instrumentalen Ensemblemusik des 16. Jahrhunderts in Italien*, AnMc, no.10 (1970)

H. Leuchtmann: 'Lassos Huldigungsmotette für Henri d'Anjou 1573', *Mf*, xxiii (1970), 165

W. Mitchell: 'The Prologue to Orlando di Lasso's *Prophetiae Sibyllarum*', *Music Forum*, ii (1970), 264

C. V. Palisca: '*Ut oratoria musica*: the Rhetorical Basis of Musical Mannerism', *The Meaning of Mannerism*, ed. F. W. Robinson and S. G. Nichols (Hanover, New Hampshire, 1972), 37

H. Leuchtmann: 'Orlando di Lasso in München', *Oberbayerisches Archiv*, xcvii (1973), 1

P. Röckl: 'Das Musikleben am Hofe Wilhelms V auf der Burg Trassnitz von 1568–1579', *Verhandlungen des Historischen Vereins für Niederbayern*, xcix (1973), 88–127

J. Bernstein: 'Lassus in English Sources: Two Chansons Recovered', *JAMS*, xxvii (1974), 315

B. Meier: *Die Tonarten der klassischen Vokalpolyphonie* (Utrecht, 1974)

M. Ruhnke: 'Lassos Chromatik und die Orgelstimmung', *Convivium musicorum: Festschrift Wolfgang Boetticher* (Berlin, 1974), 291

W. Boetticher: 'Anticipations of Dramatic Monody in the Late Works of Lassus', *Essays on Opera and English Music in Honour of Sir Jack Westrup* (Oxford, 1975), 84

J. Erb: *Parody Technique in the Magnificats of Orlando di Lasso* (diss., Harvard U., 1975)

J. Haar: 'A Madrigal Falsely Ascribed to Lasso', *JAMS*, xxviii (1975), 526

H. Leuchtmann: *Orlando di Lasso* (Wiesbaden, 1876–7)

H. Gross: *Klangliche Struktur und Klangverhältnis in Messen und lateinischen Motetten Orlando di Lassos* (Tutzing, 1977)

H. Leuchtmann: 'Orlando di Lasso als Ritter des Goldener Sporns', *Musik in Bayern*, xiv (1977), 94

D. Arnold: 'The Grand Motets of Orlandus Lassus', *Early Music*, vi 1978), 170

K. Hübler: 'Orlando di Lassus Prophetiae Sybillarum oder Über chromatische Komposition im 16. Jahrhundert', *Zeitschrift für Musiktheorie*, ix (1978), 29

G. R. Hoekstra: 'An Eight-voice Parody of Lassus: An Introduction and the Complete Music of André Pevernage's "Bon jour mon coeur" ', *Early Music*, vii (1979), 367

J. Roche: *Lassus* (London, 1982)

C. Wearing: 'Orlandus Lassus (1532–1594) and the Munich Kapelle', *Early Music*, x (1982), 147

227

WILLIAM BYRD

Joseph Kerman

CHAPTER ONE

Early years

I **Origins and early compositions**
Among the great Renaissance composers, the origins and
early life of only Josquin Desprez are as obscure as those
of William Byrd. The year of his birth can be established
with reasonable certainty as 1543, because on 15
November 1622 he described himself in his will as 'in
the 80th yeare of myne age'. But nothing is known of
his birthplace or his parentage.

It is very strange, as his biographer and the first great
editor of his music E. H. Fellowes remarked, and perhaps even unsettling, to find nothing about his birthplace or parentage in the pedigree recorded in the Her-
alds' Visitation of Essex a few years after his death.
Byrd may in fact have come from Lincoln, where the
surname 'Byrd' is not uncommon and where he received
his first appointment at the age of 19 or 20. But he
must have been brought up in London, for he was a
pupil of Tallis (this was stated by another Tallis pupil,
the courtier and amateur composer Sir Ferdinando
Heybourne, in 1575, and repeated by Anthony Wood).
Several musicians named Byrd appear in mid-century
London records, and Thomas Byrd, Gentleman of the
Chapel Royal in the 1540s and 1550s, may have been
William's father.

Thomas Morley was composing at the age of 19,
Orlando Gibbons at 16. There is little doubt that some

of Byrd's surviving compositions date from his teens. The three-part *Sermone blando* for consort and the second organ *Miserere* are typical student works, involving strict or free canons over a plainsong, and the two-part organ hymns and antiphons in the manner of John Redford and Thomas Preston inhabit a different world from Byrd's other music. Among the motets attached to his name are three apparently for the Sarum liturgy; this indicates that he was composing before the death of Queen Mary, that is, before he was 16. To be sure, Thomas Byrd has been proposed as the author of *Similes illis fiant*, which is ascribed in the manuscript simply to 'Birde'; the piece, too, is part of an unusual collaborative psalm setting with two senior members of the Chapel Royal, John Sheppard and Thomas Mundy. But Thomas Byrd is not otherwise known as a composer, and *Similes illis fiant* is relatively close in style – the canons seem indicative – to *Alleluia, Confitemini Domino*, whose ascription to William is not easily shaken.

As for *Christus resurgens*, the most ambitious of Byrd's student compositions, this Easter processional antiphon provided a favourite cantus firmus for competitive setting which he might have approached as a technical exercise after the liturgical conditions for it had lapsed. In any case it is patently more primitive in style than the other cantus firmus motets. Byrd published it in 1605, together with a non-cantus firmus setting of the verse which seems to be later.

II Lincoln, 1563–70
Byrd was appointed to the position of Organist and Master of the Choristers at Lincoln Cathedral with

effect from 25 March 1563, taking on the educational duties that such a post implies. Records published by Shaw (1967) show that he was given a larger salary than usual and also received a long-term grant of a rectory at Hainton, Lincolnshire, presumably by way of extra emolument. In 1568 he married Juliana Birley at St Margaret's-in-the-Close, where two children were baptized in 1569 and 1572.

For some unspecified reason Byrd and the chapter had a disagreement in 1569, but this was smoothed over, and in 1573, after he had left for London and his successor had been appointed (at a lower salary), the chapter heeded representations from certain 'noblemen and councillors of the Queen' and agreed to continue paying Byrd. On condition that he send it 'church songs and services' from time to time, he received a quarter of his former salary up to 1581. It seems that the young Byrd was already skilled in the great Elizabethan art of applying influence and in general well able to take care of his financial affairs.

At Lincoln Byrd found his stride as a composer; the chapter knew what it was doing when it drew up its condition. Although the chronology of his music is naturally uncertain at many points, and it is only from later that we have a good number of dated sources, internal musical evidence allows us to draw up a reasonable list of works composed at Lincoln. A striking feature of this early music is the great number of styles, forms and genres that Byrd essayed and the rapid, sure moulding of them all into something individual. It is as though he had embarked on a deliberate programme of experimentation, both in the kinds of music he wrote and in the composers whose work he looked to. Tallis,

Tye, Redford, Robert White, Robert Parsons, William Hunnis and (a little later) the émigré composers Philip van Wilder and the elder Alfonso Ferrabosco served him as models, sometimes suggesting general ideas, techniques, textures or groundplans, and sometimes providing material which he could quote directly.

Of his organ music, the three linked settings of *Clarifica me, Pater*, and perhaps other works, show signs of having been composed in the Lincoln years. The third *Clarifica*, in four parts, is Byrd's first exciting composition. And at Lincoln he laid the foundations for what was perhaps to be his greatest single accomplishment, the perfection of English virginal music from primitive beginnings. In works like those described by his pupil Thomas Tomkins as 'Byrd's old fancy' and 'Byrd's old ground' (MB 62 and 86), one can see his emerging control of 'open' expansive form on the one hand and of 'closed' periodic form on the other. In an ambitious but uneven variation work, *The Hunt's Up* (MB 40; not to be confused with the patently spurious MB 41), Byrd wrestled with a longer bass pattern than those of his earlier grounds; he drew on this work for several later ones and rewrote it in later years. (This practice, incidentally, can be inferred for a surprisingly large number of his compositions.) In general, Byrd was more successful at this time in the 'open' style, as witness the brilliant keyboard Fantasia in A minor, the best of the early motets, and the In Nomine settings for consort. To judge from the few manuscripts surviving from this period, the In Nomine settings were the first of his works to circulate widely.

Byrd's earliest settings of English poems are not madrigals but strophic songs for one voice and a con-

234

sort of viols. Such songs were written in the 1560s by composers like Parsons, Richard Farrant and Nicholas Strogers, and Byrd's *Triumph with pleasant melody* is a fair example of the style at its most elementary and drab. His consort-song settings of metrical psalms, however, show a characteristic advance in their more interesting vocal lines and consistent imitative counterpoint in the string parts. Certain of these psalms, in which the stanzas end with simple choruses, come close to verse anthems – another genre developed in the early 1560s by Farrant, Mundy and Hunnis. Byrd followed them closely. His verse anthem *Alack, when I look back* takes over both words and music of a similar composition by Hunnis (see Monson, 1982).

Most of Byrd's English liturgical music (except for the Great Service) seems to have been written at Lincoln, even though apparently little polyphonic music was required there. Was he writing this music already with an eye to London? A hard look at Byrd's output of Anglican music, as Monson has pointed out, encourages the suspicion that he set out to establish his mastery in each of its genres – Preces, psalms, simple and festal services etc. – with one or two commanding works, and then cultivated them no further. This is rather different from Fellowes's picture of an unstoppable flow of sacred composition spilling ecumenically over Anglican and Catholic genres alike. In any case, Byrd's famous Short Service became a staple of the cathedral repertory and a fixture after it appeared in John Barnard's *First Book of Selected Church Musick* (1641).

Some of the Latin motets published in 1575 were evidently also written considerably earlier. These include the most subtle of Byrd's cantus firmus motets,

235

Libera me, Domine, de morte aeterna, the brilliant if naive psalm-motet *Attollite portas*, and the long tripartite collect *Tribue, Domine–Te deprecor–Gloria Patri* set in the form of the ancient votive antiphon and in a style (or rather, styles) best described as a dazzling concatenation of old and new. The astonishing eight- and nine-part settings in imitative style of Psalms cxx and xv (*Ad Dominum cum tribularer* and *Domine, quis habitabit*), which Byrd never published, also seem to date from the Lincoln years.

Another very impressive unpublished early composition, the setting of the Lamentations, is the first of many that employ fluid, dense polyphony to achieve gravity and pathos. The work lacks the smooth consistency of White's five-part Lamentations and the simple intensity of those by Tallis. In its contrapuntal sweep, however, and in the astonishing power of the rough climax on 'Jerusalem convertere', it goes beyond the range of either of the older composers.

CHAPTER TWO

Byrd in London

I **1570–80**

Byrd was sworn in as a Gentleman of the Chapel Royal in February 1570, after the accidental death of Robert Parsons. But, as was sometimes the case, the new appointee did not immediately sever his old connections. Byrd's final departure from Lincoln in December 1572 may mark the date of his extra appointment as joint organist of the chapel with Tallis, though mention of this is not found until 1575, on the title-page of their joint publication the *Cantiones* (see fig. 10).

In London, Squire remarked, Byrd 'seems rapidly to have made his way', so rapidly that one imagines he spent a good deal of time there between 1570 and late 1572 laying the groundwork. From his first years in the chapel and on through the next two decades, Byrd is found in association with important persons. Powerful Elizabethan lords figure among the dedicatees of his various publications and are known to have interceded for him on several occasions. The Earl of Worcester and the Petre family were to become his special patrons. Around 1573 or 1574 he obtained the lease of Battails Hall in Stapleford Abbot, Essex, from the Earl of Oxford, the poet; this was the first of several properties that plunged Byrd into endless litigation. Among his song texts are poems by Oxford, Sidney, Thomas Watson and Sir Edward Dyer, including some which he could only

237

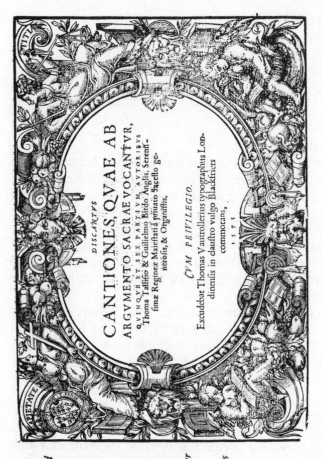

DISCANTVS

CANTIONES, QVAE AB
ARGVMENTO SACRAE VOCANTVR,
QVINQVE ET SEX PARTIVM, AVTORIBVS
Thoma Tallisio & Guilielmo Birdo Anglis, Sereniſ-
ſimæ Reginæ Maieſtati à priuato Sacello ge-
neroſis, & Organiſtis,

CVM PRIVILEGIO.
Excudebat Thomas Vautrollerius typographus Lon-
dinenſis in clauſtro vulgo Blackfriers
commorans,
1575

10. Title-page of
the 'Cantiones',
published by Byrd
and Tallis in
1575 under their
royal patent for
music printing; it
has the first
continental-style
music title-page
used in England,
adapted from
Le Roy by the
printer Vautrollier
for his London
edition of
Lassus's chansons
in 1570

238

have come by as a result of direct contact with the advanced poets of the 1570s and 1580s. The same is true of certain anonymous song texts with a decided 'literary' flavour. He provided music for Latin plays at Cambridge in 1579 and Oxford in 1592.

In 1579 the Earl of Northumberland mentioned that Byrd was teaching his daughter. Letters recently discovered by Lucy Carolan show that even before 1568 he was acting as a sort of coach to a circle of noble amateurs who were sending each other their compositions. 'I understand that youe think there was a bird-sange in my ere that made me alter my vayne', wrote Henry Lord Herbert (later Earl of Pembroke) to Henry Lord Paget. 'Yt is verye true the thing came not to youe wth owt the sight of m^r byrde, saving the last part wch he never sawe.' An undertone of respect in this correspondence confirms one's impression that Byrd moved easily among the Elizabethan aristocracy, and especially among the far from inconsiderable Catholic portions of it. Northumberland and Paget's brother Charles were both notorious conspirators on behalf of Mary, Queen of Scots.

In 1575 Byrd and Tallis secured a patent from the Crown for the printing and marketing of part-music and lined music paper, a trade with only a very limited history in England up to that time. They issued the famous *Cantiones, quae ab argumento sacrae vocantur*, comprising Latin motets for five to eight voices by both composers, and dedicated it with much ceremony to Queen Elizabeth. The prefatory matter, which includes a poem in Latin elegiacs by Richard Mulcaster, a foremost Elizabethan scholar and educator, praises the art of music, the queen and the two composers in lavish terms.

We need not take too seriously the further implication that the publication had been prepared to spread the fame of English music abroad. It has rather the air of a combination thank-offering to the queen and advertisement for the new business, furnished with patriotic rhetoric as a kind of insurance against the charge of promulgating music along with texts taken in some cases from the Roman liturgy (though to be sure, never with any explicit sectarian reference). Even the laboured title may have been composed with this in mind – 'Songs which are [strictly speaking not sacred but only] called sacred on account of their texts'.

Since Queen Elizabeth accepted the dedication of the *Cantiones*, it seems reasonable to suppose that the motets, or some of them, were sung in her Chapel Royal. They were surely written to be sung somewhere; and it is known that Elizabeth liked the Latin service. However this may be, the publication was a failure, and the chastened monopolists published nothing more for 13 years. In 1577 they complained to the queen that the patent was a source of little profit and petitioned for further benefits in terms which, said Fellowes, 'may be regarded as lacking a little in dignity'. Few Elizabethans would have regarded the matter in this light, and Byrd received the lease of the Manor of Longney in Gloucestershire – the source of another litigation in his old age. The audacity of this entire very interesting episode suggests that the driving force behind it was Byrd rather than Tallis.

His motets published in 1575 are full of musical audacities, too. Their variety of experimentation, novelty and expressive range must have dazzled contemporary musicians. Next to some of the older pieces already mentioned, which draw imaginatively on native traditions of church music, there is a newer group of penitential motets which show a significant foreign influence by way of Alfonso Ferrabosco, the prolific Italian composer (and, probably, spy) who was in England in Elizabeth's service intermittently between 1563 and 1578. (The two composers, exact contemporaries, wrote canons on the *Miserere* plainsong in a 'vertuous contention'. A seemingly unauthorized edition of these canons, *Medulla: Musicke sucked out of the sappe of two of the most famous musitians that ever were in this land*, was announced in 1603 but never published.) The son of Domenico Ferrabosco, an early madrigalist and sometime colleague of Palestrina in the Cappella Sistina choir, Alfonso as a motet composer had absorbed, a little stiffly, the early style of Lassus. Through Ferrabosco, Byrd came to understand – and became, it seems, the first English composer really to understand – classical Netherlands imitative polyphony.

One technique he learnt and used extensively was 'double imitation' (Andrews) – imitation based on a subject which, being moulded distinctively to two text fragments, breaks down into two sub-themes which can be developed and combined entirely flexibly. Byrd's *Domine, secundum actum meum* closely follows Ferrabosco's *Domine, secundum peccata mea* in this technique, though its artistic promise is perhaps realized fully only in motets of a slightly later period, such as *Domine, praestolamur* (ex.1; see Kerman, 1966). Notable here is the power Byrd achieved through the flexibility of the expositions of the first sub-theme, and the rhetorical

241

Ex.1

plan whereby the heart of the text-fragment ('adventum tuum') dominates at the end as a result of free strettos on the second. Technical innovations such as double imitation set Byrd's motets for the 1575 *Cantiones* apart from their neighbours by Tallis, fine as they are, as also from Byrd's own earlier work such as the big psalm settings or the Lamentations.

Equally new features in English composition were the use of highly expressive subjects in Byrd's penitential motets in the *Cantiones* volume of 1575, their long fluent paragraphs constructed in reference to melodic and harmonic goals, and the power with which these paragraphs are often balanced one with another. Ponderous though

242

they may be, and sometimes rough in counterpoint, these motets always convey more urgency and weight than do their models in Ferrabosco, something that is even more true of *Emendemus in melius*, an unusually intense (and concise) essay in affective homophony. This motet Byrd placed at the head of his first group in the publication, and it is one that is often found in copies by contemporary scribes.

Another very popular piece, the variations for five-part consort on the ground *Browning my dear*, was already being copied into manuscripts around 1580. The fecundity of invention shown throughout the 20 variations is astonishing, though hardly more so than the sheer contrapuntal brilliance and the secure layout of the architectural design. Large-scale keyboard master-pieces that represent a comparable level of technique are the Passing Measures Pavan and Galliard (based on the *passamezzo antico* ground) and the variations on the melody *Walsingham*. The development that led from *The Hunt's Up* to these works can be traced through several other grounds and variations, presumably dating from the 1570s.

In this decade Byrd also started his marvellous series of pavans and galliards for keyboard. 'The first that ever hee made' (MB 29), according to the Fitzwilliam Virginal Book (also according to the numbering in My Ladye Nevells Booke), exists in a version for five-part consort, and other early examples may be suspected of having a similar origin (MB 17 and 23). The result of this is a clear, solid basis in polyphony which provides unique richness in almost all Byrd's pavans and galliards – and a striking contrast or counterpoise to the brilliant, plastic figuration of the *repetenda*, or strain-variations. In addition, dance form offered him the opportunity for endless subtle manipulations of different rhythms and different phrase lengths, all within the prescribed limits of three times eight or (usually) three times 16 bars. It was a form that proved to be especially congenial to Byrd's genius.

II 1580–91

In this decade the musical harvest was even richer than it had been before, and it was richly gathered in in the great retrospective collections of his music that Byrd prepared between the years 1588 and 1591. It is natural to see these years as marking the end of one phase of his career. To envisage a 'period' as beginning around 1580 is admittedly more arbitrary. As it happens, the date 1581 is attached to some motets in a new style and also to the song *Why do I use my paper, ink and pen*, which sets a known seditious poem on the brutal execution on Tyburn Hill of Father Edmund Campion and two other Jesuits in that year (the stanzas Byrd set were not, of course, seditious ones). This event shook all England, not only the Roman Catholic community, and set off the grim chain of Elizabethan religious persecutions. It seems likely that for Byrd, as for many other English Catholics, 1581 became a year of decision and renewed commitment. At all events from around this time his involvement with the Catholic cause grew more serious.

Almost the only extant letters from Byrd are petitions (dated 1581) for assistance for a Catholic family in need as a result of persecution (see fig.11). At this period he lived in the parish of Harlington; here Juliana Byrd was cited for recusancy from 1577 on, usually in conjunc-

11. Autograph letter (17 Oct 1581) from Byrd petitioning for assistance for the Tempest family

tion with John Reason, a servant. During a raid on a Catholic household in 1583, Reason was caught while riding in to deliver a letter from Byrd along with some music. Though Byrd himself was not cited until 1585, lists of suspected recusant gathering-places name his house as early as 1580. In later years the composer and his family were repeatedly presented as recusants and once, in 1605, as long-time 'seducers' in the Catholic cause; at this time they were said to be excommunicated. Most striking of all is Byrd's recorded presence at a Berkshire house party in 1583 to welcome two of the most notorious of Jesuit missionaries, Fathers Henry Garnet and Robert Southwell, the poet. Only someone regarded (and trusted) very highly by the Catholic party would have been invited on this occasion. Byrd played the organ at another gathering at which Garnet was present, in 1605.

However, the report by Father Weston in 1586 that Byrd had sacrificed everything for his religion, including his position in the Chapel Royal, is puzzling if not altogether mistaken. This was the worst period for English Catholics, and it has been hazarded that he may have been forced into temporary semi-retirement; it was at just this time that his house at Harlington was twice searched and he was first presented for recusancy – perhaps because he was there rather than in London. In 1587 he was bound in recognizance of £200 to answer for his recusancy at Harlington (*CSPD*, cc no.59). But in 1586 and 1588 he was composing such 'official' pieces as *Rejoice unto the Lord* for Accession Day and *Look and bow down* on the defeat of the Spanish Armada (to words by Queen Elizabeth). Byrd and members of his family were marked down yearly for crippling fines for recusancy, but there appear to have been special concessions, for in a petition to the Earl of Salisbury (Hatfield House, Cecil Papers, Petitions 52), Byrd asked 'the Counsailes letter to Mr Atturney Generall to like effect and favor for his recusancye as the late gratious .Q.[ueen] and her Counsaile gave him'. Whether this favour stemmed from Elizabeth's own fondness for music we do not know, though it is pleasant to think so. What we do know is that Byrd had powerful friends. In 1605 he dedicated book 1 of the *Gradualia* to a member of the Privy Council, Northampton, thanking him specifically for assistance to himself and his family in need.

The Latin motet is intimately identified with Roman Catholicism, and it seems clear that at this time Byrd cultivated the form in a spirit of religious loyalty. Otherwise his increased output of motets in this decade – three times as many as he had written before – is difficult to explain. There were few opportunities in England for the public performance of Latin motets, especially with texts of the sort often chosen by Byrd. Many of these pieces must, in fact, be suspected of offering specific comfort to the English Catholic community. Some motets lament for Jerusalem at the time of the Babylonian captivity, some pray that the congregation may be liberated, others ring changes on the theme of the coming of God. In a few the hidden reference seems to be even more direct. Reading in *Deus, venerunt gentes* of the servants of the Lord whose bodies are thrown to the beasts of the earth and the fowls of heaven, to the shame of the psalmist, and in *Circumspice, Hierusalem* of the banished children of Jerusalem who return from the east bringing gladness, we can scarcely help thinking of Campion, Garnet, Southwell and the other Jesuit missionaries and martyrs.

By design, of course, the texts in question consist of blameless Bible extracts and the like. The hypothesis of a hidden meaning is not something that can be proved. Two considerations weigh in its favour, however. One is that Byrd also conveyed unmistakable pro-Catholic sentiments in certain English songs. The other is the large proportion of motet texts open to such an interpretation: about a third of the total.

The basic style of the new motets stems from the rich imitative polyphony of the earlier penitential motets. The counterpoint is now wonderfully supple and there is freer alternation between polyphony, semichoir work and homophony or half-homophony, notably in the frequent ending appeals 'Miserere', 'Domine, ne moreris', etc – always an impressive and moving feature of the motets in which they occur. The pieces are smoother and less ponderous than before, though many are still of monumental proportions. The 'Babylon' motets, all of which are very long, depart from this stylistic norm. In *Tribulationes civitatum* and *Ne irascaris, Domine* we hear for perhaps the first time Byrd's characteristic mild major-mode sonorities, with warm 6ths and 3rds and drawn-out pedal or ostinato effects, while in *Vide, Domine, afflictionem nostram* Phrygian progressions agitate the largely homophonic texture: an extreme, almost manneristic composition. *Ne irascaris* is found in two manuscripts dated 1581 and in many others. Purcell's copy of it has been preserved, and its second part, at least, is still very widely sung (*Civitas sancti tui*; in English, *Bow thine ear*).

It has recently been pointed out that *Civitas sancti tui*

is modelled on van Wilder's *Aspice, Domine*, a motet that circulated widely in England (Humphreys, 1979–80), that the Sanctus of Byrd's four-part mass is derived from Taverner's 'Meane' Mass (Brett, 1981) and that two of Byrd's late pavans and galliards (no.3 in C and no.2 in F) actually adopt ideas from younger composers, John Bull and Morley respectively (Neighbour, 1978). Almost certainly there is still much to be learnt about Byrd's relation to other composers, native and foreign, in the later as well as in the earlier periods of his career.

Of the greatest interest is an exchange of motets between Byrd and Philippe de Monte in 1583–4, attested to by the scribe of London, British Library, Add. MS 23264. Monte sent Byrd an eight-part motet with words selected from Psalm cxxxvii: 'By the waters of Babylon, there we sat down, yea, we wept . . . How shall we sing the Lord's song in a strange land?'. Using the same psalm, Byrd replied: 'How shall we sing the Lord's song in a strange land? If I forget thee, O Jerusalem, let my right hand forget her cunning' and to drive the point home he included in his motet a three-part canon by inversion.

He made a new effort to launch himself into the world of publishing in 1587. Both Tallis and Vautrollier, the printer of the 1575 *Cantiones*, had recently died, leaving Byrd in sole possession of the patent and perhaps also free to make more advantageous business arrangements. With the printer Thomas East as his assignee, Byrd now presided over the first great years of English music printing – great years in spite of his evident determination not to flood the market. When his patent expired in 1596 and went to Morley, an increased amount and a broader range of music began to be published. Byrd must have exerted strict control or even censorship during his years as monopolist.

His great initial success was the *Psalmes, Sonets and Songs* of 1588. This is only the third book of English songs ever known to have been published. The prefatory matter includes (besides the well-known 'Reasons . . . to perswade every one to learne to singe') a clear explanation that most of the songs had originally been for one voice and instrumental consort but had been adapted to words in all the five parts. Indeed, earlier consort-song versions of them survive in manuscript. By rescoring them, Byrd presumably meant to capitalize on the new vogue for madrigals, but he did not hesitate to designate the original sung line as 'the first singing part' in almost all cases.

The contents consist of grave 'Psalmes' and 'Songes of Sadnes and Pietie' and lighter 'Sonets and Pastorales', such as *Though Amaryllis dance in green* and *I thought that Love had been a boy*. Some were written in the 1580s (e.g. the fine Campion song and the two Sidney elegies) but an earlier date is quite possible for others, such as the ten metrical psalms and the *Lullaby*. So famous was this piece that the whole publication came to be known as 'Byrd's Lullabys'. It was intabulated for keyboard (probably not by Byrd) and mentioned in a letter of September 1602 by Worcester, who wrote rather grumpily that while Irish tunes were just then all the rage at court, 'in winter lullaby an owld song of Mr Birde wylbee more in request as I thinke'.

The 1588 set sold out and East actually printed two further editions in the same year, or at least before 1593. Byrd prepared a second songbook for publication in 1589, *Songs of Sundrie Natures*. This time he chose and converted only a few consort songs from his remaining stock; he seems to have composed a good deal of new music and also cast around for material of 'sundrie natures'. There is music for three, four, five and six parts. The book includes a consort song in its original form for voices and instruments, two carols, and the large and very fine verse anthem *Christ rising*, which was rewritten for the publication.

Although Byrd produced two excellent madrigals described as 'in the Italian vein' for the poet Thomas Watson's *First Sett of Italian Madrigalls Englished* (1590), in praise of 'Eliza ... beauteous Queen of Second Troy', the polyphonic songs published in 1589 are only slightly touched by the madrigal style which was fascinating England at that time, but which Byrd obviously found basically unsympathetic. If Henry Peacham is to be trusted, the chanson-like *Susanna fair* (no.2) and *The Nightingale* were written in another 'friendly aemulation' with Ferrabosco, that is, before 1578 (when Ferrabosco left England). The Ferrabosco chansons had just been printed in Nicholas Yonge's translated madrigal anthology *Musica transalpina* (1588), together with Byrd's rather curious consort song *The fair young virgin* on 'La virginella' from *Orlando furioso* – fitted with voices in all five parts and 'brought to speake English with the rest', as the title-page proudly announces.

In 1589 Byrd put out the first of his two new collections of motets. The *Cantiones sacrae* (for five voices), dedicated to Worcester, assembles motets which with few exceptions had been circulating in manuscript over the previous ten years or so, though for publication

Byrd touched them up slightly. The second book of *Cantiones sacrae* (for five and six voices) is more miscellaneous than the first, like the second of the English songbooks. It includes some rather old pieces such as *Domine, exaudi* and *Cunctis diebus* and some rather new ones such as *Domine, non sum dignus*, *Haec dies* and the popular *Laudibus in sanctis*. The unusual half-madrigalian style of the last motet was adopted to match the text, a 'literary' paraphrase of Psalm cl in Latin elegiac verse.

Byrd's fifth collection was not a publication but a manuscript, My Ladye Nevells Booke, dated 1591. (One branch of the Nevell family lived at Uxbridge, near Harlington, but the lady in question has not been identified for certain.) In this book Byrd preserved and, to an extent, ordered the best of his virginal music then written. It opens with two grounds composed specially for Lady Nevell – brilliant, concise pieces which were evidently Byrd's last essays in this ancient form. There follow two illustrative pieces, *The Battle* and *The Barley Break*, one a sort of 16th-century *Wellingtons Sieg* and the other a spring shower of irresistible little dance phrases. A little later comes a carefully chosen series of nine pavans, mostly with galliards, including the impressive canonic Pavan (MB 74) and the Pavan and Galliard Kinborough Good (a lady's name). Byrd included a number of quite old pieces that he still regarded highly, but he omitted the enormous early fantasias in favour of new examples of a more deft and concise nature (MB 25 and 46). Again, these appear to be the last keyboard fantasias that he composed.

One of Byrd's most imaginative compositions, the Quadran Pavan and Galliard, was not included in My

Ladye Nevells Booke, though as a companion piece to the Passing Measures Pavan and Galliard (the Quadran is based in a complex way on the *passamezzo moderno* ground) it is probably not much later. 'Excellent For matter', said Tomkins of this piece – a sample of typical English understatement – in contradistinction to the Quadran Pavan by Bull, which he considered 'Excellent For the Hand'. Another major work that did not find a place in the comprehensive anthologies of the time is the Great Service. Its mastery and its exuberance of style suggest a date of composition in the 1580s.

CHAPTER THREE

Late years

In 1593 Byrd moved further away from London to a rather large property in Stondon Massey, Essex, between Chipping Ongar and Ingatestone. Ingatestone and nearby Thorndon were the two seats of his patrons the Petres. It seems likely that Byrd and his family now joined the Catholic community presided over by the Petres and took part regularly in the undercover masses held at Ingatestone Hall. For these masses he composed some, if not all, of the *Gradualia*, as he makes clear in the dedication of book 2 to Lord Petre of Writtle (the contents have 'mostly proceeded from your house' and, having been 'plucked as it were from your gardens', are 'mostly rightfully due to you as tithes'). Byrd's famous settings of the Ordinary of the Mass were also probably written in the first instance for the Petre establishment.

Records of his immediate family are scarce, but from the inevitable recusancy entries it can be inferred that his first wife Juliana had died in about 1586 and his second wife Ellen in about 1606. His children were Christopher (*b* 1569; *d* before 1615), who married a granddaughter of Sir Thomas More; Elizabeth (*b* 1572); Thomas (1576–*c*1652), a godson of Tallis and also a musician, who spent some time at the Jesuit college at Valladolid; Rachel and Mary. 'Olde Mr Burdes three daughters' were cited as recusants in 1597 and should therefore have been at least 16 at that time; on the other hand, Mary in 1604 was described as 'puella'.

Presumably Byrd now spent less and less time in London. His name appears in none of the 20-odd lists of witnesses and petitioners recorded in the Cheque Book of the Chapel Royal from 1592 to 1623, only in two formal registers of all the members. He continued to compose, but his main efforts were directed away from London, where in any case new musical fashions reigned with which he was out of sympathy. A great deal of his time was consumed in litigation concerning the numerous leases he had acquired by grant or purchase. No fewer than six cases are known in which he was a principal, some of them very voluminous; the one concerning the Stondon Massey property dragged on for 17 years. The extensive extracts from legal documents quoted by Fellowes (*William Byrd*, pp.3ff, 11ff, 19ff) make very interesting reading.

In these documents Byrd does not always appear in too favourable a light, even after we have discounted the bias of his adversaries. As a litigant he was most tenacious, and indeed almost everything we know about his career suggests that he was an exceedingly tough-minded individual. It is like Byrd to have included the psalmist's vengeful verse 'Remember, O Lord, the children of Edom in the day of Jerusalem' in the 'Babylon' motet for Monte, one of his most personal. In his will there is pointed reference to a past quarrel with his daughter-in-law Catherine and to 'the undutifull obstinancie of one whome I am unwilling to name'. Obstinacy perhaps ran in the family – in personal affairs, in litigation and in religion.

After 1590 Byrd's attitude towards Latin sacred music underwent a significant change. The early motets were monumental and expressive; they were also personal in the sense that the texts represented the free choice of Byrd or his patrons – penitential meditations or outbursts in the first person singular as well as prayers, exhortations and protests on behalf of the Catholic community. He now started work on a grandiose scheme to provide music specifically for Catholic services. The texts were of course drawn from the appropriate sections of the liturgy, and the musical settings became much less monumental, in view of the liturgical context. This was a new way to serve the recusants' cause: practical, less personal, less self-indulgent. One wonders if it was forcefully suggested to Byrd by his Jesuit friends.

If this music was really to serve a practical purpose it had to be published. This took courage, even allowing for Byrd's connections in high places and the fact that he was in charge of music publishing. The three masses were printed between *c*1593 and *c*1595 separately, that is, in very slim books, without any title-pages (but coolly attributed to Byrd on all the pages; the publication dates, the subject of considerable speculation in the past, were established by Clulow using close bibliographical analysis). With the *Gradualia* of 1605, these halfhearted efforts at concealment were abandoned and the Catholic aspects of the book spelt out, indeed brazened out, in full detail. The political climate may well have appeared favourable in early 1605, but things changed with the Gunpowder Plot and there is record of someone being arrested for possessing *Gradualia* part-books. Byrd seems merely to have withdrawn the edition and stored the pages. He issued a second volume of *Gradualia* in 1607 and reissued both, with new title-pages, in 1610.

In musical style, the five-part mass is much simpler

and more concise than any of the five-part motets in the *Cantiones sacrae*. The three- and four-part masses are simpler still. They have relatively little word repetition, even in the shorter mass movements, and there is no place for the extended polyphonic periods that had given such intensity and grandeur to the earlier music. Despite some very well placed exceptions, such as the wonderful 'Dona nobis pacem' points in the four- and five-part masses, Byrd tended to avoid explicitly expressive setting, concentrating instead on more neutral, 'classic' musical material moulded with extreme care and beauty. In form, the masses are original, owing nothing to the imitation ('parody') technique that was universal on the Continent. Their head-motifs and frequent semichoir excursions recall English masses of a much earlier period.

Book 1 of the *Gradualia* contains music for three, four and five parts, book 2 for four, five and six (the concluding six-part mass for Sts Peter and Paul was evidently conceived as a gesture of Catholic solidarity and compliment to Petre – possibly for his ennoblement in 1603). An understanding of the collection presupposes close familiarity with the Roman liturgy that it serves. Many of the 100 items contained in the two *Gradualia* books should be regarded not as motets but rather as motet sections to be shuffled around, divided up and recombined according to the liturgical situation. The way in which this should be done is shown in the list of works. Byrd's total programme involved the provision of complete mass propers (introit, gradual, tract or alleluia, offertory, communion) for the major feasts of the church year, Marian feasts and Marian votive masses. When the same text occurs on two liturgical

257

occasions, he did not compose new music for the second but directed that his first setting should be transferred – sometimes with omissions or additions – from earlier in the book. (His rubrics are not complete or wholly consistent, but they are adequate to make his intention plain, as Jackman first showed.) Hence the 'motets' as printed are not always what they seem. To mention an extreme case, *Diffusa est gratia* should never be sung in its printed form, which is an artificial composite of several sections to be selected from in three different ways for three different services (see the list of works, under the Purification, Annunciation and Assumption).

To allow for such transfers, if for no other reason, the Propers and groups of related Propers hold to the same mode and vocal scoring. There are no other explicit unifying factors among the constituent pieces beyond a strong consistency of style, which incidentally shows that they were composed within a relatively short period (this is not true of the relatively small number of non-liturgical pieces included in the publications). The sustained effort represented by the *Gradualia* goes far beyond anything Byrd had attempted in his youth or middle years. Impressive, too, is the intricacy of the scheme, the sheer extent of it (it is larger than that of any analogous continental project) and the quality of the execution. The music is fluid, concise and effortless; simple binary structures and light homophonic phrases abound. Byrd was entirely at home with texts of a new kind, ecstatic and devotional in place of the predominantly penitential and lamenting texts of the earlier *Cantiones sacrae*.

Ex.2, from the gradual for the Nativity of the BVM, shows a typically quiet but subtle binary opening. The

Ex.2

text might conceivably have been treated in 'double imitation', but Byrd now had no time for this leisurely technique – new text fragments are starting to crowd in as early as bar 5 – and he used it only exceptionally in the late period. Even more sharply 'motivic' are the famous 'alleluia' phrases, of which the *Gradualia* provides over 80 examples and for which Byrd developed an extraordinary variety of symmetrical and sequential structures. The alleluias in *Sacerdotes*

259

Domini, Non vos relinquam orphanos, Constitues eos and other *Gradualia* numbers are among Byrd's most haunting passages.

One would dearly like to know in just how many Jacobean households Catholic Mass was celebrated in choir with music from the *Gradualia*. Appleton Hall in Norfolk was one, the home of Edward Paston, member of a distinguished family best known for the 15th-century 'Paston Letters'. At court in the 1570s Paston had been known as something of a poet, but he had soon retired to the quiet life of a country squire, a life that allowed him to practise the old religion with less interference and to indulge his hobbies, poetry and especially music. He had a mania for copying music; perhaps a third of all the surviving manuscripts of the time were written by his personal scribes, and we know from his will that cupboardsful of others existed which are now lost. A dozen anonymous consort songs in these manuscripts were identified as Byrd's by Dart and Brett. Several of the songs have topical poems by Paston which can be dated from 1596 to 1612, and the music shows that in his late years Byrd was constantly developing the consort-song style towards new flexibility and elaboration.

On Paston's instructions, no doubt, Byrd did not include any of these songs in his next and last published songbook, *Psalmes, Songs and Sonnets* (1611). The 67-year-old composer was engaging in a new flurry of publication; the years 1610–12 also saw the third edition of the 1589 songbook, reissues of the *Gradualia*, and *Parthenia*. The 1611 book includes jubilant full anthems (really motets in English), mournful verse anthems, six-part consort songs and polyphonic songs for three to five voices which are appreciably more madrigalian than those of 1589 (but still not very Italianate). In this thoroughly miscellaneous collection Byrd also included two fantasias for consort, one in four parts and one in six, perhaps with the idea of preserving the best of a genre that had not been anthologized in the period around 1590. He missed out the very fine five-part canonic Fantasia in C, of which a keyboard version had appeared in My Ladye Nevells Booke.

The published fantasias seem to date from the 1590s. In the six-part one, and in another similar work in manuscript, Byrd worked out a remarkable large-scale form consisting of what are in essence linked movements, contrasting with one another and culminating in a galliard followed by a coda. The manuscript fantasia also includes snatches of pre-existing melodies – *Greensleeves* and perhaps others – as also happens in several other of the consort and keyboard pieces. This phenomenon should be considered along with Byrd's celebration of popular songs in his variation sets. He was closer to 'folksong', it would seem, than any of the other great composers of early times.

Byrd's late keyboard music is full of new fantasy and new subtlety. He turned to writing mostly pavans and galliards, though three of the most imaginative variations also appear to date from after 1590, *Go from my window*, *John come kiss me now* and *O mistress mine, I must*. When at last he found occasion to have some keyboard music published, in *Parthenia*, *c*1612/13, jointly with Bull and Gibbons, he included only pavans and galliards and some short matching preludes. The Pavan and Galliard Sir William Petre spans the entire late period. Presumably it was written in 1591, for it was included in My Ladye Nevells Booke as a last-minute addition outside the main series of pavans; 20 years later it was the one old composition to be printed in *Parthenia*. The cogent linear and contrapuntal articulation of this superb dance pair can be gathered from ex.3, the opening strain of the pavan, without the ornamented *repetendum*; only a much longer example could show how, beyond this, keyboard texture is used in a much more integral fashion than before.

Ex.3

Keyboard figuration, too, became more flexible in the works dating from Byrd's late years, no doubt under the impetus of younger members of the English virginal school that Byrd had founded. The intricate Galliard Mistress Mary Brownlow and the limpid Pavan and Galliards The Earl of Salisbury, which appeared for the first time in *Parthenia*, show new prospects opening up to Byrd's imagination in the very last of his keyboard compositions.

His last printed works were four quiet sacred songs contributed to Sir William Leighton's *Teares or Lamentacions of a Sorrowful Soule* in 1614. Byrd died at Stondon Massey on 4 July 1623, a man of some means, and was presumably buried in the parish churchyard according to the wish expressed in his will, though the grave has not been located. The will also states that he had apartments in the London house of the Earl of Worcester, suggesting that he may have served as a personal musician – by then emeritus, no doubt – in the retinue of his old patron. He also had a chamber in the Petres' house at West Thorndon. The only known portrait of Byrd dates from about 1729 and is not to be trusted.

CHAPTER FOUR

Byrd in his time and ours

Byrd retained a fondness for the jog-trot 'plain style' poetry of the 1560s throughout his life, from the earliest consort songs to the pieces written for Leighton. This may serve as a reminder that, although he composed steadily throughout Elizabeth's reign and well into James's, he was essentially an early Elizabethan figure. He belonged to the generation of Sidney, Hooker and Nicholas Hilliard, not that of Shakespeare, Dowland and Bacon. He was as impervious to late Elizabethan elegance, euphuistic or Italianate, as he was to the subsequent Jacobean 'disenchantment'. Decorum, solidity and a certain reticence of expression were qualities that were prized in his formative years, qualities that came to him naturally.

He belonged to the pioneer generation that built Elizabethan culture. In music, Byrd did this alone, for unlike Tallis before him and Morley after, he had no immediate contemporaries of any stature (except of course Ferrabosco). The essential work was completed by the time of the Armada, as he himself seems to have acknowledged by his retrospective anthologizing at that time. He lived to write some of his greatest music later, but his younger contemporaries could not learn from this in the same way that they had from the earlier path-breaking compositions.

In recording his death, the ordinarily laconic Cheque

Book of the Chapel Royal described him as 'a Father of Musick'. To another contemporary admirer he was 'Brittanicae Musicae Parens'. While Byrd's versatility as a composer is often mentioned, and quite rightly, it is less often pointed out how much he indeed fathered for English music. With his motets, first of all, he achieved nothing less than the naturalization of the high Renaissance church style. The true power and expressiveness of imitative counterpoint had never been channelled in native composition before his motets of the 1575 *Cantiones*. As has been remarked, he rather stood back from the madrigal; but he was the first English composer who employed word illustration extensively – in motets of the 1580s such as *Deus, venerunt gentes* and *Vigilate*. He found the English song in the 1560s in a dishevelled state and pulled it together to produce a rich and extensive repertory of consort songs, a form that was very personal to Byrd and found no serious imitators. Its influence on the lute air, however, was palpable, and a relative of the consort song, the verse anthem, might be said to constitute Byrd's most lasting legacy to English music, at least in one sense. Verse anthems, of which he had provided the most authoritative models – he even wrote a 'verse' service – were composed and sung widely during his lifetime and for long after it.

He kindled English virginal music from the driest of dry wood to a splendid blaze that crackled on under Bull and Gibbons and even lit some sparks on the Continent. Even his later music for consort, which was overshadowed at the turn of the century by the new fantasias of John Coprario and the younger Alfonso Ferrabosco, provided a seminal idea of considerable importance. The crystallization of dance movements out of the sections of Byrd's two six-part fantasias looks forward to the fantasy suites of the 1620s and beyond.

Byrd's earlier music for consort represents a culmination of an older tradition. Brought up during the reign of Queen Mary, perhaps even in her Chapel Royal, he had live roots in Tudor soil. Traditional elements live on in his music along with innovatory ones: the Redfordian flashes in even some of the later keyboard works, the echoes of Robert Fayrfax and Taverner in some of the *Gradualia* motets, and especially certain technical features such as 'irregular' dissonance treatment, 6-5 harmonic progressions, and unison ostinatos or rotas. There are pieces in which these features have to a large extent been filtered out, such as *Siderum rector* from the 1575 *Cantiones* and the four-part mass, but Byrd deliberately returned to a more archaic, rougher technique as better suited to the grain of his musical personality. Sometimes he turned archaic features to exquisite effect. The point about the familiar beginning of *Ave verum corpus* from the *Gradualia* is not simply that it illustrates 'the vicious English taste for false relations', as Tovey was pleased to call it, but that this is used in such a fresh way.

Byrd's musical mind is as hard to characterize in a few words as that of any other of the great composers. Though he was 'naturally disposed to Gravitie and Pietie', in Peacham's famous phrase, there is no music at the time that projects such exuberance and gaiety as his marvellous English motets published in 1611, his sparkling keyboard galliards and his blithe 'pastorals' in the old consort-song tradition. He was always doing something unexpected. He is probably to be regarded as one of the more intellectual of composers, and yet he also had a magic touch with sonority, as witness such diverse works as the pellucid *Callino casturame*, the *Browning* for consort, *Iustorum animae* from the *Gradualia* and *Domine, quis habitabit*, a motet (in manuscript) for nine voices including three basses.

One admires most, perhaps, his manifold ways of moulding a phrase, a period or a total piece. Line, motif, counterpoint, harmony, texture, figuration can all be brought into play, and they are brought not singly but in ever new combinations. Form was expression for Byrd, and the extraordinary variety of effect that he obtained in his pieces stemmed from his fertile instinct for shape, for musical construction.

Morley and Tomkins were his pupils. If, as seems likely, Peter Philips, Thomas Weelkes and Bull were too, Byrd's direct impact on English composition can be seen to have assumed almost Schoenbergian proportions. Much of his teaching must surely be preserved in Morley's *Plaine and Easie Introduction to Practicall Musicke*, 1597, which also contains some of the many remarkable tributes to Byrd known from the period. His contemporary reputation was not as commanding as, say, that of Sidney in another artistic field or Josquin in another century. But it was still something new in English music, and there can be little doubt that it went along with a sense of artistic mission on Byrd's part that was also new. We can detect this in the way he went about anthologizing his best work, in his frequent rewriting of old pieces, and in his tendency to go back to a problem that he had not quite mastered in one piece and attack it in another: *Tribue, Domine* and *Infelix ego*, *The Hunt's Up* and *Hugh Aston's Ground*, the two six-part consort fantasias.

After Byrd's death it was his Anglican music that survived. Interest in his Latin church music was revived by the antiquarians who scored many of his motets in the 18th century. In the 1840s the Musical Antiquarian Society issued scores of the five-part mass and book 1 of the *Cantiones sacrae*, with bowdlerizations by Rimbault and editorial lectures by the insufferable Horsley. The modern revival of this music dates essentially from Terry's regime at Westminster Cathedral in 1901–24, when it seems that the entire corpus was sung, and the subsequent publication of *Tudor Church Music*, including much of the Latin church music and all of the English. Thanks to the efforts of many conductors in the intervening generations, Byrd now has a special place in the hearts and the ears of English and American choral singers. According to Squire (*Grove 4*), it was the attention drawn to Byrd in the 1880s and 1890s that began the 'recent revival of interest in the music of Tudor and Jacobean composers'.

Burney printed *The Carman's Whistle*, and Ambros wrote luminously of Byrd's keyboard music. But the general appreciation of this can hardly be said to have begun until the landmark edition of the Fitzwilliam Virginal Book by Fuller Maitland and Squire in 1899, reinforced by Hilda Andrews's edition of My Ladye Nevells Booke in 1926. Meanwhile the three English song-books were published in Fellowes's English Madrigal School (only the *Songs of Sundrie Natures* had been obtainable before, in Arkwright's Old English Edition). A complete edition was undertaken by Fellowes late in life (1937–50): at last virtually all of Byrd's music was made available in one place, in a form designed to encourage performance. Fellowes's editorial work, however, lacked sophistication, and a revision by a new generation of scholars was begun as early as 1962.

Fellowes's *William Byrd* presents extensive biographical material and a useful preliminary survey of the music. H. K. Andrews made an exhaustive study of *The Technique of Byrd's Vocal Polyphony*. A comprehensive study of Byrd's music is in preparation by Philip Brett, Joseph Kerman and Oliver Neighbour.

WORKS

Editions/ *The Collected Works of William Byrd*, ed. E. H. Fellowes (London, 1937–50) [F]; rev. under general ed. T. Dart (London, 1962–70) [D]

W. *Byrd: English Church Music, Part I*, ed. P. C. Buck and others, TCM, ii (1927) [TCM ii]
W. *Byrd: Gradualia, Books I and 2*, ed. P. C. Buck and others, TCM, vii (1927) [TCM vii]
W. *Byrd: Masses, Cantiones and Motets*, ed. P. C. Buck and others, TCM, ix (1928) [TCM ix]
W. *Byrd: Psalms Sonnets and Songs of Sadness and Piety*, ed. E. H. Fellowes, rev. P. Brett, EM, xiv (2/1963) [= D xii]
W. *Byrd: Songs of Sundry Natures*, ed. E. H. Fellowes, rev. P. Brett, EM, xv (2/1962) [= D xii]
W. *Byrd: Psalms, Songs and Sonnets*, ed. E. H. Fellowes, rev. T. Dart, EM, xvi (2/1964) [= D xiv]
W. *Byrd: Keyboard Music I*, ed. A. Brown, MB, xxvii (1969, rev. 2/1976)
W. *Byrd: Keyboard Music II*, ed. A. Brown, MB, xxviii (1971, rev. 2/1976)
The Byrd Edition, general ed. P. Brett (London, 1970–) [B] [incl. D xv, xvii]
W. *Byrd: Music for the Lute*, ed. N. North (London, 1976) [15 transcrs. for lute of kbd and vocal works, and doubtful works]

* – inc. but can be reconstructed   † – known in earlier consort song version, pubd in B xvi

Numbers in right-hand margins denote references in the text.

PRINTED LATIN MUSIC

Cantiones, quae ab argumento sacrae vocantur, 5–8vv (London, 1575), with Tallis [C], F i, TCM ix, B i   235, 237–40, 238, 242, 265, 266

Liber primus sacrarum cantionum [Cantiones sacrae], 5vv (London, 1589) [CS i], D ii   251–2, 258, 268

Liber secundus sacrarum cantionum [Cantiones sacrae], 5–6vv (London, 1591) [CS ii], D iii, B iii   252, 257

Mass, 4vv, c1592–3, F i, 30, TCM ix, 17, B iv, 24   249, 256–7, 266
Mass, 3vv, c1593–4, F i, 1, TCM ix, 3, B iv, 1   256–7
Mass, 5vv, c1595, F i, 68, TCM ix, 36, B iv, 63   256–7, 268

Gradualia ac cantiones sacrae, 3–5vv (London, 1605) [G vol./part no.] F iv–v, TCM vii   247, 256–60, 266, 267

Gradualia seu cantionum sacrarum, liber secundus, 4–6vv (London, 1607) [G ii], F vi–vii, TCM vii   256–60, 266

A list of contents of the Gradualia is given to show the various mass cycles which Byrd had in mind. Motets and motet sections moved from their original positions are in brackets.

Vol.i: Part I, 5vv
Purification of the BVM: 1. int, Suscepimus Deus, v. Magnus Dominus; [grad, Suscepimus Deus . . . terrae, from 1;] 2. grad v., Sicut audivimus; 3. all v., Senex puerum portabat . . . regebat, replaced in Lent by 4. tr, Nunc dimittis servum tuum; [off, Diffusa est gratia, from 22;] 5. comm, Responsum accepit Simeon   258

Nativity of the BVM: 6. int, Salve sancta parens (without 'alleluia'), v. Eructavit cor meum: 7. grad, Benedicta et venerabilis; 8. grad v., Virgo Dei genetrix; 9. all v., Felix es, sacra virgo; 10. off, Beata es, virgo Maria (without 'alleluia'); 11. comm, Beata viscera (without 'alleluia')

Saturday Lady Masses in Advent: 12. int, Rorate coeli, v. Benedixisti Domine; 13. grad, Tollite portas, v. Quis ascendit; 14. all v., Ave Maria . . . fructus ventris tui (correct liturgical text: Ave Maria . . . in mulieribus, as in 20); [off, 14. Ave Maria (without 'alleluia')] 15. comm, Ecce virgo concipiet (without 'alleluia')

Saturday Lady Masses from Christmas to Purification: 16. int, Vultum tuum (without 'alleluia'), [v. Eructavit, from 6;] 17. grad, Speciosus forma, [v. Eructavit, from 6,] Lingua me; 18. all v., Post partum; 19. off, Felix namque es; [comm, 11. Beata viscera (without 'alleluia')]

Saturday Lady Masses from Purification to Easter: [int, 6. Salve sancta parens (without 'alleluia'), v. Eructavit; grad, 7–8. Benedicta es, v. Virgo Dei genetrix;] all, Virga Jesse, from 20, replaced in Lent (rubric wrongly placed before 20 in original) by 21. tr, Gaude Maria; [off, 19. Felix namque es; comm, 11. Beata viscera (without 'alleluia')]   258

Saturday Lady Masses in Paschal time: [int, 6. Salve sancta parens, v. Eructavit; alls, 20. Alleluia, Ave Maria, Alleluia, Virga Jesse (correct liturgical order is Alleluia, Virga Jesse. Alleluia, Ave

Maria); off, 10. Beata es, virgo Maria; comm, 11. Beata viscera]

Saturday Lady Masses from Pentecost to Advent: [int, 6. Salve sancta parens (without 'alleluia'), v. Eructavit; grad, 7-8. Benedicta et venerabilis; all, 18. Alleluia, Post partum; off, 14. Ave Maria ... ventris tui (without 'alleluia'); comm, 11. Beata viscera (without 'alleluia')]

Annunciation of the BVM: [int, 16. Vultum tuum ('alleluia' only in Paschal time), v. Eructavit, from 6;] 22. grad, Diffusa est gratia, v. Propter veritatem, runs into tr, [22.] Audi filia (without 'alleluia'); grad and tr replaced in Paschal time by [alls, 20. Alleluia, Ave Maria. Alleluia, Virga Jesse; off, 14. Ave Maria; comm, 15. Ecce virgo ('alleluias' only in Paschal time)]

Assumption of the BVM: 23. int, Gaudeamus omnes, [v. Eructavit, from 6; grad, Propter veritatem, v. Audi filia ... speciem tuam. Alleluia, from 22;] [23.] all v., Assumpta est Maria ... angelorum; 24. off, Assumpta est Maria ... Dominum; 25. comm, Optimam partem elegit

Non-liturgical: 26. Adoramus te, Christe; 27. Unam petii a Domino; 28. Plorans ploravit

Feast of All Saints: 29. int, Gaudeamus omnes, v. Exultate iusti; 30. grad, Timete Dominum, v. Inquirentes autem, runs into all, [30.] Alleluia, Venite ad me; 31. off, Iustorum animae; 32. comm, Beati mundo corde

Part II, 4vv

Corpus Christi: 1. int, Cibavit eos, v. Exultate Deo; 2. grad, Oculi omnium, v. Aperis tu manum tuam, runs into all, [2.] Alleluia, Caro mea; 3. off, Sacerdotes Domini; 4. comm, Quotiescunque manducabitis; at Benediction of the Blessed Sacrament: 5. seq, Ave verum corpus; 6. hymn, O salutaris hostia; 7. ant, O sacrum convivium; 8. hymn, [Pange lingua ... misterium] Nobis datus

Miscellaneous and office texts: 9. Ecce quam bonum est; 10. Christus resurgens; 11. Visita quaesumus, Domine; 12. Salve regina; 13. Alma Redemptoris mater; 14. Ave regina caelorum; 15. In manus tuas, Domine; 16. Laetania; 17. Salve sola Dei genetrix

Purification of the BVM: 18. ant, Senex puerum portabat ... adoravit; 19. ant, Hodie Beata Virgo Maria
20. Deo gratias

Part III, 3vv

Marian hymns: 1. Quam terra, pontus, aethera; 2. O gloriosa Domina; 3. Memento, salutis auctor; 4. Ave maris stella

Chants for the Easter season: 5. Regina coeli; 6. Alleluia, [Vespere autem sabbati] quae lucescit; 7. Haec dies; 8. Angelus Domini descendit de coelo; 9. Post dies octo; 10. Turbarum voces in passione Domini secundum Ioannem
11. Adorna thalamum tuum

Vol.ii: 4vv

Nativity of our Lord Jesus Christ: 1. int, Puer natus est, v. Cantate Domino; 2. grad, Viderunt ... omnis terra, v. Notum fecit Dominus; 3. all v., Dies sanctificatus; 4. off, Tui sunt coeli; 5. comm, Viderunt ... Dei nostri; 6. ant, Hodie Christus natus est; 7. ant, O admirabile commercium (Magnat for Circumcision, not Christmas): 8. re, O magnum misterium; 9. repetendum and v., Beata virgo

Epiphany: 10. int, Ecce advenit dominator Dominus, v. Deus iuditium; 11. off, Reges Tharsis; 12. comm, Vidimus stellam

Votive Mass of the Blessed Sacrament (for main chants see Corpus Christi, G i/II 1-4): 13. tr, Ab ortu solis, v.2, 14. Venite, comedite panem meum (replaces all in Lent); 15. grad v., Surge, illuminare, Ierusalem (should follow 10 as grad v. for Epiphany); 16. alls, Alleluia, Cognoverunt (replaces grad Oculi omnium in Paschal time); Alleluia, Caro mea; 17. ant, Ego sum panis vivus; 18. ant, O quam suavis est; 19. hymn, Iesu nostra redemptio

5vv

Easter day: 20. int, Resurrexi, v. Domine probasti me; 21. grad, Haec dies, v. Confitemini Domino, runs into all v., [21.] Pascha nostrum ... Christus. Alleluia; 22. seq, Victimae paschali laudes; 23. off, Terra tremuit; 24. comm, Pascha nostrum ... veritatis. Alleluia

Ascension of our Lord: 25. int, Viri Galilei, v. Omnes gentes, plaudite; 26. all, Alleluia, Ascendit Deus; 27. all v., Dominus in Sina; 28. off, Ascendit Deus; 29. comm, Psallite Domine; 30. ant, O Rex gloriae

Pentecost: 31. int, Spiritus Domini, v. Exsurgat Deus; 32. all, Alleluia, Emitte spiritum tuum; 33. all v., Veni, Sancte Spiritus, reple; 34. off, Confirma hoc, Deus; 35. comm, Factus est repente de coelo

258

258

OTHER ENGLISH MUSIC

Title	No. of vv	Source	Modern edition	Remarks
A feigned friend	4	PSS ii 11	D xiv, 54	
Ah, golden hairs	1, 4 viols	*GB-Lbm, Och, Ob*	B xv, 51	Consort song; text after J. de Montemayor
Ah, youthful years	1, 5 viols	PSS ii 31	D xiv, 225	
Alack, when I look back	—	*Lbm*	B xvi, 175	Consort song; lute arr. only
	1/5, org	*DRc, Lbm, Lcm, Llp, Ob, Och, Ojc, T*	F xi, 98, TCM ii, 223	Anthem; text: W. Hunnis
All as a sea	5	*US-NYp* Drexel 4180-84	B xi, 93	Also as consort song
All ye people, clap your hands [= Alleluia, Ascendit Deus]	5	*US-NYp* Drexel 4180-84	D xii, 150	
Although the heathen poets	5	PSS i 21	D xii, 110	Fragment
Ambitious love	5	PSS i 18	D xii, 90	
An aged dame	1, 4 viols	*GB-Lbm, US-CA*	B xv, 119	Consort song; text: G. Whitney
And think ye, nymphs, to scorn at love?	5	SSN 42–3	D xiii, 245	
An earthly tree (chorus Cast off all doubtful care)	2/4, 4 viols	SSN 40, 25	D xiii, 145	'A Carowle for Christmas day'
Arise, Lord, into thy rest	5	PSS ii 18	D xiv, 88	Ps cxxxii.8–9
Arise, O Lord, why sleepest thou? [= Exsurge]	5	*GB-Cp, Ob*	—	

Title	No. of vv	Source	Modern edition	Remarks
Arise, O Lord, why sleepest thou?	5-6	Cpc, Cu (formerly EL), DRc, GL, Lbm, Lcm, Llp, Och, Ojc, T, Y, US-NYp	F xi, 148, TCM ii 227, B xi, 1	Anthem; Ps xliv.23-4, lxxix.9
As Caesar wept	1, 4 viols	GB-Lbm, Ob, US-CA	B xv, 54	Consort song
As I beheld I saw a herdman wild	5	PSS i 20	D xii, 101	Ps cxliii.1-2
Attend mine humble prayer	3	SSN 7	D xiii, 38	
Awake, mine eyes	4	PSS ii 12	D xiv, 59	Ps cxxxiii.1-2
Behold how good a thing	6	SSN 38-9	D xiii, 225	Consort song; lute arr. only
Behold, how good	—	GB-Lbm	B xvi, 175	
Behold, I bring you [= Ne irascaris]	5	Cp	—	
Behold, now praise the Lord [=Laudate pueri]	6	Lbm, T	F xvi, 138	
Behold, O God, the sad and heavy case [= Now Israel may say]	2/5, org	DRc	F xi, 103, TCM ii, 233, B xi, 104	Anthem
Be not wroth very sore [= Civitas sancti tui]	5	Lsp, Ob, US-AUS		Arr. probably by Aldrich (see US-AUS, Gosling MS)
Be unto me, O Lord, a tower of strength	4	1614'	F xi, 1	
Blame I confess [= Remember, Lord]	1, 4 viols	GB-Och	B xv, 56	Consort song
Blessed art thou, O Lord [= Tribulatio proxima est]	5	Y M.29(S)		One part only
†Blessed is he that fears the Lord	5	PSS i 8	D xii, 44	Ps cxii
Bow thine ear [=Civitas sancti tui]	5	Cfm, WB	F xi, 155	248-9
†Care for thy soul	5	PSS i 31	D xii, 165	
Cease, cares (another chorus to An Earthly tree)	—	Lbm Add.31992	B xvi, 176	Consort song; lute arr. only
Christ rising again	6	SSN 46-7	D xiii, 280, B xi, 120	'The Easter Anthem'; text: I Corinthians xv.20-22, Romans vi.9-11; also in earlier version 251
Come help, O God	5	1614'	F xi, 8	
Come, jolly swains	4	PSS ii 13	D xiv, 63	
Come, let us rejoice unto our Lord	4	PSS ii 16	D xiv, 75	Ps xcv.1-2
Come, pretty babe	1, 4 viols	US-NYp	B xv, 59	Consort song
†Come to me, grief, for ever	5	PSS i 34	D xii, 190	
Come, woeful Orpheus	5	PSS ii 19	D xiv, 98	

Title	Voices/viols	MS sources	Printed edn	Collected edn ref	Notes
Compel the hawk to sit	5		SSN 28	D xiii, 178	Text: T. Churchyard
†Constant Penelope	5		PSS I 23	D xii, 117	Text after Ovid: Heroïdes i.1–8
Content is rich	1, 4 viols	GB-Lbm, US-CA	PSS ii 22	B xv, 63	Consort song; anon. in sources
Crowned with flowers	5	GB-Lbm, Lcm, US-CA		D xiv, 125	Consort song in memory of Queen Mary I
Crowned with flowers and lilies	1, 4 viols	GB-Lbm, US-CA		B xv, 100	Consort song
Delight is dead	2, 3 viols	GB-Lbm, Lcm, US-NYp		B xv, 107	Consort song
Depart, ye furies	—	GB-Lbm		B xvi, 177	Consort song; lute arr. only
E'en as in seas	1, 4 viols	Lbm		B xv, 66	Consort song; anon. in source
Even from the depth	5		PSS i 10	D xii, 53	Ps cxxx.1
•Exalt thyself, O God	6	Ojc, T, WO Ms A3.3 (T part and inc. score), Y		F xvi, 140 (Ojc only), Y; B xi, 11	Ps lvii.6, 9–12
Fair Britain isle	1, 4 viols	Lbm		B xv, 124	Consort song, on the death in 1612 of Henry, Prince of Wales; anon. in source
†Farewell, false love	5		PSS I 25	D xii, 131	Text attrib. Raleigh
From Citheron the warlike boy is fled	4		SSN 19–21	D xiii, 105	
From depth of sin	3		SSN 6	D xiii, 32	Ps cxxx.1–2
From virgin's womb (chorus Rejoice, rejoice)	1/4, 4 viols		SSN 35, 24	D xiii, 135	'A Carowle for Christmas day'
•Have mercy on us, Lord	1, 4 viols	Lbm		B xv, 8	Consort song; Ps lxvii
•Have mercy upon me, O God	1/6, 4 viols		PSS ii 25	D xiv, 154	Ps li.1–2
Hear my prayer	1/5, org	1641[5]: org, DRc, Lcm, Llp, Ob, Och, Ojc, T, Y, US-NYp		F xi, 122, TCM ii, 238, B xi, 129	Anthem, 'For a meane alone'; Ps cxliii.1–2
Help, Lord, for wasted are those men	5		SSN 17	D xii, 38	Ps xii
Help us, O God	6	GB-Cpc, DRc, GL, Lbm, Llp, Och, Ojc, T, Y, US-NYp		B x, 6	Ps lxxix.9; 2p. of Arise, O Lord, often alone in MSS
He that all earthly pleasure scorns	1, 4 viols	GB-Lbm		B xv, 128	Consort song; anon. in source
How long shall mine enemies triumph	5	Cp, DRc, Lbm, Och, Ojc, SHR, T, Y, US-CA, NYp		F xi, 12, TCM ii, 242, B xi, 25	Anthem; Ps xiii.2–5
†How shall a young man	5		PSS i 4	D xii, 20	Ps cxix.9–16
How vain the toils	1, 5 viols		PSS ii 32	D xiv, 233	

Title	No. of vv	Source	Modern edition	Remarks
O Lord, turn thy wrath [= Ne irascaris]	5	1641⁵		
	5	PSS i 6	D xii, 32	Ps xv
†O Lord, who in thy sacred tent	5	GB-Och, T	B xv, 1	Consort song; Ps xv
O Lord, within thy tabernacle	5	Lbm, US-CA	F xvi, 34	
O sweet deceit	5	PSS i 35	D xii, 194	Text attrib. E. Dyer
†O that most rare breast	5	GB-Lbm, Ob, US-CA	B xv, 28	Consort song
O that we woeful wretches	1, 4 viols	GB-Lbm, Lcm, US-CA	B xv, 31	Consort song; anon. in sources
Out of the orient crystal skies	1, 4 viols	PSS i 16	D xii, 78	Text: Sidney
†O you that hear this voice	5	SSN 27	D xiii, 168	
Penelope that longed for the sight	5	PSS ii 29	D xiv, 199	Ps cxvii
Praise our Lord, all ye Gentiles	6	1641⁵; GB-Cpc, DRc, GL (Bassus), Lbm, Llp, Ob, Och, Ojc, Y, US-NYp	F xi, 52, TCM ii, 277, B xi, 69	Anthem: 'The fourth Prayer after the Communion before the Blessing'
Prevent us, O Lord	5			
†Prostrate, O Lord, I lie	5	PSS i 27	D xiii, 143	
Rejoice, rejoice: see From virgin's womb	4	SSN 24	D xiii, 141	
Rejoice unto the Lord	1, 4 viols	GB-Lbm, T, US-CA	B xv, 37	Consort song, 1586
Remember, Lord [= Blame I confess]	—	GB-Lbm, US-CA	B xv, 56	Consort song, inc; only title remains
Retire, my soul	5	PSS ii 17	D xiv, 81	Ps xxxii.1-2
Right blest are they	3	SSN 2	D xiii, 7	
Save me, O God, for thy Name's sake	5	GB-Cpc, Cu (formerly EL), DRc, Lbm, Ob, Och, Ojc, T, WB, Y, US-NYp	F xi, 57, TCM ii, 266, B xi, 75	Anthem; Ps liv.1-4
†See those sweet eyes	5	SSN 29, 34	D xiii, 188	
Sing joyfully unto God our strength	6	1641⁵; org: GB-Cp, Cpc, Cu (formerly EL), DRc, GL (Bassus), Ob, Och, Ojc, T, Y, US-NYp	F xi, 90, TCM ii, 288, B xi, 82	Anthem; Ps lxxxi.1-4
Sing we merrily unto God	5	PSS ii 20-21	D xiv, 106	Ps lxxxi.1-2
Sing ye to our Lord	3	PSS ii 6	D xiv, 24	Ps cxlix.1-2
Sith death at length	1, 4 viols	GB-Lbm, US-CA	B xv, 78	Consort song
*Sith that the tree	1, 4 viols	GB-Lbm	B xv, 81	Consort song; 2p. in lute arr. only

†Susanna fair	5	PSS i 29	D xii, 154	Text after G. Guéroult: Susanne ung jour	
Susanna fair	3	SSN 8	D xiii, 46	Text after G. Guéroult: Susanne ung jour	251
The eagle's force	3	PSS ii 1	D xiv, 1	Text: T. Churchyard	251
The fair young virgin [= La virginella]	5	1588³⁹	F xvi, 1	Text after Ariosto	
The greedy hawk	3	SSN 14	D xiii, 77	Text: G. Whitney	
•The Lord is only my support	1, 4 viols	Lbm	B xv, 5	Consort song; Ps xxiii	
The man is blest	1, 4 viols	Lbm, T	B xv, 11	Consort song; Ps cxii	
The match that's made	5	PSS i 26	D xii, 137		
The nightingale	3	SSN 9	D xiii, 52		251
The noble famous queen [= While Phoebus us'd to dwell]	1, 4 viols	Lbm, US-CA	B xv, 97	Consort song, on the death of Mary, Queen of Scots	
This day Christ was born	6	PSS ii 27	D xiv, 178	'A Carroll for Christmas Day'	
This sweet and merry month of May	6	1590³⁹	D xiv, 240	Text attrib. T. Watson	
This sweet and merry month of May	4	1590³⁹, PSS ii 9	D xiv, 42	Text attrib. T. Watson	250
†Though Amaryllis dance in green	5	PSS i 12	D xii, 60	Consort song; anon. in source	
Though I be Brown	1, 4 viols	GB-Lbm	B xv, 144	Anthem, 'A Prayer for the King'; text: Hunnis	
Thou God that guid'st	2/5, org	1641⁸; org: Cu (formerly EL), DRc, Lcm, Llp, Och, Ojc, T, Y, US-NYp	F xi, 128, TCM ii, 296, B xi, 148		
•Thou poet's friend	1, 4 viols	GB-Lcm	B xv, 84	Consort song	
Triumph with pleasant melody	1, 4 viols	Lbm, Ob, Och	B xv, 43	Consort song	
•Truce for a time	1, 4 viols	Lbm, Ob	B xv, 87	Consort song	
Truth at the first	1, 4 viols	Lbm, US-CA	B xv, 90	Consort song; anon. in sources	
Turn our captivity, O Lord	6	PSS ii 30	D xiv, 211	Ps cxxvi.5-7	
Unto the hills mine eyes I lift	6	SSN 45	D xiii, 264	Ps cxxi	
Upon a summer's day	3	SSN 12-13	D xiii, 68		
Wedded to will is witless	5	PSS ii 23	D xiv, 134		
Weeping full sore	5	SSN 26	D xiii, 155		
What is life?	4	PSS ii 14	D xiv, 68		
What pleasure have great princes?	5	PSS i 19	D xii, 96		
What pleasure have great princes?	5	GB-Lbm	B xvi, 60	Anon. MS composition in anon. Lbm copy of PSS i	
•What steps of strife	1, 4 viols	Lbm, US-CA	B xv, 93	Consort song	

Title	No. of vv	Source	Modern edition	Remarks
What vaileth it	6	GB-Lbm, US-CA	F xvi, 59	Text: Sidney
What wights are these?	—	GB-Lbm	B xvi, 181	Consort song; lute arr. only
†When first by force	5	SSN 31	D xiii, 199	Text of consort song version: I that sometime a sacred maiden Queen
When I was otherwise	5	SSN 30	D xiii, 194	
When younglings first on Cupid fix their sight	3	SSN 10–11	D xiii, 59	
†Where Fancy fond	5	PSS i 15	D xii, 74	
Where the blind	1, 4 viols	GB-Lbm, US-CA	B xv, 146	Consort song; anon. in sources
While Phoebus us'd to dwell [= The noble famous queen]	1, 4 viols	GB-Lbm, Och	B xv, 97	Consort song
While that a cruel fire	—	Lbm	B xvi, 181	
While that the sun	4	SSN 23	D xiii, 129	
†Who likes to love	5	PSS i 13	D xii, 64	Consort song; lute arr. only
Who looks may leap	3	PSS ii 5	D xiv, 18	Text: G. Whitney 'A Dialogue between two Shepherds'
Who made thee, Hob, forsake the plough?	2, 4 viols	SSN 41	D xiii, 241	244, 250
†Why do I use my paper, ink and pen?	5	PSS i 33	D xii, 183	Text attrib. H. Walpole
With lilies white	1, 4 viols	Lbm	B xv, 149	Consort song; anon. in source
With sighs and tears	—	Lbm	B xvi, 182	Consort song; lute arr. only
Wounded I am	4	SSN 17–18	D xiii, 94	
Wretched Albinus	1, 4 viols	Lbm, US-CA	B xv, 152	Consort song; anon. in sources
Ye sacred muses	1, 4 viols	GB-Lbm, US-CA	B xv, 114	Consort song; elegy for T. Tallis (d 1585)

CANONS

Most of the canons in F xvi are now thought to be spurious; see Brett (1972)

Canon two in one 'per arsin et thesin', D xvi

Canon six in one (and four in two) D xvi

243, 267

CONSORT MUSIC

(all published in B xvii; p. nos. in parentheses)

Fantasias, grounds and dances:

Browning a 5 (39)

Fantasia a 3 in C, no.1 (2)

Fantasia a 3 in C, no.2 (4)   268

Fantasia a 3 in C, no.3 (6)   268

Fantasia a 4 in a, inc. (11)   243

Fantasia a 4 in G [= In manus tuas, Domine], one part only (147)

Fantasia a 4 in g, PSS ii 15 (7)

Fantasia a 5 in C [= kbd fantasia in C, MB 26] (19)

Fantasia a 6 in F [= Laudate, pueri, Dominum], inc. (48)

Fantasia a 6 in g, no.1 (53)

Fantasia a 6 in g, no.2, PSS ii 26 (63)

Pavan a 5 in c [= kbd pavan in c, MB 29] (73)   243

Pavan and galliard a 6 in C (75)

Prelude [and Ground] (29)

BIBLIOGRAPHY

W. B. Squire: 'A Father of Music', *Musical Review*, i (1883), 299, 317, 331

E. H. Fellowes: *The English Madrigal Composers* (Oxford, 1921, 2/ 1948/*R*1975)

H. B. Collins: 'Byrd's Latin Church Music', *ML*, iv (1923), 254

E. H. Fellowes: *William Byrd: a Short Account of his Life and Work* (Oxford, 1923, 2/1928) [superseded by Fellowes (1936)]

W. H. Hadow: 'William Byrd, 1623–1923' [British Academy Lecture, 27 April 1923], *Collected Essays* (London, 1928), 41

F. Howes: *William Byrd* (London, 1928)

E. J. Dent: 'William Byrd and the Madrigal', *Festschrift für Johannes Wolf* (Berlin, 1929), 24

E. H. Fellowes: *William Byrd* (London, 1936, 2/1948)

——: *English Cathedral Music from Edward VI to Edward VII* (London, 1941, rev. 5/1969)

J. A. Westrup: 'William Byrd (1543–1623)', *ML*, xxiv (1943), 125

T. Dart and P. Brett: 'Songs by William Byrd in Manuscripts at Harvard', *Harvard Library Bulletin*, xiv (1960), 343

J. Kerman: 'Byrd's Motets: Chronology and Canon', *JAMS*, xiv (1961), 359

H. K. Andrews: 'Transposition of Byrd's Vocal Polyphony', *ML*, xliii (1962), 25

J. Kerman: *The Elizabethan Madrigal: a Comparative Study* (New York, 1962)

——: 'The Elizabethan Motet: a Study of Texts for Music', *Studies in the Renaissance*, ix (1962), 273–305

H. K. Andrews: 'Printed Sources of William Byrd's "Psalmes, Sonets and Songs" ', *ML*, xliv (1963), 5

J. L. Jackman: 'Liturgical Aspects of Byrd's *Gradualia*', *MQ*, xlix (1963), 17

J. Kerman: 'On William Byrd's *Emendemus in melius*', *MQ*, xlix (1963), 431

H. K. Andrews: 'The Printed Part-books of Byrd's Vocal Music', *The Library*, 5th ser., xix (1964), 1

P. Brett: 'Edward Paston (1550–1630): a Norfolk Gentleman and his Musical Collection', *Transactions of the Cambridge Bibliographical Society*, iv (1964), 51

——: *The Songs of William Byrd* (diss., U. of Cambridge, 1965)

J. G. O'Leary: 'William Byrd and his Family at Stondon Massey', *Essex Recusant*, vii (1965), 18

H. K. Andrews: *The Technique of Byrd's Vocal Polyphony* (London, 1966/*R*1980)

Bibliography

P. Clulow: 'Publication Dates for Byrd's Latin Masses', *ML*, xlvii (1966), 1

J. Kerman: 'Byrd, Tallis, and the Art of Imitation', *Aspects of Medieval and Renaissance Music: a Birthday Offering to Gustave Reese* (New York, 1966), 519

P. le Huray: *Music and the Reformation in England, 1549–1660* (London, 1967), chap.8

O. Neighbour: 'New Consort Music by Byrd', *MT*, cviii (1967), 506

H. W. Shaw: 'William Byrd of Lincoln', *ML*, xlviii (1967), 52

O. Neighbour: 'New Keyboard Music by Byrd', *MT*, cxii (1971), 657

P. Brett: 'Word-setting in the Songs of Byrd', *PRMA*, xcviii (1971–2), 47

——: 'Did Byrd write "Non nobis, Domine"?', *MT*, cxiii (1972), 855

I. Holst: *Byrd* (London, 1972)

J. Caldwell: *English Keyboard Music before the 19th Century* (London, 1973)

J. Kerman: 'William Byrd, 1543–1623', *MT*, cxiv (1973), 687

——: 'Old and New in Byrd's Cantiones sacrae', *Essays on Opera and English Music in Honour of Sir Jack Westrup* (Oxford, 1975), 25

C. Monson: 'Byrd and the 1575 Cantiones sacrae', *MT*, cxvi (1975), 1089; cxvii (1976), 65

A. Roberts: 'Byrd's Other Conceite', *MT*, cxvi (1975), 423

N. Bergenfeld: *The Keyboard Fantasy of the Elizabethan Renaissance* (diss., New York U., 1978)

O. W. Neighbour: *The Music of William Byrd*, iii: *Consort and Keyboard Music* (London, 1978)

D. Humphreys: 'Philip van Wilder: a Study of his Work and its Sources', *Soundings*, no.8 (1979–80), 13

J. Kerman: 'William Byrd and the Catholics', *New York Review of Books*, xxvi/8 (1979), 32

C. Monson: 'The Preces, Psalms, and Litanies of Byrd and Tallis: another "Virtuous Contention in Love" ', *MR*, xl (1979), 257

E. Morin: *Essai de stylistique comparée: les variations de William Byrd et John Tomkins sur 'John come kiss me now'* (Montreal, 1979)

P. Brett: 'Editing Byrd', *MT*, cxxi (1980), 492, 557

——: 'Homage to Taverner in Byrd's Masses', *Early Music*, ix (1981), 169

J. Kerman: *The Music of William Byrd*, i: *The Masses and Motets* (London, 1981)

E. E. Knight: 'The Praise of Musicke: John Case, Thomas Watson, and William Byrd', *CMc* (1981), no.30, p.37

C. Monson: 'Through a Glass Darkly: Byrd's Verse Service as Reflected in Manuscript Sources', *MQ*, lxvii (1981), 64

——: 'Authenticity and Chronology in Byrd's Church Anthems', *JAMS*, xxxv (1982), 280

R. Turbet: *A Hundred Years of Byrd Criticism, 1883–1982* (diss., U. of Aberdeen, 1983)

TOMÁS LUIS DE VICTORIA

Robert Stevenson

CHAPTER ONE

Life

Tomás Luis de Victoria, the greatest Spanish composer of the Renaissance, was born in Avila in 1548, the seventh of 11 children of Francisco Luis de Victoria and Francisca Suárez de la Concha, who married in 1540. There were important relatives on both sides of the family. For example, three of his Suárez de la Concha cousins won success, Cristóbal as a naval commander, Hernando as a Jesuit pioneer in Mexico and Baltasar as a merchant in Florence, where he married Grand Duke Cosimo I de' Medici's sister-in-law and was ennobled. The uncle on his father's side after whom Victoria was named was a lawyer who pleaded cases before the royal chancery at Valladolid; he entered the priesthood after his wife's death and in 1577 was installed as a canon of Avila Cathedral. Victoria's father died on 29 August 1557, and another uncle, Juan Luis, who was also a priest, took charge of the orphaned family.

Victoria learnt the rudiments of music as a choirboy at Avila Cathedral under the *maestros de capilla* Gerónimo de Espinar (1550–58) and Bernadino de Ribera (1559–62); Ribera and his successor, Juan Navarro (1564–66), were among the leading Spanish composers of their time. The cathedral organists during this period were Damián de Bolea and Bernabé del Aguila. Victoria may also have known Antonio de Cabezón, who played at the cathedral in November 1552 and again in June

291

1556; Cabezón's wife came from Avila, and their family residence from about 1538 to 1560 was not far from Victoria's. Victoria's classical education probably began at S Gil, a school for boys founded at Avila by the Jesuits in 1554. The school enjoyed a good reputation from the beginning, and S Theresa of Avila insisted that her nephews attend it; in April 1557 S Francisco de Borja visited Avila to inspect it and to encourage other Jesuit establishments in the town.

After his voice had broken, Victoria was sent to the Jesuit Collegio Germanico, Rome, which had been founded in 1552. He may have been enrolled by 25 June 1563, though 1565 is a more probable date (see Casimiri). The 200 students at the college were of two kinds, a small group of young men in training for the German missionary priesthood and a much larger number of English, Spanish and Italian boarders, whose fees helped maintain the college; Victoria was among the latter group and was specifically enrolled as a singer. Here, if not already at S Gil, he achieved fluency in Latin. In the dedication of his first collection of motets (1572) he acknowledged his debt to Otto Truchsess von Waldburg, Cardinal-Archbishop of Augsburg, who with King Philip II had been a chief benefactor of the college. Victoria surely knew Palestrina, who at the time was *maestro di cappella* of the nearby Seminario Romano, and may even have been taught by him. He was the only peninsular composer before Manuel Cardoso to master the subtleties of Palestrina's style, as is evident in even his earliest publications.

For at least five years from January 1569 Victoria was singer and organist at S Maria di Monserrato, the Aragonese church at Rome in which the two Spanish popes are buried; his monthly salary was one scudo. From 1568 to 1571 he may also have been *maestro* of the Truchsess's private chapel (Jacobus de Kerle had left the post by 18 August 1568). In September or October 1571 the rector of the Collegio Germanico engaged him to teach music to interested boarders at a monthly salary of 15 julios paid out of students' fees. In 1573 the college authorities decided to separate the Italian boarders from the German seminarians, and on 17 October a parting ceremony was held, during which Victoria's pupils and others sang his specially composed eight-part psalm *Super flumina Babylonis*. After the reorganization he was retained to teach the German seminarians, with whom he was able to converse in Latin, and was appointed *maestro di cappella*. The new rector, Michele Lauretano, paid him two scudi a month, increased to three in April 1574. On 9 January 1574 Pope Gregory XIII gave the Collegio Germanico the Palazzo di S Apollinare as their new home and on 15 April 1576 the adjoining church. A bull of the latter date prescribed that the student body sing the entire Office on at least 20 days of the church year. Victoria continued as *maestro di cappella* of the Collegio Germanico until 26 December 1576 or possibly a few months longer – his successor was in office by 20 September 1577. In 1575 he graduated from minor orders to the priesthood: Bishop Thomas Goldwell, the last surviving member of the pre-Reformation English hierarchy, ordained him deacon on 25 August and priest three days later. The ceremonies took place at the English church on the Via di Monserrato.

Victoria next joined the Congregazione dei Preti dell' Oratorio, a newly formed community of lay priests led by S Filippo Neri, and on 8 June 1578 he received a chaplaincy at S Girolamo della Carità, which he held until 7 May 1585. During these years he published five sumptuous volumes in folio, one each of hymns, *Magnificat* settings and masses, an Office for Holy Week and an anthology of motets; the last-named contained two motets by Francisco Guerrero, who was a personal friend, and one by Francesco Soriano. From 1579 to 1585 he derived his personal income largely from five Spanish benefices conferred by Gregory XIII (S Miguel at Villalbarba, S Francisco and S Salvador at Béjar, S Andrés at Valdescapa and another rent in the diocese of Osma), which produced a total of 307 ducats a year. While a chaplain at S Girolamo della Carità, and even earlier, he further increased his income by occasionally serving at S Giacomo degli Spagnoli. Each year from 1573 to 1577 this church paid him four scudi for Corpus Christi services; in 1579 he received six scudi and 60 baiocchi and in 1580 nine scudi and 60 baiocchi; on 18 November 1582 he and a number of choristers received nine scudi for celebrating the victory by Spanish naval forces at the Battle of Terceira, in the Azores.

In the dedication of *Missarum libri duo* (1583) to Philip II, Victoria expressed his desire to return to Spain and to lead a quiet life as a priest. The king, as a reward for his homage, named him chaplain to his sister, the Dowager Empress María, daughter of Charles V, wife of Maximilian II and mother of two other emperors, who from 1581 lived in retirement with her daughter Princess Margarita at the Monasterio de las Descalzas de S Clara at Madrid. The convent was established in 1564 by Juana de la Cruz, sister of S Francisco de

Borja, and liberally endowed by Charles V's daughter Juana, who married John III of Portugal; it housed 33 strictly cloistered nuns, who heard Mass daily in an exquisite small chapel attended by priests who were required to be accomplished singers of plainchant and polyphony. Victoria served the dowager empress from 1587 at the latest until her death in 1603, with an annual salary of 120 ducats, and he was *maestro* of the convent choir until 1604. From then until his death he held the less arduous post of organist, earning 40,000 maravedís in each of his first two years in it and 75,000 a year thereafter. The chaplains enjoyed a number of benefits, including a personal servant, meals served in their private quarters adjacent to the convent and a month's holiday each year. Until 1601 they were all required to participate in the daily singing of two masses, one a votive mass with deacon and sub-deacon. At the time of Victoria's arrival the choir comprised 12 priests (three to a part) and four boys. Instrumentalists were engaged for Easter and for Corpus Christi and its octave. In 1601 a royal decree provided for a bassoonist, who was to play in all musical services, and for two clergymen chosen for their excellent voices to replace three of the foundation's 12 chaplains. At the same time the number of choirboys was increased to six; they were required to practise daily and to learn plainsong, polyphony and counterpoint from the *maestro*.

Life at the convent held such advantages for Victoria that no cathedral post could tempt him – in 1587, for example, he turned down invitations from Seville and Saragossa to become *maestro de capilla* there. The élite of Madrid often went to services at the convent, where his works were regularly sung. It is doubtful whether

12. Autograph letter (14 Jan 1582) from Victoria at Rome to the Seville Cathedral chapter: Victoria reminds the chapter that through Francisco Guerrero he had sent them two years ago his [1576] Masses. He had not thanked them for the money gift they had sent him. He now sends them another publication printed at his own expense in Rome, a book of psalms, hymns, Magnificats in all [8] tones, and four Salves à 5 and à 8 [1581]. He hopes this volume of vespers music for feast days throughout the year will prove serviceable. The notes are large enough for all the singers to see. He wishes all his works to find use in Seville Cathedral

any cathedral would have allowed him the extended leave that the convent gave him in 1592 to enable him to supervise the printing at Rome of his *Missae ... liber secundus*, which he dedicated to María's son Cardinal Alberto. On 18 July 1593 his motet *Surge Debora et loquere canticum* was performed in his presence by the Collegio Germanico during Mass and Vespers at S Apollinare to celebrate the defeat of the Turks at Sisak. On 2 February 1594 he joined the cortège at Palestrina's funeral. A royal warrant of 21 January 1594 authorized the Spanish ambassador at Rome to pay him 150 ducats owing to him from a benefice at Córdoba. He returned to Madrid in 1595.

María bequeathed three chaplaincies to the convent, one of which went to Victoria, who thereby continued to receive his salary of 120 ducats after her death. Most of his income, however, derived from his numerous simple benefices, whose yearly revenue had grown by 1605 to 1227 ducats through the addition of pensions from the dioceses of Córdoba, Segovia, Sigüenza, Toledo and Zamora. On 1 October 1598 he engaged Julio Junti de Modesti of Madrid to produce 200 copies of a collection of polychoral masses, *Magnificat* settings, motets and psalms in partbooks, which eventually appeared in 1600. The printer, who was paid 2500 reales in three instalments, was himself allowed an additional 100 copies to sell, beginning 12 months after publication. The masses of this collection were extremely popular at the time, but they are rarely performed today. The nine-part *Missa pro victoria* was a favourite work of Philip III; the eight-part *Missa 'Ave regina coelorum'* and *Missa 'Alma Redemptoris mater'* were so popular in Mexico City that in 1640 they had to be recopied by hand because the original partbooks were worn out. Victoria or his agents sent sets to such distant places as Graz, Urbino and Bogotá, Colombia. In accompanying letters he asked for contributions to cover printing costs and in at least one instance solicited money to secure the release of a younger brother from prison. His strong family ties were specially evident during the last years of his life, when two of his brothers and two of his sisters lived in Madrid; one of the brothers, Agustín, was also a chaplain of the Descalzas convent. Victoria died near the convent in the chaplains' residence, on 20 August 1611. He was buried at the convent, but his tomb has not been identified.

CHAPTER TWO

Works

I General characteristics

Victoria not only left far less music than Palestrina or
Lassus but also limited himself to Latin sacred texts. He
had a habit of reissuing works that he had already
published: more than half the contents of five of his 11
prints had appeared in earlier prints, and of prints subsequent to his first only the first consists almost entirely
of newly published music. Moreover, unlike Palestrina,
he succeeded in publishing, usually in a luxurious
format, nearly the whole of what is now recognized as
his authentic oeuvre. Thus the first seven volumes of the
eight-volume complete edition of 1902–13 consist
wholly of music published during his lifetime; some of
that in the eighth is spurious.

Victoria's posthumous reputation has largely rested
on some plangent motets in his first publication (1572)
and on the *Officium defunctorum* of 1605, composed on
the death of the Empress María. Such memorable
motets as *O vos omnes* and *Vere languores nostros* and a
passage such as the setting of the words 'nihil enim sunt
dies mei' in *Versa est in luctum* from the Office of the
Dead do indeed have a poignancy rarely encountered in
other music of the period. Poignancy and mystical fer-
vour are, however, not the only emotions in Victoria's
music, nor indeed the predominant ones. His contemporaries and immediate successors certainly saw a dif-

ferent side of his artistic nature. One astute critic who knew his whole oeuvre as few do today was John IV of Portugal, who, noting in his *Defensa de la música moderna* (1649) that he instinctively leant more towards the joyful than to the sad, observed that 'although there is much in his Holy Week volume [1585] that exactly suits the text, nonetheless his disposition being naturally sunny he never stays downcast for long'. John IV also gave the lie to another misconception about Victoria still prevalent in the 20th century when he endorsed the liberal use of instruments to double the vocal lines, and there is other contemporary evidence confirming that doubling was widely practised in his works circulating in Spain.

II Masses

Further confirmation of Victoria's generally cheerful disposition can be found in his own motets that he chose as the bases of his parody masses. He based seven of his masses on his own motets – *Ascendens Christus*, *Dum complerentur*, *O magnum mysterium*, *O quam gloriosum*, *Quam pulchri sunt*, *Trahe me post te* and *Vidi speciosam*; the masses are parodies of motets for Ascension, Pentecost, the Circumcision, All Saints, the Conception, any Lady feast and the Assumption respectively. Five of these motets end with exultant 'Alleluias'. His three masses based on his own Marian antiphons *Salve regina*, *Alma Redemptoris* and *Ave regina*, as well as the *Missa 'Laetatus sum'*, based on his own psalm, display similarly positive qualities. Three other parody masses are based on works by Guerrero, Morales and Palestrina respectively. The *Missa pro victoria* is one of several Spanish battle masses based on Clément Janequin's *La guerre*.

There are 20 authentic masses by Victoria, all published during his lifetime. 15 are parodies, four are
paraphrases (*'Ave maris stella'*, *De Beata Maria
Virgine*, *Pro defunctis* of 1583 and the mass sections of
the *Officium defunctorum*), and one, *Missa quarti
toni*, is mostly a free mass, which does, however, at the
close of both Gloria and Credo ('Amen') quote verbatim
the music of the last appearance of 'ipsum quem genuit
adoravit' in his Purification motet *Senex puerum portabat*. The four masses first published in the 1600
miscellany contrast in a number of ways with those
published earlier: they are for two or three choirs, one
of which has an organ accompaniment, and all four are
in an undeviating F major. There are subtle structural
differences too, such as the greater use of free episodic
material, and the repetition of polyphonic blocks. These
are sometimes from movement to movement: for
instance, in the *Missa pro victoria*, first Kyrie, bars 1–
8 = Agnus Dei, bars 1–8; second Kyrie, 36–
42 = Agnus Dei, 16–22; Gloria, 1–3 = Credo, 83–5;
Gloria, 28–34 = Agnus Dei, 8 (beat 3) –15 (beat 3); and
Gloria, 59–76 = Credo, 133–50. But there are also
repetitions within the same movement: in the *Missa pro
victoria*, Gloria, bars 59–64 = bars 67–72; Credo,
133–8 = 141–6; and Sanctus, 21–5 (beat 1) = 25–9
(beat 1) = 47–51 (beat 1) = 51–5 (beat 1). Another
feature of Victoria's late masses is his frequent recourse
to triple metre: whereas *'Ave maris stella'* and *'Dum
complerentur'* (both 1576) do not contain a single bar of
triple time, the 1600 masses are full of them, the *Missa
pro victoria* alone containing 134.

A prominent stylistic trait in masses from all periods
of Victoria's career, and in other works, too, is the kind
of tonal fluctuation represented by melodic progressions

such as F–G–F♯, F♯–G–F♮ and E–F–E♭, which are not found in, for example, the works of Palestrina or Guerrero (ex.1). He anticipated both when in 1576 he chose to base a mass on one of his own motets (*Dum complerentur*). In his middle-period masses, however, he shared with Guerrero a fondness for paired imitation. His masses are on the whole much more concise than Palestrina's or Guerrero's; this is particularly true of those in the 1592 and 1600 volumes. Unlike Palestrina,

Ex.1

he broke up his masses with frequent emphatic cadences. He often wrote functional rather than modal harmony, even in the *Missa quarti toni*. The modes that he used in his parody masses have been tabulated by Rive (1969), who drew attention to the high incidence of the Dorian and Ionian modes (six and five masses respectively) compared with the Mixolydian (three masses), a tendency also found in his other music. His chromatic alterations in his parodies, especially the later ones, make the Dorian mode sound increasingly like a minor key and the Ionian more and more like a major key.

III Magnificat settings

The principal source of Victoria's *Magnificat* settings is his 1581 collection, which contains 16 of them, including the six already published in 1576; the two polychoral settings in his 1600 volume are based in part on works from the two earlier books. Despite containing some of his finest inspirations, his *Magnificat* settings of 1581 never found as much favour in Spanish dominions as those of Morales or even Guerrero. Only in Italy did they continue in much demand after the printed copies were exhausted; for example, in Italy in 1594 a 60-folio manuscript choirbook containing his *Magnificat* settings from the 2nd to the 7th tone was expensively copied for presentation to the Bishop of Casale Monferrato (a copy is in the library of the conservatory in Milan).

In contrast with the *Magnificat* settings composed by Morales, Guerrero and Palestrina, Victoria's settings are greatly coloured by *musica ficta*: for example, in his odd-verse *Magnificat* on the 7th tone (1581) he called for 69 accidentals, whereas Palestrina prescribed only 16 in his corresponding setting (1591). Like his masses of 1600, the two *Magnificat* settings in that volume show differences from the earlier settings: they are more concise, include more triple time and light parlando rhythms and fewer unaccented passing notes, and display a new aversion to canon (there is only one, and that is optional).

IV Hymns

Victoria's hymns have also proved to be far less popular than they deserve. The principal source is the set of 32 in his 1581 volume, where the texts and chronological order are basically the same as in Guerrero's *Liber*

13. *Opening of Victoria's Lamentations 'Incipit lamentatio Jeremiae' from his 'Officium Hebdomadae Sanctae' (Rome: Alessandro Gardane, 1585)*

vesperarum (1584) and Palestrina's *Hymni totius anni* (1589). Like Guerrero he provided polyphony for the even-numbered strophes (Palestrina's hymns are basically settings of the odd-numbered ones). In their final verses Guerrero and Palestrina frequently resorted to canon and increased the numbers of voices from four to five, but Victoria shunned canon altogether and sometimes heightened final verses by returning to a four-part texture after reducing it to three voices in some middle strophes. He included two settings of *Pange lingua*, the second of which is marked 'more hispano' because it is based on the peninsular melody, not the Roman.

V Music for Holy Week

Victoria's *Officium Hebdomadae Sanctae* (1585), comprising nine Lamentations, 18 responsories, two Passions and various other pieces, includes some of his most admired music, much of it of a plangent austerity. So austere indeed did Mendelssohn find Victoria's *St John Passion* when it was sung in the Cappella Sistina on Good Friday of 1831 that he wrote his teacher Zelter a complaining letter (dated 16 June 1831). He took particular exception to the setting of the crowd's calling for Christ's crucifixion, finding it insufficiently energetic; on the other hand, the Passion music has also been criticized in modern times for being too 'dramatic'.

Among the other contents of the *Officium Hebdomadae Sanctae*, the Lamentations have received the most critical attention. Not only does the music's sorrowful quality completely accord with the text, but the Lamentations also reveal the most overtly Spanish traits (their Spanish plainsong melodies are discussed in Cramer's edition).

In accordance with both the Spanish and Roman customs they are mainly chordal, but Victoria showed great ingenuity in varying the textures through scalic passages and contrasts of high and low voices. The responsories are also mainly homophonic, but by contrast the *St Matthew Passion*, for Palm Sunday, contains some contrapuntal writing, including canon. The Lamentations also exist in earlier form (Rome, Biblioteca Apostolica Vaticana, C.S.186); the significant differences between this and the printed version have been studied by Rive (1965) and by both Rubio and Cramer (in their editions; 1977, 1982). As Rive (the first to study the two versions intensively) reported:

between the date of the first beginning of compositions and the date of publication in 1585, Victoria's technique of composition made tremendous advances. His re-working of earlier music shows greater conciseness in melodic organization, a keen insight into the problems of apt setting of text and a greater appreciation of harmonic organization, movement, and purpose.

VI Sequences and antiphons
Victoria wore his learning lightly in his three scintillating eight-part sequences, *Lauda Sion* (1585), for Corpus Christi, *Victimae paschali* (1600), for Easter, and *Veni, Sancte Spiritus* (1600), for Whitsun. The Easter sequence, one of his most ebullient works, is closer in spirit to a popular villancico than almost any of his other short works and emphasizes the drama of the question-and-answer text. It moves from triple to duple metre in a most attractive manner and soars to a climax of unrestrained joy in the final 'Alleluias'. The play of syncopated homophony at bars 36–46 of the Corpus Christi sequence echoes the strains of revelry found in the earliest surviving *guineos*.

The fact that Victoria composed no fewer than four different settings of *Salve regina* (two for five voices and one each for six and eight voices) and two each of *Alma Redemptoris*, *Ave regina* and *Regina coeli* (each pair for five and eight voices respectively) shows the importance that he attached to the Marian antiphon. The individuality of the *Salve regina* settings is remarkable, considering that they are all in the same mode and on the same plainsong. The number of manuscript copies of them both in the Iberian peninsula and in the New World argues that they enjoyed great popularity in Victoria's own day and in the early 17th century.

Their influence in Italy was also great. For example, the 'Et Jesum' from Victoria's six-voice *Salve regina* in the 1572 publication was found by Roland Jackson as an anonymous item in a manuscript (Chicago, Newberry Library, Case MS VM2092.4M329) and proposed by him as a work by Marenzio because of stylistic affinities (1971; he included it in Marenzio's *Opera omnia*, CMM, lxxii/1, 1978, as a doubtful work). Subsequently however Jackson inclined to the view that since Victoria's printed *Salve regina* preceded anything published by Marenzio, the stylistic affinity instead points up an unsuspected relationship between the two composers, and he concluded (1980) that the motets that Marenzio presumably wrote in Rome in the 1570s may have been influenced by Victoria.

VII   Psalms

All of Victoria's published psalms are polychoral. The only one not for two choirs is *Laetatus sum*, which is for three, and it is also unique in starting in triple metre, which in the others is employed only in the final 'Gloria Patri'.

Just as he frequently republished his motets, so also his polychoral psalms. His *Liber primus* (1576) contains *Nisi Dominus* (Psalm cxxvi) and *Super flumina Babylonis* (Psalm cxxxvi); in an appendix to his folio book of hymns of 1581 he repeated *Nisi Dominus* and added the double-choir *Dixit Dominus, Laudate pueri* and *Laudate Dominum omnes* (Psalms cix, cxii, cxvi). Two years later his *Motecta* (1583) contained repetitions of all the previously published double-choir psalms, plus the triple-choir *Laetatus sum* (Psalm cxxi) on which he was to base a parody mass published at Madrid in 1600. Except for *Super flumina Babylonis*, the first five verses of which he composed for the parting of Italian and German students at the Collegio Germanico (17 October 1573), he set all the verses in his polychoral psalms. To avoid any hint of monotony in these through-composed pieces he constantly alternated between the choirs, and in the longer psalms included some verses for single choir or soloists.

Victoria's miscellaneous Madrid print of 1600 again repeated all the previously published psalms, but he also added an organ part which duplicates and on occasion simplifies the vocal parts for the first choir. The substitution of the organ part for the first choir parts made it possible for smaller musical establishments, with only enough voices to constitute a second choir, to perform the polychoral psalms. Better still, in places that could afford the expense of two or three choirs, the vesper psalms were given added colour by the extra organ part. In addition to psalms for Vespers, the 1600 volume contains one for Compline, the previously unpublished double-choir *Ecce nunc* (Psalm cxxxv).

As if a total of seven polychoral through-composed

psalms did not sufficiently cater for the need, Victoria also prepared for publication in Rome a collection of ten vesper psalms for modest four-part choir which were copied in manuscript by his colleague at the oratory, Francisco Soto de Langa. These psalms are easier than the polychoral ones and are plainsong-based; the first eight open with a plainchant half-verse enunciating the Gregorian psalm-tone. Victoria's fastidiousness comes to light in his handwritten plea to Soto de Langa begging him to be very careful with word-placement, and he also exercised his usual care with accidentals. Fischer (1975) remarked on Victoria's willingness to sharpen the G in the 4th tone, not only at cadences but also elsewhere. For internal reasons such as their conciseness, and because Victoria could not be in Rome to oversee their printing, Fischer dated them from after 1592. Apparently, however, Victoria's desire that they should be printed was never fulfilled.

VIII Assessment

After their publication and detailed analysis, the ten manuscript vesper psalms may suffer the same fate as the hymn *Jesu dulcis memoria* and the *Missa Dominicalis*, which, though included by Pedrell in the last volume of the *Opera omnia*, are now deemed by all scholars to be spurious. Certainly the *Missa 'Pange lingua'*, ascribed to Victoria in Choirbook 5 at Cuenca Cathedral, is not by him but by Juan Pérez Roldán. From time to time isolated works ascribed to Victoria continue to turn up, especially in Italian archives; but the best proof that the works published by him in his lifetime constitute his oeuvre as he wished it known rests on the constant republication of motets, *Magnificat* settings and other works that he

309

supervised himself. Whatever he himself chose to keep retouching and republishing can never justly take second place to an isolated work left unpublished at his death.

Several earlier historians and anthologists expressed a preference for Victoria's motets, often at the expense of all his other works. It is easy to see the attractions of so intensely passionate a work as *Vere languores nostros*, and there are many other arresting ones. Several include descriptive writing of a madrigalian nature prompted by the words; examples include the rising scales at 'surge' in *Nigra sum sed formosa* and at the beginning of *Ascendens Christus in altum*. Victoria sometimes used expressive melodic intervals, such as the diminished 4th in *Vere languores nostros* (ex.2*a*) and *Sancta Maria, succurre miseris* and in the *Ave Maria* for double choir (ex.2*b*), another trait reminiscent of madrigalian music and consistent with the relatively small role played by plainsong in his motets. In contrast with Palestrina, he did not hesitate to introduce chromaticisms (exx.3*a–c*). Several works begin with paired

Ex.2

(a) *Vere languores nostros*

310

Assessment

Ex.3

(a) *Vidi speciosam*, 6vv

(b) *Magnificat septimi toni*

(c) *Missa 'Salve regina'*

Ex.4 *Missa 'Simile est regnum coelorum'* (Kyrie I)

311

imitation, such as the Kyrie of his *Missa 'Simile est regnum coelorum'*, based on Guerrero's motet (ex.4). However, in contrast with Guerrero, only a few of Victoria's motets include extensive use of canon.

Victoria's published works that have never yet been given the benefit of adequate recorded performances include all his organ-accompanied polychoral masses that were first published in 1592 and 1600. On his own written testimonial his *Missa pro victoria* attracted Philip III's special attention. In a stunning defence of this unjustly neglected work, Gudmundson (1976) showed that it not only anticipated Baroque splendours but also that it was solidly grounded in aesthetic and philosophical principles of the highest order.

Editions: T. L. de Victoria: *Opera omnia*, ed. F. Pedrell (Leipzig, 1902–13/R1965) [P]

T. L. de Victoria: *Motetes*, ed. S. Rubio (Madrid, 1964) [R] [based chiefly on 1603 edn. of 1583 Motecta, variants annotated; incl. 7 motets from MS sources]

T. L. de Victoria: *Opera omnia*, ed. H. Anglés, MME, xxv, xxvi, xxx, xxxi (1965–8) [A]

Numbers in right-hand margins denote references in the text.

(published in Rome unless otherwise stated)

[33] Motecta, 4–6, 8vv (Venice, 1572) [1572] — 292, 299

Liber primus: qui missas, psalmos, …aliaque complectitur, 4–6, 8vv (Venice, 1576) [incl. 7 works from 1572 edn.] [1576] — 296, 303, 308

Cantica beatae virginis vulgo Magnificat, una cum 4 antiphonis [8 settings] beatae virginis per annum, 4, 5, 8vv (1581) [incl. 6 Magnificat, 3 Marian antiphons from 1576 edn.] [1581a] — 294, 303

[32] Hymni totius anni secundum sanctae romanae ecclesiae consuetudinem, 4vv, una cum 4 psalmis, pro praecipuis festivitatibus, 8vv (1581, 2/1600 without 4 psalms) [incl. psalm from 1576 edn.] [1581b] — 294, 296, 303, 308

[9] Missarum libri duo, 4–6vv (1583) [incl. 5 from 1576 edn.] [1583a] — 294

[53] Motecta, 4–6, 8, 12vv (1583, 2/1589a with 8 motets rev., 3/1603) [1583 incl. 33 from 1572 edn. (12 rev.) and 13 from 1576 Liber primus; 3/1603 does not incl. revs. of 1583 or 1589a] (see Introduction to MME, xxvi, 11) — 294, 308

[37] Motecta festorum totius anni cum communi sanctorum, 4–6, 8vv (1585?) [incl. 25 from previous edns; 3 not by Victoria.] [1585a] — 294

[37] Officium Hebdomadae Sanctae, 3–8vv (1585) [incl. 2 from 1572, 1 from 1576, 1 from 1583 edns.]; ed. S. Rubio (Cuenca, 1977), ed. E. C. Cramer (Henryville, 1982) [1585b] — 294, 304, 305

[7] Missae, una cum antiphonis Asperges, et Vidi aquam totius anni: liber secundus, 4–6, 8vv (1592) [incl. 1 mass from 1583 edn.] [1592] — 297, 302

[32] Missae, Magnificat, motecta, psalmi et alia quam plurima, 3, 4, 8, 9, 12vv (Madrid, 1600) [incl. 19 works from previous edns.] [1600] — 297, 301, 302, 303, 308

Officium defunctorum: in obitu et obsequiis sacrae imperatricis, 6vv (Madrid, 1605) [1605] — 299, 301

MASSES — 301–2

Alma Redemptoris mater, 8vv (2 choirs), org, 1600 (on own antiphon, 1581a); P iv, 99 — 297, 300

Ascendens Christus, 5vv, 1592 (on own motet, 1572); P ii, 162 — 300

Ave maris stella, 4vv, 1576; P ii, 1; A xxv, 1 — 301

Ave regina coelorum, 8vv (2 choirs), org, 1600 (on own antiphon, 1581a); P vi, 1 — 297, 300

De Beata Maria Virgine, 5vv, 1576; P ii, 93; A xxv, 58 — 301

Dominicalis, 4vv, E-TO (spurious, see R. Casimiri, NA, x, 1933); P viii, 5 — 309

Dum complerentur, 6vv, 1576 (on own motet, 1572); P iv, 29; A xxx, 87 — 300, 301, 302

Gaudeamus, 6vv, 1576 (on Morales's Jubilate Deo, 1538); P iv, 1; A xxv, 99 — 300, 301, 302

Laetatus sum, 12vv (3 choirs), org, 1600 (on own psalm, 1583b); P vi, 59 — 300, 308

O magnum mysterium, 4vv, 1592 (on own motet, 1572); P ii, 69 — 300

O quam gloriosum, 4vv, 1583a (on own motet, 1572); P ii, 56; A xxx, 30 — 300

Pange lingua, 4vv, CUi (spurious, also attrib. J. Pérez Roldán, SE) — 309

Pro defunctis, 4vv, 1583a; P vi, 102 — 301

Pro defunctis, 6vv, 1605; P vi, 124

Pro victoria, 9vv (2 choirs), org, 1600 (on Janequin, La guerre, 1528); P vi, 26 — 297, 300, 301, 302

Quam pulchri sunt, 4vv, 1583a (on own motet, 1572); P ii, 38; A xxx, 1 — 300

Quarti toni, 4vv, 1592 (on own motet, Senex puerum portabat, 1572); P ii, 81 — 301, 302

Salve regina, 8vv (2 choirs), org, 1592 (on own antiphon, 1576); P iv, 72 — 300

Simile est regnum coelorum, 4vv, 1576 (on F. Guerrero, 1570); P ii, 21; A xxv, 31 — 312

Surge propera, 5vv, 1583a (on Palestrina, 1563); P ii, 119; A xxx, 49

Trahe me post te, 5vv, 1592 (on own motet, 1583b); P ii, 145 — 300

Vidi speciosam, 6vv, 1592 (on own motet, 1572); P iv, 56 — 300

MAGNIFICAT SETTINGS, ETC

(verses set polyphonically given in parentheses)

Magnificat primi toni (odd), 4vv, 1576; P iii, 1 — 303

Magnificat primi toni (even), 4vv, 1576; P iii, 6

313

Laudate Dominum omnes gentes (Ps cxxi), 8vv (2 choirs), org, 1581b; P vii, 20 — 308

Laudate pueri Dominum (Ps cxii), 8vv (2 choirs), org, 1581b; P vii, 11

Miserere mei Deus (Ps i), 8vv (2 choirs), 1585b; P v, 147

Nisi Dominus (Ps cxxvi), 8vv (2 choirs), org, 1576; P vii, 43 — 308

Super flumina Babylonis (Ps cxxxvi), 8vv (2 choirs), 1576; P vii, 53; A xxxi, 129 — 293, 308

10 psalms (cix, cx (2 settings), cxii, cxv, cxvi, cxxvi, cxlvii), 4vv, I-Rn (see Fischer)

MOTETS

P based on 1572 edn.; R based on 3/1603 edn.

Ardens est cor meum, 6vv, 1576; P i, 133; R iii, no.34; A xxxi, 78

Ascendens Christus in altum, 5vv, 1572; P i, 53; R ii, no.26; A xxvi, 44 — 300, 310

Ave Maria, 4vv; P viii, 4; R iv, no.46

Ave Maria, gratia plena, 8vv (2 choirs), org, 1572, 1600 (org in 1600 edn. only); P i, 146; R iv, no.44; A xxvi, 118 — 310

Beata es Virgo Maria, 6vv, D-Mü; ed. S. Rubio, Antologia polifónica sacra, ii (Madrid, 1956), 61 [transposed up a major 3rd]; R iv, no.51 [original pitch]

Beati immaculati, 4vv, MÜs; ed. S. Rubio, Antología polifónica sacra, ii (Madrid, 1956), 328; R iv, no.47

Benedicam Dominium, 4vv; P viii, 2; R iv, no.48

Benedicta sit Sancta Trinitas, 6vv, 1572; P i, 118; R iii, no.35; A xxvi, 88

Congratulamini mihi, 6vv, 1572; P i, 129; R iii, no.40; A xxxi, 82

Cum beatus Ignatius, 5vv, 1572; P i, 72; R ii, no.25; A xxxi, 63

Date ei de fructu, 4vv, I-Fc E. 117 (no.26 of Motetti a piu voci di diversi autori, discovered by E. C. Cramer)

Descendit angelus Domini, 5vv, 1572; P i, 77; R ii, no.28; A xxxi, 56

Doctor bonus amicus Dei Andreas, 4vv, 1572; P i, 3; R i, no.2; A xxvi, 30

Domine in virtute tua, 8vv, MÜs; R iv, no.52

Domine non sum dignus, 4vv, 1583b; P i, 39; R i, no.16; A xxxi, 12

Dum complerentur dies Pentecostes, 5vv, 1572; P i, 59; R ii, no.27; A xxvi, 54 — 300

Duo seraphim clamabant, 4vv, 1583b; P i, 36; R i, no.14; A xxxi, 4

Ecce Dominus veniet, 5vv, 1572; P i, 67; R iii, no.24; A xxvi, 37

Ecce sacerdos magnus, 4vv, 1585a; P i, 46; R ii, no.20; A xxxi, 31

Ego sum panis vivus, 4vv, MÜs; ed. S. Rubio, Antologia polifónica sacra, i (Madrid, 1954), 281; R iv, no.49

Estote fortes in bello, 4vv, 1585a; P i, 41; R i, no.17; A xxxi, 23

Gaude, Maria virgo, 5vv, 1572; P i, 82; R iii, no.31; A xxxi, 53

Gaudent in coelis animae Sanctorum, 4vv, 1585a; P i, 44; R i, no.19; A xxxi, 28

Hic vir despiciens mundum, 4vv, 1585a; P i, 48; R ii, no.21

Iste sanctus pro lege, 4vv, 1585a; P i, 43; R i, no.18; A xxxi, 26

Magi viderunt stellam, 4vv, 1572; P i, 14; R i, no.7; A xxvi, 10

Ne timeas, Maria, 4vv, 1572; P i, 22; R i, no.10; A xxxi, 15

Nigra sum sed formosa, 6vv, 1576; P i, 136; R iii, no.41; A xxxi, 97 — 310

O decus apostolicum, 4vv, 1572; P i, 9; R i, no.4; A xxvi, 34

O doctor optime, 4vv, E-Bc; ed. in Rubio (1949); R iv, no.50

O Domine Jesu Christe, 6vv, 1576; P v, 119; R iv, no.43; A xxxi, 75

O Ildephonse, 8vv (2 choirs), org, 1600; P i, 153; R iv, no.45

O lux et decus Hispaniae, 5vv, 1583b; P i, 85; R iii, no.29; A xxxi, 71

O magnum mysterium, 4vv, 1572; P i, 11; R i, no.6; A xxvi, 7 — 300

O quam gloriosum est regnum, 4vv, 1572; P i, 1; R i, no.1; A xxvi, 27 — 300

O quam metuendus est, 4vv, 1585a; P i, 51; R ii, no.23

O regem coeli, 4vv, 1572; P i, 29; R i, no.5; A xxvi, 1

O sacrum convivium, 4vv, 1572; P i, 34; R i, no.15; A xxxi, 8

O sacrum convivium, 6vv, 1572; P i, 122; R iii, no.36; A xxvi, 93

O vos omnes, qui transitis per viam, 4vv, 1572; P i, 27; R i, no.13; A xxvi, 17 — 299

Pueri Hebraeorum, 4vv; R i, no.11

Quam pulchri sunt gressus tui, 4vv, 1572; P i, 6; R i, no.3; A xxvi, 20 — 300

Quem vidistis, pastores, 6vv, 1572; P i, 90; R iii, no.32

Resplenduit facies ejus, 5vv, 1585a; P i, 88; R iii, no.30 — 310

Sancta Maria, succurre miseris, 4vv, 1572; P i, 19; R i, no.9; A xxxi, 19

Senex puerum portabat, 4vv, 1572; P i, 17; R i, no.8; A xxvi, 24 — 301

Surge Debora et loquere canticum, lost, cited in Casimiri, p.158 — 297

Surrexit Pastor Bonus, 6vv, 1572; P i, 126; R ii, no.33; A xxvi, 83 — 300

Trahe me post te, 6vv, 1583b; P i, 140; R iv, no.42

Tu es Petrus, 6vv, 1572; P i, 105; R iii, no.37; A xxxi, 101

BIBLIOGRAPHY

F. X. Haberl: 'Tomas Luis de Victoria: eine bio-bibliographische Studie', *KJb*, xi (1896), 72

P. Wagner: *Geschichte der Messe* (Leipzig, 1913), 421ff

H. Collet: *Victoria* (Paris, 1914)

R. Mitjana: *Estudios sobre algunos músicos españoles del siglo XVI* (Madrid, 1918), 229ff

F. Pedrell: *Tomás Luis de Victoria Abulense* (Valencia, 1918)

J. B. Trend: *The Music of Spanish History to 1600* (London, 1925), 154ff

W. D. Hirschl: *The Styles of Victoria and Palestrina: a Comparative Study, with Special Reference to Dissonance Treatment* (diss., U. of California, Berkeley, 1933)

R. Casimiri: '*Il Vittoria*: nuovi documenti per una biografia sincera', *NA*, xi (1934), 111–97

F. Hernández: 'La cuna y la escuela de Tomás L. de Victoria', *Ritmo*, xl/141 (1940), 27

E. Young: *The Contrapuntal Practices of Victoria* (diss., U. of Rochester, NY, 1942)

H. von May: *Die Kompositionstechnik T. L. de Victorias* (Berne, 1943)

S. Rubio: 'Una obra inédita y desconocida de Tomás Luis de Victoria', *La ciudad de Dios*, clxi (1949), 525–59

——: 'Historia de las reediciones de los motetes de T. L. de Victoria y significado de las variantes introducidas en ellas', *La ciudad de Dios*, clxii (1950), 313–51

N. Saxton: *The Masses of Victoria* (diss., Westminster Choir College, Princeton, 1951)

G. Reese: *Music in the Renaissance* (New York, 1954, rev. 2/1959), esp. 599ff

A. Salazar: 'Victoria o el fin de una época', *Revista musical chilena* (1954), no.46, p.37

H. Federhofer: 'Graz Court Musicians and their Contributions to the "Parnassus Musicus Ferdinandaeus" (1615)', *MD*, ix (1955), 243

J. Subirá: 'La música en la Capilla y Monasterio de las Descalzas Reales de Madrid', *AnM*, xii (1957), 149, 165

P. Boepple: 'Seeing the Light: Victoria's Melody is Clue to his Music', *New York Times* (25 Jan 1959), section 2, p.9

H. Taubman: 'Works of Victoria: Dessoff Choirs Offer Program of Spaniard', *New York Times* (29 Jan 1959), 18

R. Stevenson: 'Missa pro defunctis (RCA Victor LM 2254)', *MQ*, xlvi (1960), 414

S. Rubio: 'A los 350 años de la muerte de Tomás Luis de Victoria', *La ciudad de Dios*, clxxiv (1961), 693–727

317

Victoria

R. Stevenson: *Spanish Cathedral Music in the Golden Age* (Berkeley and Los Angeles, 1961), 343–480
——: 'The Bogotá Music Archive', *JAMS*, xv (1962), 302, 310
R. G. Villoslada: 'Algunos documentos sobre la música en el antiguo Seminario Romano', *Archivum Historicum Societatis Iesu*, xxxi (1962), 108, 112
T. N. Rive: *An Investigation into Harmonic and Cadential Procedure in the Works of Tomás Luis de Victoria, 1548–1611* (diss., U. of Auckland, 1963)
——: 'Verdict on Victoria', *Caecilia*, xci/3 (1963), 91
D. Stevens: 'Spanish Cathedral Music', *MT*, civ (1963), 187
T. N. Rive: 'Victoria's *Lamentationes Geremiae*: a Comparison of Cappella Sistina MS 186 with the Corresponding Portions of *Officium Hebdomadae Sanctae* (Rome, 1585)', *AnM*, xx (1965), 179–208
R. Stevenson: 'Estudio biográfico y estilístico de T. L. de Victoria', *Revista musical chilena* (1966), no.20, p.9
✓ ——: 'Tomás Luis de Victoria: Unique Spanish Genius', *American Choral Review*, viii (1966), no.3, pp.1, 7; no.4, pp.1, 6, 18
——: 'Victoria, Tomás Luis de', *MGG* [incl. fuller bibliography]
An Alphabetical Index to Tomás Luis de Victoria, Opera Omnia, ed. Bibliography Committee, Music Library Association, New York (Ann Arbor, 1966)
H. Anglès: 'Tomás Luis de Victoria', *NOHM*, iv (1968), 398
F. Burkley: 'Priest-composers of the Baroque: a Sacred–Secular Conflict', *MQ*, liv (1968), 169, 184
J. A. Kriewald: *The Contrapuntal and Harmonic Style of Tomás Luis de Victoria* (diss., U. of Wisconsin, 1968)
H. Anglès: 'Problemas que presenta la nueva edición de las obras de Morales y de Victoria', *Renaissance-muziek 1400–1600: donum natalicium René Bernard Lenaerts* (Louvain, 1969), 21
T. Rive: 'An Examination of Victoria's Technique of Adaptation and Reworking in his Parody Masses, with Particular Attention to Harmonic and Cadential Procedure', *AnM*, xxiv (1969), 133
T. Culley: *Jesuits and Music, i: A Study of the Musicians connected with the German College in Rome during the 17th Century and of their Activities in Northern Europe* (Rome, 1970)
R. Stevenson: 'Tomás Luis de Victoria', *Heterofonia*, iii/13 (1970), 10
R. Jackson: 'Two Newly-found Motets by Marenzio(?)', *JAMS*, xxiv (1971), 103
S. Rubio: 'Felipe Pedrell, editor de *Opera omnia* de Tomás Luis de Victoria', *AnM*, xxvii (1972), 39
R. Stevenson: 'Mexican Colonial Musical Manuscripts Abroad', *Notes*, xxix (1972–3), 213
E. C. Cramer: *The 'Officium Hebdomadae Sanctae' of Tomás Luis de*

318

Bibliography

Victoria: a Study of Selected Aspects and an Edition and Commentary (diss., Boston U., 1973)

R. V. Shalley: *A Comparative Study of Compositional Technique in Selected Paraphrase Masses of Cristóbal de Morales and Tomás Luis [de] Victoria* (diss., U. of Cincinnati, 1973)

R. Stevenson: 'The Toledo Manuscript Polyphonic Choirbooks and some other Lost or Little Known Flemish Sources', *FAM*, xx (1973), 107

K. Fischer: 'Unbekannte Kompositionen Victorias in der Biblioteca nazionale in Rom', *AMw*, xxxii (1975), 124

S. Rubio: *Juan Vázquez, Agenda defunctorum: Estudio técnico-estilístico y transcripción* (Madrid, 1975), 70 [comparison of MS and 1585 edn. of Victoria's Lamentations]

E. C. Cramer: 'The Significance of Clef Combinations in the Music of Tomás Luis de Victoria', *American Choral Review*, xviii/3 (1976), 3

H. E. Gudmundson: *Parody and Symbolism in Three Battle Masses of the Sixteenth Century* (diss., U. of Michigan, 1976)

S. Rubio, ed.: *Tomás Luis de Victoria: Officium Hebdomadae Sanctae* (Cuenca, 1977) [introduction, 1–134]

J. López-Calo, ed.: *Catálogo del Archivo de música de la Catedral de Ávila* (Santiago de Compostela, 1978), 290ff

R. Stevenson: 'Sixteenth- through Eighteenth-century Resources in Mexico – Part III', *FAM*, xxv (1978), 185

——: 'Recientes disertaciones sobre música española', *Revista musical chilena* (1979), no.145, p.126

M. V. Hall: 'Bach, Britten and Victoria', *MT*, cxxi (1980), 87

R. Jackson: 'Comments and Issues', *JAMS*, xxxiii (1980), 211

J. Roche: 'Renaissance Polyphony', *MT*, cxxi (1980), 640

J. Torres: *Cincuenta años de música (1929–1979): Índices generales de la Revista Musical Ilustrada 'Ritmo'* (Madrid, 1980), 114 [lists 21 articles on Victoria pubd in *Ritmo*]

S. Rubio: 'Dos interesantes cartas autógrafas de T. L. de Victoria', *Revista de musicología*, ii (1981), 333

E. C. Cramer, ed.: *Officium Hebdomadae Sanctae*, Institute of Mediaeval Music, Musicological Studies, xxi/1–4 (Henryville, 1982) [introduction]

S. Rubio: 'La Misa "Pro Victoria" de Tomás Luis de Victoria', *Ritmo*, lii/518 (1982), 12

L. Hernández: 'Samuel Rubio: una vida para la música: Estudio bio-bibliográfico', *Revista de musicología*, vi (1983), 55, 61, 70, 72, 88, 92

J. E. Ayarra Jarné: 'Carta de Tomás Luis de Victoria al Cabildo sevillano', *Revista de musicología*, vi (1983), 143 [see fig.12 above, p.296]

319

Index

Index

Index

Index

Index